BOOKS BY EDWARD HOAGLAND

Novels

Cat Man
The Circle Home
The Peacock's Tail

Essays and Journalism

Notes from the Century Before:
A Journal from British Columbia
The Courage of Turtles
Walking the Dead Diamond River

WALKING THE DEAD DIAMOND RIVER

WALKING THE DEAD DIAMOND RIVER

EDWARD HOAGLAND

RANDOM HOUSE · NEW YORK

Acknowledgment is made to the magazines in which these essays, sometimes shortened, first appeared. "Walking the Dead Diamond River," "Of Cows and Cambodia," "In the Toils of the Law," and "The Midnight Freight to Portland" are from *The Atlantic Monthly*. "Passion and Tensions," "Women Aflame," "Splendid, With Trumpets," "Jane Street's Samurai," "On the Question of Dogs," "The Assassination Impulse," "Meatcutters Are a Funny Bunch," "Marriage, Fame, Power, Success," and "The New England Wilderness" were published in *The Village Voice*. *Life* published "Two Clowns." *Audience* published "City Rat," "Fred King on the Allagash," and "Heart's Desire." "Tiger Bright" is from *Esquire*. "Hailing the Elusory Mountain Lion" appeared in *The New Yorker*.

The author also wishes to acknowledge with thanks assistance from the Creative Artists Public Service Program of the New York State Council on the Arts during the time this book was completed.

Library of Congress Cataloging in Publication Data

Hoagland, Edward.
Walking the Dead Diamond River.

I. Title.
PS3558.0334W3   814′ . 5′4   72–10806
ISBN 0–394–48361–8

FOR ROSS WETZSTEON,
JOHN BERRYMAN,
EDWIN HONIG AND
STEELE COMMAGER

CONTENTS

WALKING
THE DEAD
DIAMOND
RIVER

OF COWS
AND
CAMBODIA

During the invasion of
Cambodia, an event which may rate little space when
recent American initiatives are summarized but which for
many of us seemed the last straw at the time, I made an
escape to the woods. The old saw we've tried to live by
for an egalitarian half-century that "nothing human is
alien" has become so pervasive a truth that I was worn to
a frazzle. I was the massacre victim, the massacring
soldier, and all the gaudy queens and freaked-out hipsters
on the street. Nothing human *was* alien; I'd lost the essential anti-egalitarian ability to tune out on occasion, and
everything was ringing in my ears. Of course, even my
flight itself was part of a stampede of people who were
doing the same; and since my wife and I happened to be
involved in a kind of low-grade marital crisis, too, for all
my dovish politics, during my last few days in the city I
had been going to mean and bloody movies and reading
dirty books, as I usually do when in a trough of depression.

I have a hundred acres, mostly woodland, which I'm

informed is probably generating enough oxygen for eighteen hundred people to breathe. I don't institute many
improvements, both because of my ignorance and because,
for instance, instead of chopping deadwood for the stove,
for twelve dollars I can buy sufficient stove-sized scrap
from the bobbin-and-dowel mill down the road to cook
and heat the house four months. A ten-mile stretch of
Vermont state forest adjoins my land, and there is more
forest beyond, so what I really do is walk. An old overgrown stagecoach road which has been kept open by
hunters' jeeps and loggers' wagons winds with appropriate
slow grandeur up through a pass and down into a wild
valley, where there are several ponds and much birdlife
and an abandoned log shack or two. A long brook rattles
through the undergrowth and evergreens for miles, and
the ridges roll up to haystack humps and aggregate themselves into the broad miniature mass of Mount Hor, which
on its other side looks off a giddy cliff into a spring-fed
lake several miles long. There is a smugglers' cave beside
the lake where silks and whisky used to be stored; the
Canadian border is only fifteen miles away, and for a
whole summer a revenuer slept in a hammock in the
woods along the shore, posing as a poet but listening for
sounds. Another nearly lost, forgotten smugglers' camp—
this dating from the Civil War, complete with cemetery
and cellar holes—lies up behind an opposing mountain
across the lake. Around on my side of Mount Hor a deep,
traditional sort of cave corkscrews into the mountain a
hundred feet or more, a place where hunters lived, and
once an eccentric called Leatherman, who wore skins and

4

lived off whatever he could catch or kill. Hor is a fastness for bears. I've heard descriptions of how six of them have died of gunshot wounds in the valley below. The surviving bears, like shy, fleet Indians still holding out, sometimes hoot to their mates at dusk in June—a single quiet hoot with a growl at the end, which distinguishes the sound from an owl's call. Plenty of deer skirt through, and on the mountainside you can find boggy glades where single deer have made their beds in the fine grassy patches, leaving the imprint of themselves after they run. There are frogs on the paths—occasionally a charged, invigorated snake with a frog in its mouth. I've seen mink holes along the brook, and glimpsed a pair of tiny shrews playing at the entrance to their burrow. The porcupines, after huddling in congregations through the winter, spread out and fight for territory during the spring, with piercing, nasty screams, though in the evening you can hear them chewing bark high in the spruces, their teeth sounding gravelly-voiced.

My collie, Bimbo, who accompanies me, tangles with mystery creatures like mother raccoons fifty yards back in the brush. He has enough finesse not to get torn by them or squirted by skunks, and kills woodchucks with a chop of his jaws and a snap of his head, mouthing them hungrily to break the bones, lingering over the body and salivating. But then he lets them fall and, trotting home, finishes off last night's helping of dry dog chow instead. Before I adopted him, he wolfed down crusts of bread on his visits to the house, running four miles for the privilege. Though he is uncompromising with strangers, he's almost overly loyal to me, having had so many other masters that he keeps a weather eye peeled for the day when he may find himself alone, starving again. He sticks beside me in the woods rather than ranging out, but chases any deer we see with businesslike directness wholly wolfish for the moment, testing the air before finally happily lying down in a stream, and by his manner telegraphs the different creatures whose tracks he smells. He avoids gun-carrying people, having seen some shooting, and is afraid of thunder, indicating its approach before I hear it come. He is most cheerful in the morning, as if the day as it advances saddens him—he points up a somber nose. But he's a great ground-scratcher after urinating and a dramatic posturer with other dogs, his sense of self perhaps enhanced because he lives in isolation in the country and meets few other dogs. He fights sharply and seems to take a rich and realistic view of the citizenship of all the animals in the world, making no unnatural distinctions between those wild and tame. Cows, cats and fishers intrigue him equally. Meadow mice are a pleasure to hunt, but in bear country he doesn't wag his tail as much and walks with gingerly circumspection through the smashed berry thickets, the rank and muddy wallows. When we set out, he springs with all four feet off the ground and catches my hand in his mouth, and when we get back to the house he pulls off the burrs that have stuck to me, breathing lovingly. There are two things difficult about him. He personalizes cars, and chases them with an inimical bold heroism, since he's been hit three times. And in an apparent attempt to aggrandize himself, he loves to roll on the moldering bones of redoubtable strange animals. Worse than just using a dead deer, he singles out a picnicker's ordure to roll in if he can, smearing his fluffy fur with excrement, wearing it like epaulets, as the most mythic material of all. Afterward he romps and struts; it gives him a tremendous lift to smell so thickly like a man.

Besides believing nothing human should be alien, we used to aspire to another condition: as D. H. Lawrence said, we must *live more intensely*. We thought that, vague and dreamy, we were letting life slide by. But I was joining a mass swing of people looking for country acreage who had begun to feel so hard-pressed that their main effort was just to disengage themselves. They were of different politics and different vocations, yet some of them felt that if they lived any more intensely, they might have to be hospitalized.

Although we're swamped in populace and intensity, a few ridges over from me was a commune—twelve or fifteen persons in their twenties whose response to these dilemmas was more hair of the dog. Instead of barricading themselves behind thousands of acres of forestland, as I was trying to do, they intended to chum and combine with some of these overnumerous souls. And with the aspens trembling, field flowers blooming, the blue sky and the lavish landscape, their admirable experiment seemed to be working out. The children were sunburned and muscular, doing without diapers and caring for each other. They lived in a Children's Tent, and while there was some uncertainty and ear-pulling, mostly they roamed

7

between adventures, catching toads, feeding the hens. The grownups slept in pairs tucked into plastic lean-tos or hunters' tents under the spruces—there was one lofty-looking tepee. They had a geodesic dome which wowed their visitors and was intended to be transformed into a candle factory eventually, as well as a roomlike area covered with sheets of plastic draped over poles where the cooking was done, and a large produce garden that didn't succeed, owing to the acid soil.

Consistent with their life style, they tried to welcome strangers, even explaining their beliefs to sightseers if asked to, or letting a hitchhiker camp with them for a week or so on a probationary basis. Since several were veterans of an ill-fated commune further south in the state which had turned into a kind of motel for traveling hippies, this time they'd bought enough land for an agricultural existence, but without buildings, so that in these first months nobody could stay over unless he bestirred himself at least to pitch a tent. They built an outhouse, chicken house and cow shed, repaired their road, attempted to incorporate as a private elementary school so they could educate their own children, avoided obtrusive drug use, helped their neighbors hay in exchange for the loan of farm equipment, and wisely went to meetings of the local Grange so that the local people could see firsthand that they were not dragons. The men were fit-looking—the long hair didn't appear to be a mark of bereavement—and the girls eloquent, graceful, appealing; they had big eyes, and as in many communes, they got the job of dealing with outsiders. I felt wistful when I dropped in.

8

Obviously, no notable amount of work was being done. Everyone went off on jaunts into the countryside or swam or gathered firewood or sat talking all day in the cook tent, fixing salads of sorrel, lamb's-quarters and wild mustard leaves with little berries and raw eggs stirred in. They made butter and ice cream and pots of sugared oatmeal, and boiled milkweed and fried cornbread. It was a summer idyll. Lying underneath the trees, they never did get the log house built that they had planned.

By October, like grasshoppers who'd danced the harvest time away, they were looking for winter quarters to rent, stung by the frosts, worried for their children's health. It developed that the townspeople were not so friendly after all; nothing was available. They were college folk, so they weren't really going to have to stay and freeze, but it was interesting to note that the most favorably disposed faction in town were older persons who could remember living off the land and looking rather ragged themselves during the Great Depression. Also, the oldsters connected the rootless appearance of these hip types with the itinerant loggers from French Canada in earlier days—long-haired, linguistically a puzzle, with underfed dependents —and therefore weren't afraid of them.

This corner of Vermont is without industry, and when a summer resident shows up again the following spring the winter news of friends and neighbors is likely to be bad—bad luck, bad health—because so many younger people clear out, and there is hardly any way for a man who has stayed around to have advanced himself. Seventy-five years ago the town had factories manufacturing cheese, knickers, shoes and butter tubs, and what was then the longest power line east of the Rockies. Seventeen miles long, it carried 800 kilowatts and was the hobbyhorse of the inventive-minded middle class, although at that time farm boys still went into the woods after spruce chewing gum, which they cut off the trees with sharpened poles and steamed and sold downtown for a dollar a pound. Later they saved their gum money to buy battery radios and "windchargers," noisy windmills that turned and turned on the roof of the house and kept the batteries charged.

Since then whole settlements have disappeared in the outlying sections of town, and the country has grown so wild that one of the postal clerks has killed twenty-three bears so far. The saying is that you need only soak your feet in a bucket and set the salty water out by the back door for deer to drift right up to drink. A deer is just a joker like oneself; he's not much better at hearing a man move toward him in the woods than the man may be at hearing him.

Like most of the other abandoned farms, mine has its residue of projects that failed: a stunted orchard, an attempt at raising Christmas trees. The soil was marginal, and the family tried to keep goats at one time, and they had cows but the barn burned. Failure makes some men rough on their wives. There are stories of how the man who lived here during the thirties wouldn't bother to cut the stovewood short enough to fit the kitchen stove, wouldn't even cut down more than a week's supply, in case, as he said, he died; his wife could cut down her own trees after that. By and by he did die, and she moved off the place, saying that she was sick and tired of "staring at that damn mountain." Another, more sensible enterprise of theirs had been raising hunting dogs.

Woodcock fly up; a little fox runs down the road. In the springtime, when I arrive, being in my own fields is plenty for me—airing the house and stepping in and out, discovering again that the night sky exhibits stars by the thousand if they aren't blotted out by lights. No matter how brutal the winter has been (last Christmas fifty inches of snow fell in a single week), the grass is coming up like kettledrums; birches and pines, which grow as much as three feet in a year, are mustering themselves and shooting up. Goldfinches pick apart the dandelions; sapsuckers chisel for bugs underneath the maple bark. I roast potatoes to eat in their jackets like rolls and take walks on the drizzly evenings, listening to my brook, admiring the treetops against the sky, comparing spruce with fir, red spruce, white spruce, red pine, white pine. I watch the bats over Little Fish Pond, hearing trout jump that sometimes sound so big I step back under the trees, afraid somebody is heaving stones.

The young men hunt hard in season, turning their attention to the sport, but the old men think about it all the time; it is an elixir to them. They seem to feel they'll live longer if they are still able to shoot, as though in dealing death they are immortal for the moment. Far from shying from the ghastly antics of the dying deer, they recount these covetously, like a formula that may stave off the same collapse in themselves—the creature jerking its legs up

11

as it fell, twitching and groaning on the ground. These tales can extend through half an afternoon, each man has killed so many deer, often outwitting the game warden too. Porcupines and groundhogs can be hunted much of the year, and some people do so when times are grim, either for the relish of the kill and as a means of staving death off, or else for food. When neighbors quarrel, they hear each other next morning out in the woods shooting small game; and in the fall, when the hayfields are mown and visibility is good, they both lay up a store of gutted groundhogs, later grinding the meat with onions, apples and sunflower seeds into a matchless burger steak. Years ago people put up barrels of salted smelt caught in the spawning season, bins of root vegetables, canned green tomatoes, and grated horseradish cut with turnip. Then in midwinter, after letting a barrel of hard cider freeze, they'd drill a hole in the middle and tap the nearly pure alcohol, which made a man's heart feel as if it were wrapped in soft cotton.

In farming country old people are not sequestered away, and when somebody dies nearly everyone knew him. Only last week in the drugstore he may have crossed his fingers and said with a mild smile that he was hoping for a clean bill of health from the doctor. The butchering, the weighing of each cow's fate every few months, also makes death a familiar companion. Not every cow that doesn't freshen promptly is sent to slaughter, but she goes "down the road," to bob in terror under the auctioneer's prodding. It's personal—rather like a slave auction, perhaps. "What a pretty lady this is! Look at the teats on her! Keep her in the pasture this summer, and then if you don't like her, cut her throat in the fall!" Milk farmers are involved in all the intricacies and ambiguities of life-and-death power, and generally are glad to be. Since they work mostly around the barn, they're paler than the farmers who grow crops. Not until the 1960 census did Vermonters come to outnumber their cows, and several say the reason they were in no hurry was that they simply *liked* cows. In the isolated gores and valleys cows were a kind of harem. They could withhold or volunteer part of their milk, and if well soothed and happy they gave more. Even with machine-milking, the udders need a good old-fashioned warm-fingered stroking beforehand, and when a cow is bred artificially, the technician massages her cervix as well as squirting in the semen. After he leaves, a skillful farmer will squat down for a while and in a friendly fashion rub and squeeze her teats.

Against the sense of exuberant release I felt on long walks in the woods was the knowledge that this in fact was just a hermetic patch of wilderness with highways on all sides, scarcely larger than a park: it was a ship in a bottle, and I was only hiding out. The commune idealists, who read *The Whole Earth Catalog* as a life's chart, seemed doctrinaire, not easy company, so on days when I wasn't out with the dog hunting for smugglers' camps, I started accompanying an artificial inseminator from Newport Center named Donald Nault on his regular rounds. I had the frivolous notion that I might be watching the way human procreation would eventually be carried on, each liberated woman choosing semen that suited her from a listing of donor traits. Instead, the cows, pinned in their stanchions, looked around at us like immobilized moose turning to watch the wolves approach to eat. But as Nault kneaded them the experience became less unpleasant or fearsome, obscurely peaceful. They visibly relaxed, as though an ill wind had blown through the barn but had left them unharmed.

Nault has five kids and lives in a frail-looking frame house, shingled gray and set on a hilltop that overlooks most of his working territory, which is twenty-five miles square. His wife is a stocky, pretty woman, an ironist, a pertinacious mother, who stuffs bitterns and flying squirrels to decorate the living room. He is a good explainer and seems to smile more than most people do, although he's perfectly prepared to yell. He's gangly and has short gray hair and the open-faced look of a high-school science teacher, with thin-rimmed glasses, a spacious physiognomy but narrow bones. His voice is flat-timbred and dispassionate-sounding; he breaks his vowels in half, twanging the halves in different tones. He keeps bees and hunts with bow and arrow for hobbies, and works in the 4-H program, a much more freewheeling proposition than scouting, being geared to what farm youngsters can do off in the boondocks by themselves. Like the bulk-milk pickup drivers, the feed dealers and John Deere men, he's one of the county's peripatetics. According to tax figures, his corner of it has seventy-six hundred cattle, of which he services about half (the rest still rassle with his competitor, the bull). Even allowing for the heifers that are too young to breed, this means he services at least ten cows a day because he does free repeat breedings when the first doesn't take. He's off three days a month, including Sundays, but gets no other vacation, and is paid at the rate of $2.80 per cow. The fee the farmer pays is $7.

I learned about the business, along with a good deal of outright gynecology, riding around with Nault from farm to farm, seeing the lightning rods atop red barns and white houses (summer people reverse the colors—red houses and white barns). The farmers took no more notice of us than of meter readers, and though the days turned out to be rawer than I'd expected, with sometimes after-births and once a dead calf on the floor, there was the pleasure of the pasturage and rollercoaster woods and the big-siloed, spruced-up farms lying in front of the dramatic silhouette of the Green Mountains, Jay Peak jutting up immediately in front.

Besides enjoying the guided tour, I was glad for the friendship between Nault and myself. We were contemporaries and whatever we didn't have in common tended not to come up. But the hard monotony of bread-winning communicated itself too, just as it does whenever one absorbs the routines that another person must live by. We'd pull up by a milkhouse, built of cement for easy cleaning, with cold spring water tumbling into black slate sinks and a torpedolike five-hundred-gallon milk cooler gleaming, milk stools hanging up beside breeding charts and bacteria counts sent by the creamery. The milkhouse is for people, but the dark barn, drafty and partitionless, smells of fermenting silage and wet, fleshly herd politics. The cows have topknots where they've been dehorned and side-set eyes, trusting noses and flappy ears.

Nault steps into his rubber boots and syringes semen into a catheter, which he holds crosswise in his mouth while working with his hands. He is medical in manner, not chieftainish like the farmers, and though I admired the delicacy with which he handled the task, I pitied him the tedium of pounding round and round between a hundred farms year after year, none his. Some of the fellows envy him his free-lance life, however. Leaping land values, the overall slide toward change, cause a hollering across the countryside. Farmers think of retiring on the money their acreage would bring; yet dairying really has never been more profitable, they say. A hundred pounds of milk will buy two hundred pounds of grain, but a cow only needs to eat about a pound of grain for every three or four pounds of milk she produces during the winter months, or one to nine or ten pounds when she is pasturing. This is the ratio that matters. Also, about one acre of grazing ground and one of hay are necessary to support a cow in New England, and so if she brings in a yearly profit of perhaps two hundred dollars after all expenses, then each acre is worth a hundred dollars a year to the farmer and he will only continue keeping cows as long as that hundred dollars does not seem too paltry a sum when measured against the prices the land speculators offer him.

Whereas in the old days a man might dabble in winter logging or the Christmas-tree business or maple sugaring and take the chance that a few cows would catch pneumonia while he was gone, now it's best to be a specialist, with all the thorny breeding questions and mastitis and Bang's disease and vibriosis to watch for. Little farms must have the same expensive milk-handling equipment as big ones, so that the little operators are being bought out. Efficiency demands that they get rid of the mediocre milkers, then feed the good producers all the protein they will eat, whether in the form of short early-cut hay and high-value alfalfa and clover, or store-bought nutrients like beet pulp, citrus rinds, and chopped-up corn, wheat, barley, oats and molasses ground together. Most of the cattle Nault breeds are black-and-white Holsteins, which yield an average of 14,900 pounds of milk a year, far out-performing the brown-and-white Guernseys or Jerseys. Genetically Holsteins are also more trustworthy than Guernseys and, being big, are worth two hundred dollars as beef just as they stand. Jerseys do keep a hold on some farmer's affections because they're quite emotional and heated, yet small, easy to manage, and their milk tests high in butterfat, which means a premium is paid.

The landscape grew more familiar as we tooled around Nault's territory. Sometimes, during the afternoon, we went right back to the same farms, driving through gray rain squalls, past fields of timothy, rye grass and vetch, and stands of lusciously foliaged trees in the townships of Troy and Coventry. We saw Canadian Frenchmen with De Gaulle's nose at the age-old New England occupation of gathering stones. We passed the house of the district's healer, a seventh son of a seventh son, who can cure everything from dropsy to the twist in the postman's hip, which got out of its socket as the poor guy leaned from his driver's seat to reach the mailboxes. This healer is a

17

rough type and doesn't pray beside his customers; he simply puts his hand on the ailing area and holds it there for ten or fifteen minutes, telling raunchy jokes meanwhile.

Once we passed a mink farm, consisting of cage-filled sheds and several horses waiting in a vacant lot to be killed, cut up and fed to the mink, then drove up the first grade of the mountains to a brown slumping home isolated in deep woods, with a toolshed in back where a brown cow was tied. No grownups were around. A girl of twelve, who had been left in charge, came out of the house, handed Nault seven one-dollar bills and watched him work. Afterwards we coasted back to moneyed, rolling pasturelands, with immense barns equipped with stanchions by the hundred, all electrically hooked to the fire alarm so that the cows would be freed automatically in case of a disaster. Indeed, the latest innovation is to dispense with stanchions entirely, letting the creatures mill as they wish about the barn, only walking them through a "milking parlor" twice a day, because the more benign they feel, the more milk they will brew.

These new procedures naturally discourage the *machismo* bent of many farmers, which is why lots of them still keep bulls. The snorting beast costs hundreds of dollars to feed, more than the farmer saves in breeding fees, and it inhabits a stall where otherwise he could stable a milker. Yet some people will alternately utilize Nault's super variety of semen and their own yokel bull, and then, to his consternation, instead of raising the fine new calves which have the perfected genes for future stock and selling off the quirky local progeny, as often as not a man will keep his own bull's calves and send Nault's scientific infants straight to the butcher's block.

I am describing what I did in the aftermath of the Cambodia invasion, not a story with an end but of interest to me because it is what I would do again in the event of other invasions, or practically any other kind of trouble; it is the only thing that I can think of. I liked being poised near the Canadian border the way I was, and found that ducking quickly into the woods and living by myself had helped: up early, aware of other creatures besides man, with the sky-clock of sun and stars.

After hiking awhile around Mount Hor, I began going across the road to explore a large steep formless upland known as Robbins Hill, after a rifle-toting family of Raggedy Anns who have disappeared. I'd been learning to recognize the common trees, and a riotous arboretum of these were crowded together on Robbins Hill in what was an orgy for me. Young trees, particularly, send me into a hustle of needle-squeezing, bark-tapping and branch-waggling. I can't believe how straight and true to type they are, how springy to the touch and brown and green. To discover so many examples together in deep grass—lacy cedars next to hemlocks next to wavy larch and beech and yellow birch—was grounds for glee. Laughing to myself, I rushed from one to another, touching the leaves—perfect little maples, perfect little balsam firs. There was a flowering shrub called moose missy by the old people and a flower that they called frog's mouth.

Now this was all escapism—a word that's going to

19

lose its sting. I was escaping to recuperate, my ears grateful for the quiet of the woods. My wife flew up to join me as soon as she could, and except for her company, I found the old people best to be with, rather than those my own age, saddled with mortages and emphatic politics. My neighbors told me about fermenting beer forty or fifty years ago that had a head so thick they could write their names in it or spoon it off for sandwich filling. They'd make next Christmas's plum pudding on Christmas Eve, to marinate in brandy for twelve months, and serve last year's. The husband remembers skidding logs down off Robbins Hill with oxen one winter after a forest fire. The fire leapt across the road on some loose birch bark that caught the wind, and he remembers how pathetically the porcupines squealed as it caught up with them. There was only one farrier in the county, a man named Duckless, who shoed oxen for icy winter work; he did it as a kind of stunt. Oxen are stiff-legged and can't lift their legs as a horse can, so he employed a block and tackle and canvas sling to hoist them up. Since they are cloven-hoofed, each foot needed two shoes. The dogs would collect from the farms nearby as if a bitch had come in heat. Dogs love a blacksmith's visits because they chew on the hoof parings—the parings are taffy to them.

My friend Paul Sumner went foxing with his dog as a youngster, following the fox for many winding miles and hours. He'd get twenty-five dollars for the skin at a time when the daily wage at the sawmills was less than a dollar and fifty cents. A fisher skin was worth still more. He had a Long Tom rifle which had a kick that knocked

him down and a bolt action so loud that if he missed
when he was deer shooting, the animal would stop running and listen, mystified by the strange sound. There
were ten Sumner children, and necessarily the boys
hunted for meat. They'd get one rabbit started, and in
dodging about, it would scamper through every other
good rabbit hiding place, scaring up a throng. After each
snowstorm the father would tramp around the swamp,
leaving a great circle of snowshoe tracks beyond which
the younger kids were not supposed to go. Though they
were very poor, the saying was that no woman could be
admitted into heaven who cut more than four pieces from
a pie. Paul still makes his own bullets, weighing out the
grains of powder as some men roll their cigarettes. He
used to make shot for his shotgun by mincing up a flattened pipe, and would hike off for days with a bait pail
and traps into the Big Woods over in Essex County,
carrying a few bottle caps with wax and string in them
to heat the kindling for his fire on a wet night, later
pouring his supper grease on the next morning's firewood.
He remembers Halley's Comet in 1910, having climbed
Mount Hor especially to see it, sleeping on the crest and
watching a duckhawk fly up at dawn out of a tree and
kill a fast-flying duck with such impact that both of them
fell from the sky. He remembers fishing in Canada and
catching northern pike four feet long. If the line broke,
by jinks, he says, the fisherman jumped in the lake and
wrestled with the fish, almost like another man. The
blueberries were as big as thumbs and turned the hill-
sides blue.

He tells the legend of how oak trees acquired scalloped leaves. There was a man who signed a pact with the Devil according to which, after enjoying his handsome looks and riches, he would have to give himself up "when the oak lost its leaves." But oaks never do lose all their leaves; some cling stubbornly to the trees all through the winter until fresh foliage sprouts in the spring. And so the Devil, who was a bad loser, ran around and round the archetypal oak, chewing on its leaves, marking the edges with his teeth.

In the cavalry down in Brownsville, Texas, after World War I, Paul used to feed his horses sugar cane for a treat. His barracks mates kept an ocelot for a mascot; and there was a pet terrier in a bar they patronized which was so tough the customers would throw a tennis ball at it as hard as they could, down the aisle between the tables and the bar, and the dog, bounding in the air, would catch it on the fly. Back in Vermont, Paul, who was always a fisherman, located an old quarry hole with bass swimming at the bottom of it. A man lived nearby in a tar-paper shack, ten feet by six and all grown over with blackberries—"The house was only standing up because the termites inside were holding hands." It stood under a fine white pine that the fellow called his "sunflower tree" because the needles seemed so radiant when the light was right. He raised tomatoes on the remains of a defunct outhouse and baked his bread in loaves so big around, a slice was the size of a pane of glass. He spent his days bucking firewood for money, though flourishing his rifle when people came to pick it up (he'd grab a broomstick and aim with that if they were kids). He was so fussy that he wouldn't let anybody touch his cartridges, afraid they'd leave some sweat on them and tarnish the parts of his gun, and yet his house was stuffed with junk, scarcely allowing room for the bed and stove. He never washed his dinner plate, just dumped more food on it, but every few weeks he would scrape off the detritus and fry that too, calling it "stodge."

Another character on that road was the Turkey Buyer, who ranged about the state in a truck carrying gobblers. When he passed a farm that raised the birds he would screech to a stop, jump out, run up to the door and tell the farmer that one of the turkeys from his truck had got out of its crate and scurried in among the farmer's turkeys; would he please help catch it? Together they would catch one of the farmer's turkeys, and then the Turkey Buyer, with many thanks, would drive away.

Dan Tanner was a neighbor of Paul's too. Dan was a seven-footer who had once killed a bear which went after a string of fish he'd caught by stabbing it with a sharp stick of heartwood just underneath the arm. He was exceedingly tough; his wife, Abbey, used to wash the blood off all the men he licked. A good trout brook made up in their back field, most of it underground for the first mile. Nevertheless, there were some holes you could fish through and catch short little trout, discolored from not having seen the sun. Tanner ran a still that cooked his booze so hot, the pots and tubing jounced. He set aside a jug for Saturday and one for Sunday, but usually he'd finish Saturday's before sunset, vomit it up and finish Sunday's too. He didn't trouble very much about the law and feuded with the game warden. One time in the winter when the warden was trailing him,

Dan carefully tossed the doe he'd killed behind a rock
and turned downhill, taking small steps, down to a brook,
then walked backwards in his own tracks, stepping exactly in each step, and hopped behind a dead spruce on
the ground, where he lay still. Pursuing him, the warden
passed by and looked in vain for Tanner's tracks across
on the other side of the brook. Thirsty, he stooped to
drink, and Tanner fired a shot into the water just underneath his nose.

Paul, who is a father, a widower, is a less violent man.
He suffers from angina but cuts pulpwood for a living at
nineteen dollars a cord. One corner of his farm is about
to be razed for an interstate highway, and parallel with
that will be a power line, so his years of retirement will
probably be spent between these fierce belts of activity.
For much of his working life he was a lineman himself
for a power company. The photos on the wall show him
in climbing boots high on a leaning pole with a tree
fallen on the line. He's got blue eyes and a jug-handle
pair of ears, a puckery, sharp-witted face, a twisty smile.
He jokes a lot, collapsing in laughter, swinging his arms,
although he has a sense of misery as well. In wintertime
he needs to shovel the snow from in front of his windows
in order to see out; it gets so deep that he can walk
right onto the roof when the ice must be scraped off. He
grows winter apples, which are not picked until after the
first snowfall. The frosts seem to condition them; that's
when the deer prefer them too.

He who fights and runs away lives on, and that's what
I had been up to. As the summer closed I went again to

the roots of the brook under Mount Hor, finding the split-pear prints of deer and listening to the ravens honk. There is a "boiling spring" that Robert Frost used to visit, according to reports. The spring no longer boils, having become choked with leaves—it never did boil in the Westerner's meaning of the word; they don't have hot springs here—but it still tastes pristine and heads a cold and lively stream. Talking with the various old men, each one with a heart condition, I sometimes felt the need for haste in gathering information: even a sense that if the fellow should suffer a stroke before my eyes, I would bend over him, urgently asking, *Where was that cave? Who was it that you said lived there?*

Each of them, after his own manner of doing things, was in the process of selling off his land—at least the relics on it, like wagonwheels—pretending that he was just trying to "get rid of the stuff," impatient that the buyer hadn't come for them, and watching as his pastures, laboriously maintained since the nineteenth century, grew back to tangled wilderness. In September I accompanied a man I am fond of into the jungle that had formerly been his lower pasture and now was on the point of being sold to me. He was in his middle eighties and walked very slowly, like a frail Galapagos turtle, looking incongruously weightless but leaning heavily while I helped him to edge through the willow-alder thickets. We looked for the old fence line, where bits of barbed wire lingered on the trees, and the stump of a black cherry tree that he thought the bears had killed, and a round rock called Whippoorwill Rock, and a big butternut, and for the place beside the stream where his brothers and he had once successfully rigged a power saw operated by a waterwheel. The alders were a jungle, yet he struggled much farther into the center of the property than I'd expected, calm and slow about it, swaying a little when the wind blew. Many landmarks had been obliterated, but he found a few. The growth was swamp grass now, smothering in spiraea brush. Remembering as he went along, he persevered so far that I was afraid that even with my help he wouldn't be able to extricate himself again.

CITY RAT

Delightedly, I used to cross Park Avenue wearing an undershirt on my way to digs far to the south and east. I could remember waiting, as a boy of eight, on almost the same street corner for the St. Bernard's school bus in a proper tweed blazer, striped tie and shiny shoes, and so this gulf between costumes seemed sweet. Sweaty, bare-shouldered, strolling the summer streets, I felt my class or creed unidentifiable, which very much pleased me. Physically I was in my prime, I liked to jog, and, long and loose like a runner, though still smooth-faced, I felt as if I were a thousand miles and a whole world away from that small boy. I'd sit around on door stoops after a walk of eighty blocks or so, up from the Battery or down from Yankee Stadium, and watch the world go by. If I'd been an out-of-towner, awed by the city, these walks would have been ideal for adjusting. Wherever I ran out of steam, I'd sit, keeping an eye peeled, and try to pretend that this was now my territory and I must figure it out quickly. It should be remembered that fifteen years ago violence in New York City was fairly well contained within a framework of teenage gangs attacking other gangs, not wayfarers; Negro bitterness bore down mainly on other Negroes, and though sometimes the Mafia in Brooklyn dumped a body on Avenue D, the Lower East Side itself and other such areas were quite peaceful.

I was in the theater district once, sitting on a stoop, enjoying the stream of life, when a brisk, well-preserved man with custom-fitted pants, a cane and good coloring halted in front of me. "Young man," he said abruptly, "are you trying to break into the theater?" Aware that it was a funny question, he raised his eyebrows while he waited, as if I'd been the one who'd asked. I was holding my knees and looking up at him. He tapped my feet with the point of his cane as though he were buying me and I was supposed to stand.

I was too nervous to answer. Superciliously he stared at me. "You'd better come along. There are a great many young men trying to get into the theater. I'm in the theater." He tapped me again. I still didn't trust myself to speak, and he glanced at my Army boots, laughed and said, "Are you a paratrooper? Come now, last chance, young man. Fame and fortune. There are a great many of you and one of me. What's going to set you apart?"

My embarrassed silence made him uncomfortable, as well as the possibility that somebody might recognize him standing there in this peculiar conversation. As he left, he called back, "Good luck, little friend, whoever you are." But I grinned more confidently at him as he got farther off, because a couple of months before I'd had my picture in *Time* as a blazing new author; perhaps he never had. That was the second fillip to wandering in my undershirt along Fifth or Park Avenue: the fact that on other days I'd be wearing a snaky gray flannel suit, slipping through the crowds in the skyscraper district, and shooting up high in a building for a swank lunch. I wasn't really masquerading as a carpenter; on the contrary, I'd made no choices yet— I was enjoying being free.

Banging around on a motor scooter down the length of Manhattan by way of the waterfront, I'd unwind in the evening after writing all day. New York was compartmentalized; Harlem was in Harlem, and on Delancey Street there were live ducks for sale, and in a shop with big windows, shoemakers cutting soles for shoes. I looked at coming attractions under the various movie marquees and watched the traffic on the stairs to a second-floor whorehouse (sailors coming down and a cop going up). Since I was both bashful and lonely, I would leave notes on the bulletin boards of some of the coffeehouses— "Typist wanted"—then wait by the telephone. The girls were under no illusions about what I was up to when they called, except that they usually did want some work out of the arrangement as well, and, unfairly enough, that's what I was reluctant to give. I kept my manuscripts in the refrigerator as a precaution against fire and was a nut about safeguarding them. Inevitably, then, the sort of girl who'd phone me blind and invite me over for a screw on the strength of a note I'd left in a coffeehouse was not a girl I'd trust my typing to.

One girl had a beachboy crouching naked on the floor painting her bathtub red when I arrived; the rest of the apartment was a deep black. Another, on Houston Street, immediately embraced me with her head swathed in bandages from the blows that her husband had bestowed the night before. Pulling the bookcases over, he'd strewn the books around, broken all the china and announced he was leaving. Nothing had been picked up since. The baby, only a year old, cried desperately in the playpen, and though his mother naturally hoped I would be able to step right into the father's role and comfort him, I wasn't that skillful. A window was broken, so it was cold. She took me to the bedroom, moaning, "Hit me! Hit me!" When things there didn't work out she led me downstairs to a kind of commune, introduced me around and announced to the members that I was impotent.

Still, I was busy, once sleeping with three different women in as many days, and covering the city better than most news reporters, it seemed to me, recognizing innumerable street nooks and faces which epitomized New York for me. Perhaps the air was rather sooty, but it didn't cause headaches or give people bleeding throats. Now I sometimes spit blood in the morning and feel raw sulfur in my gullet from breathing the air; in midtown or around Canal Street I breathe through my teeth like a survivalist who specializes in outlasting Black Lung. This morning when I went out to buy milk for breakfast I saw a clump of police cars and a yellow car which had slid out of the traffic and come to rest against the curb, empty except for a gray-looking dead man in his thirties slumped sideways

against the wheel. I stood rubbernecking next to the delicatessen owner. One night last year I'd stood in a crowd
and watched most of the building that houses his store
burn to a shell, all of us—he wasn't there—as silent and
spellbound as if we were witnessing public copulation.
Though he is not a friendly man, I like his Greek blunt-
ness and at the time I'd felt guilty to be watching as a
mere spectacle what was a catastrophe for him. But here
he was, rubbernecking at this fellow's death just like me,
only less solemnly; he chuckled, shaking his head. I kept
a straight face and felt a pang, but while I crossed the
street with the groceries and rode up in the elevator the
incident entirely slipped my mind; I didn't even mention
it when I got home.

Such imperviousness is a result of changes in the city as
well as in me. If I have lost my bloom, so has the city, more
drastically. Among the beggars who approach me, almost
weekly I see a mugger who is clearly screwing up his
nerve to do more than just *ask* for money. I have the New
Yorker's quick-hunch posture for broken-field maneuvering, and he swerves away. A minute later, with pounding
feet, there he goes, clutching a purse, with a young woman
in forlorn pursuit. Recently, riding in a bus, I saw a po-
liceman with his gun drawn and his free hand stretched
out tiptoe hastily after a suspect through a crowd and
make the nab as the bus pulled away. It's not any single
event, it's the cumulative number of them—shouted arguments, funerals, playground contretemps, drivers leaning
on their horns, adults in tears, bums falling down and hitting their heads, young men in triumph over a business

31

deal—that one sees in the course of a midday walk which veneers one with callousness.

We each work out a system of living in the city. With music, for instance. I put trumpet voluntaries on the phonograph in the morning, organ fugues after supper, and whale songs or wolf howls in the silence at night. I go to a Village bar which is like a club, with the same faces in it day after day, although as a hangout it does acquire a tannic-acid taste if you go too often because most of the people are divorced or on that road. The newspapermen see it as belonging to them; hungry poets and movie novelists view it as a literary saloon; the seamen, photographers, carpenters, folk singers, young real-estate impresarios, political lawyers, old union organizers and Lincoln Brigade veterans all individually believe it's theirs.

I'm tired of Washington Square, Tompkins Square Park, Abingdon Square, even Central Park (I lived next to it for several years and found it to be ground as overused as the banks of the Ganges are). And the last time my wife and I picnicked in Van Cortlandt Park, which is more countrified, we needed to cut at top speed through the woods to escape two men who were stalking us. Space is important to me, and each of these public resting spots has its own character and defines a particular period for me. In the early sixties I was in Washington Square, watching, among other things, the early stirrings of Negro belligerence, still indirect. It seemed to take the form of their ballplaying, sometimes one man alone, throwing a rubber ball as high as he could and catching it on the second or third bounce. They were lanky, like men just out of the

Army or prison, and when they played catch they loped all over the park, taking possession everywhere. Already they had secret handshakes and contemptuous expressions, and this gobbling up the whole park with their legs and lofting a rubber ball into the stratosphere bespoke the blocked energy, the screened anger that would soon explode. The explosion is past; new developments are brewing in these parks, but I am fatigued with watching.

The Chinese laundryman we go to is mean of heart and keeps his children home from school to iron for him while he loafs. The two girls next to us are sleeping with the super, and sit in triumph while their apartment is painted, as a consequence. Perhaps he sleeps well, but I'm almost sleepless from fighting with my wife. And there are explosions going off nightly down in the street. I have no idea what they are; years ago I would have thought just firecrackers. New York is a city of the old and young, and looking out the window, I sometimes see old people fall. One man has cancer of the mouth. When he feels well he sits outside the barber shop or in the park, not looking up, withdrawn into his memories, but seeming tranquil there; certainly nobody enjoys the sunshine more. But the next day when you walk past he is sitting quietly hemorrhaging into his handkerchief, looking at it fearfully, then boosting himself off the bench to go back to the nursing home.

In the apartment on the other side of us are two young men who entertain a lot, and one day somebody leaned out their window with a rifle equipped with a spotting scope, searching the courtyard and the street. I assumed it was a toy, but in any case I simply pulled down the

blinds; one can't react to everything. We'd had a stink in
the corridor the week before that gradually grew stronger.
It was a really hideous smell, subterraneanly terrifying,
and we and some of the neighbors began to wonder
whether somebody might not have died. It was pervasive,
hard to isolate, and we were all city procrastinators—with
so many emergencies, so many lonely people, why get
involved? At last, however, where our consciences had
failed, our noses got the better of us and we called the
cops. It turned out to be a decomposing chicken which
someone had defrosted before a trip and forgotten about.
A month or so later the same putrid smell invaded our
floor all over again. Holding our noses, we complained left
and right, trying to ignore it. Even so, again the police
had to be called. This time they found a young woman
dead of an overdose of heroin, with her headband wrapped
around her arm as a tourniquet and her cat still alive,
having managed to subsist on her body fluids.

Year round, I keep my air conditioner on, its steady hum
submerging the street sounds. But one of the neighbors
upstairs, finding this noise, too, unnerving, has lent me a
white-sound machine, an instrument which, like a sort of
aural sun lamp, manufactures a sense of neutrality and
well-being. Right now neutrality seems to be the first condition of peace; these devices have become commonplace.
People are seeking to disengage, get out of town, or at
least stay indoors and regale themselves with surfy sounds.
The question everybody is asking is, Where does one live?
New York is the action scene; one won't feel the kinesis
of the 1970s in a Sicilian fishing village, and very few

people are really quite ready to write all that off. Maybe the best of both worlds is to be a New Yorker outside New York. Anyway, I'm at my best as a traveler, and looking back when I am elderly, I may be fondest of some of my memories of hauling a suitcase along, grinning, questioning strangers, breathing the smoke of their wood fires, supported, although I was far from home, by the knowledge of where I'd come from. Arriving in Alaska, straight from New York, one feels tough as a badger, quick as a wolf. We New Yorkers see more death and violence than most soldiers do, grow a thick chitin on our backs, grimace like a rat and learn to do a disappearing act. Long ago we outgrew the need to be blow-hards about our masculinity; we leave that to the Alaskans and Texans, who have more time for it. We think and talk faster, we've seen and know more, and when my friends in Vermont (who are much wiser folk than Alaskans) kid me every fall because I clear out before the first heavy snow, I smile and don't tell them that they no longer know what being tough is.

Setting out from home for the landmark of the Empire State Building, I arrive underneath it as a countryman might reach a nearby bluff, and push on to the lions at the public library, and St. Patrick's, and the fountain in front of the Plaza. Or in fifteen minutes I can take my two-year-old daughter to the Museum of Natural History, where, after waving good-by to the subway train, she strides inside, taking possession of the stuffed gorillas, antelopes, spiny anteaters, modeled Indian villages and birds and fish—the pre-twentieth-century world cooked

35

down to some of its essentials. Six or seven puppet shows and several children's plays are being presented in the city this afternoon, and there are ships to watch, four full-scale zoos, and until recently goats, monkeys, chickens and ten horses were quartered on an eccentric half-acre a few blocks from our building. Just the city's lighted skyscrapers and bridges alone will be with my daughter forever if her first memories are like mine—she lies on her back looking upward out the window when we ride uptown in a taxi at night, with the lights opals and moons.

But is it worth the blood in the throat? Even when we go out on a pier to watch the big ships, what comes blowing in is smudgy smoke instead of a clean whiff of the sea. For me it's as disquieting as if we had to drink right out of the Hudson; our lungs must be as calloused as the soles of our feet. Is it worth seeing a dead man before breakfast and forgetting him by the time one sits down to one's orange juice? Sometimes when I'm changing records at night I hear shrieks from the street, sounds that the phonograph ordinarily drowns out. My old boyhood dreams of playing counterspy have declined in real life to washing perfume off my face once in a blue moon when, meeting an old girlfriend in a bar, I get smooched, but I still have a trotting bounce to my walk, like a middle-aged coyote who lopes along avoiding the cougars and hedgehogs, though still feeling quite capable of snapping up rabbits and fawns. Lightness and strength in the legs is important to me; like the closed face, it's almost a must for the city. There's not a week when I don't think of leaving for good, living in a *house*, living in the West,

perhaps, or a smaller town. I will never lose my New
Yorker's grimace, New Yorker's squint and New Yorker's
speed, but can't I live with them somewhere else?

PASSION
AND
TENSIONS

We look at the lidded, exhausted, discredited face of Dean Rusk, Secretary of State for eight years, and suspect that he may be a long time dying, and don't envy him the wait. Remembering the two million war dead, the marches, riots, the idealists jailed, the thousands of exiles, the wear and tear and lost hair—his busy silence then—it's hard to pity him. But he must already guess how history will deal with him, and what must be painful is to see it happen now, so very soon, before he's dead and gone. We remember, too, the sharp sarcasm toward critics of the war expressed only a few years ago by powerful figures—Clark Clifford, Averell Harriman—who later turned anti-war, when what was then established policy was questioned. They thrived; then, reversing with the tide, they continued to thrive. Even those, like the Bundy brothers, who didn't reverse with the tide have generally thrived. By contrast, the pained dissenters whom one remembers watching on the street may have found that their imaginations, which

brought alive for them the suffering that the fellows at
State and at Defense were dead to, are not as marketable.

These men of affairs, these violent monkeys! It's not a
matter of wanting to see the Bundys eat crow. Like musk
oxen, their brethren—one might say, their generation—
have closed ranks around them, which is understandable.
We wonder, though, whom to admire. Ideally, ordinarily,
one admires one's elders, their age and survival being a
kind of homely badge of achievement. If the teens are for
education, the twenties for exploration, the thirties the
best of all possible worlds, then, to generalize, the forties
are for proficiency and accomplishment and the fifties for
power and know-how—or for making one's peace with
defeat. But nowadays engineers in the high-flying fields
are not merely unemployed; they are being asked to completely rethink what they have been about throughout
their professional lives, not so much to see whether they've
done any good as whether they haven't done a great deal
of harm. Young lawyers and doctors are setting about to
try to institute the most elementary reforms in their professions. This does not involve just the usual bent of the
young for reform, but the absence of admiration of anybody for anybody. Can one think of a leader who is
widely admired, even among those his own age? (Reform-
ers—miraculous ombudsmen sprung up from nowhere,
like Ralph Nader—don't count; after all, they are simply
attempting to bring us around to square one, from
which position in time and with difficulty something
eventually may be accomplished.)

Business, military service, religion—what a shambles.

Where does this leave the multitude who have spent their working lives within the old system? Their successes, that strong middle-aged effectiveness which should be the fruition of people's lives, are called into question by the simple fact that so much of what they've been doing just doesn't work, or seems to have been *harmful*. And if we find we can't straightforwardly admire an active, successful man any more as we used to, then what do we think of the prime of life itself? What do we think of old men? What can we look forward to if, instead of a certain cheerful measure of esteem, there is ignominy in being old, if experience itself—what we go through such weary anxiety for—not only counts for nothing in the end but winds up making us objects of disparagement? When accomplishment is considered possible only among those who are young, what do we do who *are* young, or relatively young, and already know that we haven't done much, don't know how to do much, know almost nobody who has done or ever is going to do much? Sometimes one looks back in order to take stock and finds that one has arrived at the stage of life where one works oneself to exactly the same level of exhaustion each night, with children and job, but that the crowded events seem to add up only to having made several people very unhappy.

I've always had a special liking for old men. Once when as a boy I saw some friends catch a fish and clean it without first killing it, I found myself thinking that an old man wouldn't do such a thing. I listened to the stories strangers told—old people who sat next to me on a bus —and recognized that their pride in what they said was not random boasting, that a man's life story summarizes plainly enough the stamina, concentration and energy he has had over the years, as well as his luck; loyalty, friendship, sanity, imagination—those old words too. Old men are usually joyful men at heart. Ulcers and hypertension have winnowed away the more fretful fellows to the peace of the grave. Old men are those who have bobbed to the surface in time of flood, who have smiled to themselves and let their hurts heal.

Of course, I also felt the fierce desire that young people have that the older generation be made to admit its errors and have its nose rubbed in them. I wanted my parents to swallow the fact that divorce and drinking, of which they disapproved, were well on the rise among their friends. But these grudging admissions were supposed to be drawn from them in particular. *Old* people weren't enemies; I didn't insist they be humbled. I knew they ate humble pie practically all the time, that they managed shrinking stores of strength with declining faculties, and when invited out were expected to sing for their suppers with a birdy, tea-towel personality that must be discouraging if not degrading. Old age was the one time in life when bravery was expected of people as a matter of routine, and any old man had an edge on my affections when I first glanced at him, having undoubtedly seen enviable things, having held up for seven or eight decades through the same procedures of life toward which I looked apprehensively. We all liked hearing these old stories. There was a good word affectionately in currency then—old-timer.

41

I'm at what used to be called in the *Reader's Digest* a dangerous age. Nearing forty, sometimes I look around at the women I know to figure out whom I would go to if I left my wife (or she me). These notions never work out; I've been divorced once, and under the circumstances the girls I'd thought of beforehand didn't want me for even one night, and definitely not the first. This doesn't erase the fancy, though. There is B., with a wide splendid face, hair teasing her shoulders, and a big bosom, as one would want, a forceful undogmatic radical and something of a ruffian-of-the-night (if my image is correct, which it probably is not). It is a blessing of B.'s that if I were to call and she did ask me over, she would not expect me to come bearing a proposal of marriage, not being one of those women my age so bogged down in problems and appalled by them that nothing short of a proposal will calm her down. Punctual, civil men like myself, I understand from several of my friends, still run into the attitude that their dependability in regard to the surface courtesies betrays some deeper form of decency or gentility, some anachronistic sense of honor that may be seized on and put to use.

User-user link-ups like this are one of the phenomena the Women's Lib movement seeks to do away with, and, sisterhood that it is, it bolsters its sadder, more frantic membership by suggesting some reasons for their distress outside themselves. So I'm for it, realizing that when it is venomous the venom was there before. I don't agree with the women who think themselves blacks, but I'm willing to grant the organized contingent of them perhaps the degree of excitement some "Italian-Americans" feel, with their rallies and writers making hay with the Mafia-as-our-thing, an excitement not entirely spurious either. It's an excitement I even envy vaguely, as I did the similar breathless, glamorous sense of "relevance" and being top dog that bandwagon Jews on the New York scene felt a few years ago. Any relevance somebody un-excited like me felt was humbler, and since I am no more a woman than I am black or "Italian-American," any relevance that I have today continues to be humbler. Men who happen to be Wasps—not to mention hetero-sexuals—have been watching other people's excitement for a long time. We've resented the people who tried to make us foot-wipes and laughed at the ones who turned into Yahoos like any prototype Wasp just as soon as they made it big, but their excitement was fun for them.

I wouldn't be vague about envying this except that I've never been sure what it's about. During these sieges of excitement, looking at someone like me who has been excluded since birth from their group even before it be-came a group, they seem to say, Now *we* can live happy and high on the hog and fulfill ourselves as you do—male, Wasp, heterosexual, whichever you are. And I re-peat to myself, Is this really what they're excited about, these groups: that now women, "Italian-Americans," Jews, homosexuals or blacks can be happy like me, on top, cock of the walk? Good heavens, my friends, I say silently, if this is what you're suddenly so excited about, do you think it's as easy as that? Who is cock of the walk? Mc-

George Bundy was; who is now? Gloria Steinem, Huey Newton, Anthony Scotto, Norman Podhoretz? Are they more content, are they better? If happiness is being a white male Protestant, what about the stifled, ruminative, apologetic fellows I see at Christmas reunions and old-friend parties? Think again. The best of "your" writers, like James Baldwin, the best of "our" writers (we who have been unexcited throughout)—the best of *all* writers —have been ridiculing our lackluster existence since printing began. Now the Jews, tired too, have mostly joined us.

Life is lonely. Some are sinkers and some are floaters; some of us who grew up in the suburbs have moved into the inner city to enliven it for ourselves, and some who grew up in the inner city have moved out excitedly to the suburbs. Mercy on us—we exchange suits of clothes. But there is a disturbing development about Women's Lib. It's not that in their bitterness the believers may actually take their bosoms and sex away from men—comforts just as important to them as to anyone else. Instead, it's that as well as being equal they will come to regard themselves as the same, judging men by the same lights and through the same eyes as men judge each other. There will then be no softness for the fallen—which just now, when failure is so widespread as to be pandemic and when the stigma of failure is as grotesque and iron as ever, would be a wretched development. We know the shape a man out of a job assumes in other people's eyes: he's invisible, beyond hearing. He turns everybody off—everybody, that is, except for some private citizen

44

who is a woman and happens to find him attractive. Her different wavelength, the "trap of compassion," as a propagandist recently called it, or being a "loser-lover," in the current phrase, has kept her open. The same soft spot in men, cutting through the hard laminations of the way of the world, may rescue her, in turn, when she falls on her nose.

We hear about "sisters" and "brothers" everywhere, always in harsh, exclusionary terms that mock the supposed meaning of the words, much as Fundamentalists do when they call out "Brother" or "Sister" over our heads to somebody who won't roast for eternity on the coals of hell. We must hope it is easier to be old when we have become old, but in the meantime, with so much out of whack, so much defeat, so much revision going on, how lucky we are that there are two sexes and that our sympathies delve more deeply and unconventionally into the one not our own. Mercy is there when mercy's required. Otherwise we would find no bottom to land on whenever some desolate rush of fashion knocks us down.

HAILING THE ELUSORY MOUNTAIN LION

The swan song sounded by the wilderness grows fainter, ever more constricted, until only sharp ears can catch it at all. It fades to a nearly inaudible level, and yet there never is going to be any one time when we can say right *now* it is gone. Wolves meet their maker in wholesale lots, but coyotes infiltrate eastward, northward, southeastward. Woodland caribou and bighorn sheep are vanishing fast, but moose have expanded their range in some areas.

Mountain lions used to have practically the run of the Western Hemisphere, and they still do occur from Cape Horn to the Big Muddy River at the boundary of the Yukon and on the coasts of both oceans, so that they are the most versatile land mammal in the New World, probably taking in more latitudes than any other four-footed wild creature anywhere. There are perhaps only four to six thousand left in the United States, though there is no place that they didn't once go, eating deer, elk, pikas, porcupines, grasshoppers, and dead fish on the beach.

They were called mountain lions in the Rockies, pumas (originally an Incan word) in the Southwestern states, cougars (a naturalist's corruption of an Amazonian Indian word) in the Northwest, panthers in the traditionalist East—"painters" in dialect-proud New England—or catamounts. The Dutchmen of New Netherland called them tigers, red tigers, deer tigers, and the Spaniards *leones* or *leopardos*. They liked to eat horses—wolves preferred beef and black bears favored pork—but as adversaries of mankind they were overshadowed at first because bears appeared more formidable and wolves in their howling packs were more flamboyant and more damaging financially. Yet this panoply of names is itself quite a tribute, and somehow the legends about "panthers" have lingered longer than bear or wolf tales, helped by the animal's own limber, far-traveling stealth and as a carry-over from the immense mythic force of the great cats of the Old World. Though only Florida among the Eastern states is known for certain to have any left, no wild knot of mountains or swamp is without rumors of panthers; nowadays people delight in these, keeping their eyes peeled. It's wishful, and the wandering, secretive nature of the beast ensures that even Eastern panthers will not soon be certifiably extinct. An informal census among experts in 1963 indicated that an island of twenty-five or more may have survived in the New Brunswick–Maine–Quebec region, and Louisiana may still have a handful, and perhaps eight live isolated in the Black Hills of South Dakota, and the Oklahoma panhandle may have a small colony—all outside the established range in Florida,

Texas, and the Far West. As with the blue whale, who will be able to say when they have been eliminated?

"Mexican lion" is another name for mountain lions in the border states—a name that might imply a meager second-best rating there yet ties to the majestic African beasts. Lions are at least twice as big as mountain lions, measuring by weight, though they are nearly the same in length because of the mountain lion's superb long tail. Both animals sometimes pair up affectionately with mates and hunt in tandem, but mountain lions go winding through life in ones or twos, whereas the lion is a harem-keeper, harem-dweller, the males eventually becoming stay-at-homes, heavy figureheads. Lions enjoy the grassy flatlands, forested along the streams, and they stay put, engrossed in communal events—roaring, grunting, growling with a racket like the noise of gears being stripped—unless the game moves on. They sun themselves, preside over the numerous kibbutz young, sneeze from the dust, and bask in dreams, occasionally waking up to issue reverberating, guttural pronouncements which serve notice that they are now awake.

Mountain lions spirit themselves away in saw-toothed canyons and on escarpments instead, and when conversing with their mates they coo like pigeons, sob like women, emit a flat slight shriek, a popping bubbling growl, or mew, or yowl. They growl and suddenly caterwaul into falsetto—the famous scarifying, metallic scream functioning as a kind of hunting cry close up, to terrorize and start the game. They ramble as much as twenty-five miles in a night, maintaining a large loop of territory which they

48

cover every week or two. It's a solitary, busy life, involving a survey of several valleys, many deer herds. Like tigers and leopards, mountain lions are not sociably inclined and don't converse at length with the whole waiting world, but they are even less noisy; they seem to speak most eloquently with their feet. Where a tiger would roar, a mountain lion screams like a castrato. Where a mountain lion hisses, a leopard would snarl like a truck stuck in snow.

Leopards are the best counterpart to mountain lions in physique and in the tenor of their lives. Supple, fierce creatures, skilled at concealment but with great self-assurance and drive, leopards are bolder when facing human beings than the American cats. Basically they are hot-land beasts and not such remarkable travelers individually, though as a race they once inhabited the broad Eurasian land mass all the way from Great Britain to Malaysia, as well as Africa. As late as the 1960s, a few were said to be still holding out on the shore of the Mediterranean at Mount Mycale, Turkey. (During a forest fire twenty years ago a yearling swam the narrow straits to the Greek island Samos and holed up in a cave, where he was duly killed—perhaps the last leopard ever to set foot in Europe on his own.) Leopards are thicker and shorter than adult mountain lions and seem to lead an athlete's indolent, incurious life much of the time, testing their perfected bodies by clawing tree trunks, chewing on old skulls, executing acrobatic leaps, and then rousing themselves to the semiweekly antelope kill. Built with supreme hardness and economy, they make little allowance for man—they don't see him as different. They relish the flesh of his dogs, and they run up a tree when hunted and then sometimes spring down, as heavy as a chunk of iron wrapped in a flag. With stunning, gorgeous coats, their tight, dervish faces carved in a snarl, they head for the hereafter as if it were just one more extra-emphatic leap— as impersonal in death as the crack of the rifle was.

The American leopard, the jaguar, is a powerfully built, serious fellow, who, before white men arrived, wandered as far north as the Carolinas, but his best home is the humid basin of the Amazon. Mountain lions penetrate these ultimate jungles too, but rather thinly, thriving better in the cooler, drier climate of the untenanted pampas and on the mountain slopes. They are blessed with a pleasant but undazzling coat, tan except for a white belly, mouth and throat, and some black behind the ears, on the tip of the tail and at the sides of the nose, and so they are hunted as symbols, not for their fur. The cubs are spotted, leopardlike, much as lion cubs are. If all of the big cats developed from a common ancestry, the mountain lions' specialization has been unpresumptuous—away from bulk and savagery to traveling light. Toward deer, their prey, they may be as ferocious as leopards, but not toward chance acquaintances such as man. They some-times break their necks, their jaws, their teeth, springing against the necks of quarry they have crept close to—a fate in part resulting from the circumstance that they can't ferret out the weaker individuals in a herd by the device of a long chase, the way wolves do; they have to take the luck of the draw. None of the cats possess enough lung capacity for gruelling runs. They depend upon shock tactics, bursts of speed, sledge-hammer leaps, strong collarbones for hitting power, and shearing dentition, whereas wolves employ all the advantages of time in killing their quarry, as well as the numbers and gaiety of the pack, biting the beast's nose and rump—the technique of a thousand cuts—lapping the bloody snow. Wolves sometimes even have a cheering section of flapping ravens accompanying them, eager to scavenge after the brawl.

It's a risky business for the mountain lion, staking the strength and impact of his neck against the strength of the prey animal's neck. Necessarily, he is concentrated and fierce; yet legends exist that mountain lions have irritably defended men and women lost in the wilderness against marauding jaguars, who are no friends of theirs, and (with a good deal more supporting evidence) that they are susceptible to an odd kind of fascination with human beings. Sometimes they will tentatively seek an association, hanging about a campground or following a hiker out of curiosity, perhaps, circling around and bounding up on a ledge above to watch him pass. This mild modesty has helped preserve them from extinction. If they have been unable to make any adjustments to the advent of man, they haven't suicidally opposed him either, as the buffalo wolves and grizzlies did. In fact, at close quarters they seem bewildered. When treed, they don't breathe a hundred-proof ferocity but puzzle over what to do. They're too light-bodied to bear down on the hunter and kill him easily, even if they should attack—a course they seem to have no inclination for. In this century in the United States only one person, a child of thirteen, has been killed by a mountain lion; that was in 1924. And they're informal animals. Lolling in an informal sprawl on a high limb, they can't seem to summon any Enobarbus-like front of resistance for long. Daring men occasionally climb up and toss lassos about a cat and haul him down, strangling him by pulling from two directions, while the lion, mortified, appalled, never does muster his fighting aplomb. Although he could fight off a pack of wolves, he hasn't worked out a posture to assume toward man and his dogs. Impotently, he stiffens, as the dinosaurs must have when the atmosphere grew cold.

Someday hunting big game may come to be regarded as a form of vandalism, and the remaining big creatures of the wilderness will skulk through restricted reserves wearing radio transmitters and numbered collars, or bearing stripes of dye, as many elephants already do, to aid the busy biologists who track them from the air. Like a vanishing race of trolls, more report and memory than a reality, they will inhabit children's books and nostalgic articles, a special glamour attaching to those, like mountain lions, that are geographically incalculable and may still be sighted away from the preserves. Already we've become enthusiasts. We want game about us—at least at a summer house; it's part of privileged living. There is a precious privacy about seeing wildlife, too. Like meeting a fantastically dressed mute on the road, the fact that no words are exchanged and that *he's* not going to give an account makes the experience light-hearted; it's wholly ours. Besides, if anything out of the ordinary happened, we know we can't expect to be believed, and since it's rather fun to be disbelieved—fishermen know this—the privacy is even more complete. Deer, otter, foxes are messengers from another condition of life, another mentality, and bring us tidings of places where we don't go.

Ten years ago at Vavenby, a sawmill town on the North Thompson River in British Columbia, a frolicsome mountain lion used to appear at dusk every ten days or so in a bluegrass field alongside the river. Deer congregated there, the river was silky and swift, cooling the summer air, and it was a festive spot for a lion to be. She was thought to be a female, and reputedly left tracks around an enormous territory to the north and west—Raft Mountain, Battle Mountain, the Trophy Range, the Murtle River, and Mahood Lake—territory on an upended, pelagic scale, much of it scarcely accessible to a man by trail, where the tiger lilies grew four feet tall. She would materialize in this field among the deer five minutes before dark, as if checking in again, a habit that may have resulted in her death eventually, though for the present the farmer who observed her visits was keeping his mouth shut about it. This was pioneer country; there were people alive who could remember the time when poisoning the carcass of a cow would net a man a pile of dead predators —a family of mountain lions to bounty, maybe half a dozen wolves, and both black bears and grizzlies. The Indians considered lion meat a delicacy, but they had clans which drew their origins at the Creation from ancestral mountain lions, or wolves or bears, so these massacres amazed them. They thought the outright bounty hunters were crazy men.

Even before Columbus, mountain lions were probably not distributed in saturation numbers anywhere, as wolves may have been. Except for the family unit—a female with her half-grown cubs—each lion seems to occupy its own spread of territory, not as a result of fights with intruders but because the young transients share the same instinct for solitude and soon sheer off to find vacant mountains and valleys. A mature lion kills only one deer every week or two, according to a study by Maurice Hornocker in Idaho, and therefore is not really a notable factor in controlling the local deer population. Rather, it keeps watch contentedly as that population grows, sometimes benefitting the herds by scaring them onto new wintering grounds that are not overbrowsed, and by its very presence warding off other lions.

This thin distribution, coupled with the mountain lion's taciturn habits, make sighting one a matter of luck, even for game officials located in likely country. One warden in Colorado I talked to had indeed seen a pair of them fraternizing during the breeding season. He was driving a jeep over an abandoned mining road, and he passed two brown animals sitting peaceably in the grass, their heads close together. For a moment he thought they were coyotes and kept driving, when all of a sudden the picture registered that they were *cougars!* He braked and backed up, but of course they were gone. He was an old-timer, a man who had crawled inside bear dens to pull out the cubs, and knew where to find clusters of buffalo skulls in the recesses of the Rockies where the last bands had hidden; yet this cryptic instant when he was turning his jeep round a curve was the only glimpse—unprovable—that he ever got of a mountain lion.

Such glimpses usually are cryptic. During a summer I spent in Wyoming in my boyhood, I managed to see two coyotes, but both occasions were so fleeting that it required an act of faith on my part afterward to feel sure I had seen them. One of the animals vanished between rolls of ground; the other, in rougher, stonier, wooded country, cast his startled gray face in my direction and simply was gone. Hunching, he swerved for cover, and the brush closed over him. I used to climb to a vantage point above a high basin at twilight and watch the mule deer steal into the meadows to feed. The grass grew higher than their stomachs, the steep forest was close at hand, and they were as small and fragile-looking as filaments at that distance, quite human in coloring, gait and form. It was possible to visualize them as a naked Indian hunting party a hundred years before—or not to believe in their existence at all, either as Indians or deer. Minute, aphid-sized, they stepped so carefully in emerging, hundreds of feet below, that, straining my eyes, I needed to tell myself constantly that they were deer; my imagination, left to its own devices with the dusk settling down, would have made of them a dozen other creatures.

Recently, walking at night on the woods road that passes my house in Vermont, I heard footsteps in the leaves and windfalls. I waited, listening—they sounded too heavy to be anything less than a man, a large deer or a bear. A man wouldn't have been in the woods so late, my dog stood respectfully silent and still, and they did seem to shuffle portentously. Sure enough, after pausing at the edge of the road, a fully grown bear appeared, visible only in dimmest outline, staring in my direction for four or five seconds. The darkness lent a faintly red tinge to his coat; he was well built. Then, turning, he ambled off, almost immediately lost to view, though I heard the noise of his passage, interrupted by several pauses. It was all as concise as a vision, and since I had wanted to see a bear close to my own house, being a person who likes to live in a melting pot, whether in the city or country, and since it was too dark to pick out his tracks, I was grateful when the dog inquisitively urinated along the bear's path, thereby confirming that at least I had witnessed *something*. The dog seemed unsurprised, however, as if the scent were not all that remarkable, and, sure enough, the next week in the car I encountered a yearling bear in daylight two miles downhill, and a cub a month later. My farmer neighbors were politely skeptical of my accounts, having themselves caught sight of only perhaps a couple of bears in all their lives.

So it's with sympathy as well as an awareness of the tricks that enthusiasm and nightfall may play that I have been going to nearby towns seeking out people who have claimed at one time or another to have seen a mountain lion. The experts of the state—game wardens, taxidermists, the most accomplished hunters—emphatically discount the claims, but the believers are unshaken. They include some summer people who were enjoying a drink on the back terrace when the apparition of a great-tailed cat moved out along the fringe of the woods on a deer path;

a boy who was hunting with his .22 years ago near the village dump and saw the animal across a gully and fired blindly, then ran away and brought back a search party, which found a tuft of toast-colored fur; and a state forestry employee, a sober woodsman, who caught the cat in his headlights while driving through Victory Bog in the wildest corner of the Northeast Kingdom. Gordon Hickok, who works for a furniture factory and has shot one or two mountain lions on hunting trips in the West, saw one cross U.S. 5 at a place called Auger Hole near Mount Hor. He tracked it with dogs a short distance, finding a fawn with its head gnawed off. A high-school English teacher reported seeing a mountain lion cross another road, near Runaway Pond, but the hunters who quickly went out decided that the prints were those of a big bobcat, splayed impressively in the mud and snow. Fifteen years ago a watchman in the fire tower on top of Bald Mountain had left grain scattered in the grooves of a flat rock under the tower to feed several deer. One night, looking down just as the dusk turned murky, he saw two slim long-tailed lions creep out of the scrubby border of spruce and inspect the rock, sniffing deer droppings and dried deer saliva. The next night, when he was in his cabin, the dog barked and, looking out the window, again he saw the vague shape of a lion just vanishing.

A dozen loggers and woodsmen told me such stories. In the Adirondacks I've also heard some persuasive avowals —one by an old dog-sled driver and trapper, a French Canadian; another by the owner of a tourist zoo, who was exhibiting a Western cougar. In Vermont perhaps the most eager rumor buffs are some of the farmers. After all, now that packaged semen has replaced the awesome farm bull and so many procedures have been mechanized, who wants to lose *all* the adventure of farming? Until recently the last mountain lion known to have been killed in the Northeast was recorded in 1881 in Barnard, Vermont. However, it has been learned that probably another one was shot from a tree in 1931 in Mundleville, New Brunswick, and still another trapped seven years later in Somerset County in Maine. Bruce S. Wright, director of the Northeastern Wildlife Station (which is operated at the University of New Brunswick with international funding), is convinced that though they are exceedingly rare, mountain lions are still part of the fauna of the region; in fact, he has plaster casts of tracks to prove it, as well as a compilation of hundreds of reported sightings. Some people may have mistaken a golden retriever for a lion, or may have intended to foment a hoax, but all in all the evidence does seem promising. Indeed, after almost twenty years of search and study, Wright himself finally saw one.

The way these sightings crop up in groups has often been pooh-poohed as greenhorn fare or as a sympathetic hysteria among neighbors, but it is just as easily explained by the habit mountain lions have of establishing a territory that they scout through at intervals, visiting an auspicious deer-ridden swamp or remote ledgy mountain. Even at such a site a successful hunt could not be mounted without trained dogs, and if the population of the big cats was extremely sparse, requiring of them long journeys during the mating season, and yet with plenty of deer all over, they might not stay for long. One or two hundred miles is no obstacle to a Western cougar. The cat might inhabit a mountain ridge one year, and then never again.

Fifteen years ago, Francis Perry, who is an ebullient muffin of a man, a farmer all his life in Brownington, Vermont, saw a mountain lion "larger and taller than a collie, and grayish yellow" (he had seen them in circuses). Having set a trap for a woodchuck, he was on his way to visit the spot when he came over a rise and, at a distance of fifty yards, saw the beast engaged in eating the dead woodchuck. It bounded off, but Perry set four light fox traps for it around the woodchuck. Apparently, a night or two later the cat returned and got caught in three of these, but they couldn't hold it; it pulled free, leaving the marks of a struggle. Noel Perry, his brother, remembers how scared Francis looked when he came home from the first episode. Noel himself saw the cat (which may have meant that Brownington Swamp was one of its haunts that summer), once when it crossed a cow pasture on another farm the brothers owned, and once when it fled past his rabbit dogs through underbrush while he was training them—he thought for a second that its big streaking form was one of the dogs. A neighbor, Robert Chase, also saw the animal that year. Then again last summer, for the first time in fifteen years, Noel Perry saw a track as big as a bear's but round like a mountain lion's, and Robert's brother, Larry Chase, saw the actual cat several times one summer evening, playing a chummy hide-and-seek with him in the fields.

Elmer and Elizabeth Ambler are in their forties, populists politically, and have bought a farm in Glover to live the good life, though he is a truck driver in Massachusetts on weekdays and must drive hard in order to be home when he can. He's bald, with large eyebrows, handsome teeth and a low forehead, but altogether a strong-looking, clear, humane face. He is an informational kind of man who will give you the history of various breeds of cattle or a talk about taxation in a slow and musical voice, and both he and his wife, a purposeful, self-sufficient redhead, are fascinated by the possibility that they live in the wilderness. Beavers inhabit the river that flows past their house. The Amblers say that on Black Mountain nearby hunters "disappear" from time to time, and bears frequent the berry patches in their back field—they see them, their visitors see them, people on the road see them, their German shepherds meet them and run back drooling with fright. They've stocked their farm with horned Herefords instead of the polled variety so that the creatures can "defend themselves." Ambler is intrigued by the thought that apart from the danger of bears, someday "a cat" might prey on one of his cows. Last year, looking out the back window, his wife saw through binoculars an animal with a flowing tail and "a cat's gallop" following a line of trees where the deer go, several hundred yards uphill behind the house. Later, Ambler went up on snowshoes and found tracks as big as their shepherds'; the dogs obligingly ran alongside. He saw walking tracks, leaping tracks and deer tracks marked with blood going toward higher ground. He wonders whether the cat will ever attack him. There are plenty of bobcats around, but they both say they know the difference. The splendid, nervous *tail* is what people must have identified in order to claim they have seen a mountain lion.

I, too, cherish the notion that I may have seen a lion. Mine was crouched on an overlook above a grass-grown, steeply pitched wash in the Alberta Rockies—a much more likely setting than anywhere in New England. It was late afternoon on my last day at Maligne Lake, where I had been staying with my father at a national-park chalet. I was twenty; I could walk forever or could climb endlessly in a sanguine scramble, going out every day as far as my legs carried me, swinging around for home before the sun went down. Earlier, in the valley of the Athabasca, I had found several winter-starved or wolf-killed deer, well picked and scattered, and an area with many elk antlers strewn on the ground where the herds had wintered safely, dropping their antlers but not their bones. Here, much higher up, in the bright plenitude of the summer, I had watched two wolves and a stately bull moose in one mountain basin, and had been up on the caribou barrens on the ridge west of the lake and brought back the talons of a hawk I'd found dead on the ground. Whenever I was watching game, a sort of stopwatch in me started running. These were moments of intense importance and intimacy, of new intimations and aptitudes. Time had a jam-packed character, as it does during a mile run.

I was good at moving quietly through the woods and at spotting game, and was appropriately exuberant. The finest, longest day of my stay was the last. Going east, climbing through a luxuriant terrain of up-and-down boulders, brief brilliant glades, sudden potholes fifty feet deep—a forest of moss-hung lodgepole pines and firs and spare, gaunt spruce with the black lower branches broken off— I came upon the remains of a young bear, which had been torn up and shredded. Perhaps wolves had cornered it during some imprudent excursion in the early spring. (Bears often wake up while the snow is still deep, dig themselves out and rummage around in the neighborhood sleepily for a day or two before bedding down again under a fallen tree.) I took the skull along so that I could extract the teeth when I got hold of some tools. Discoveries like this represent a superfluity of wildlife and show how many beasts there are scouting about.

I went higher. The marmots whistled familially; the tall trees wilted to stubs of themselves. A pretty stream led down a defile from a series of openings in front of the ultimate barrier of a vast mountain wall which I had been looking at from a distance each day on my outings. It wasn't too steep to be climbed, but it was a barrier because my energies were not sufficient to scale it and bring me back the same night. Besides, it stretched so majestically, surflike above the lesser ridges, that I liked to think of it as the Continental Divide.

On my left as I went up this wash was an abrupt, grassy slope that enjoyed a southern exposure and was sunny and windblown all winter, which kept it fairly free of snow. The ranger at the lake had told me it served as a wintering ground for a few bighorn sheep and for a band of mountain goats, three of which were in sight. As I approached laboriously, these white, pointy-horned fellows drifted up over a rise, managing to combine their retreat with some nippy good grazing as they went, not to give any pursuer the impression that they had been pushed into flight. I took my time too, climbing to locate the spring in a precipitous cleft of rock where the band did most of its drinking, and finding the shallow, high-ceilinged cave where the goats had sheltered from storms, presumably for generations. The floor was layered with rubbery droppings, tramped down and sprinkled with tufts of shed fur, and the back wall was checkered with footholds where the goats liked to clamber and perch. Here and there was a horn lying loose—a memento for me to add to my collection from an old individual that had died a natural death, secure in the band's winter stronghold. A bold, thriving family of pack rats emerged to observe me. They lived mainly on the nutritives in the droppings, and were used to the goats' tolerance; they seemed astonished when I tossed a stone.

I kept scrabbling along the side of the slope to a section of outcroppings where the going was harder. After perhaps half an hour, crawling around a corner, I found myself faced with a bighorn ram who was taking his ease on several square yards of bare earth between large rocks, a little above the level of my head. Just as surprised as I, he stood up. He must have construed the sounds of my advance to be those of another sheep or goat. His horns had made a complete curl and then some; they were thick, massive and bunched together like a high Roman helmet, and he himself was muscly and military, with a grave-looking nose. A squared-off, middle-aged, trophy-type ram, full of imposing professionalism, he was at the stage of life when rams sometimes stop herding and live as rogues.

He turned and tried a couple of possible exits from the pocket where I had found him, but the ground was badly pitched and would require a reeling gait and loss of dignity. Since we were within a national park and obviously I was unarmed, he simply was not inclined to put himself to so much trouble. He stood fifteen or twenty feet above me, pushing his tongue out through his teeth, shaking his head slightly and dipping it into charging position as I moved closer by a step or two, raising my hand slowly toward him in what I proposed as a friendly greeting. The day had been a banner one since the beginning, so while I recognized immediately that this meeting would be a valued memory, I felt as natural in his company as if he were a friend of mine reincarnated in a shag suit. I saw also that he was going to knock me for a loop, head over heels down the steep slope, if I sidled nearer, because he did not by any means feel as expansive and exuberant at our encounter as I did. That was the chief difference between us. I was talking to him with easy gladness, and beaming; he was not. He was unsettled and on his mettle, waiting for me to move along, the way a bighorn sheep waits for a predator to move on in wildlife movies when each would be evenly matched in a contest of strength and position. Although his warlike nose and high bone helmet, blocky and beautiful as weaponry, kept me from giving in to my sense that we were brothers, I knew I could stand there for a long while. His coat was a down-

64

to-earth brown, edgy with muscle, his head was that of
an unsmiling veteran standing to arms, and despite my
reluctance to treat him as some sort of boxed-in prize, I
might have stayed on for half the afternoon if I hadn't
realized that I had other sights to see. It was not a day
to dawdle.

I trudged up the wash and continued until, past tree
line, the terrain widened and flattened in front of a preliminary ridge that formed an obstacle before the great
roaring, silent, surflike mountain wall that I liked to think
of as the Continental Divide, although it wasn't. A cirque
separated the preliminary ridge from the ultimate divide,
which I still hoped to climb to and look over. The opening
into this was roomy enough, except for being littered with
enormous boulders, and I began trying to make my way
across them. Each was boat-sized and rested upon under-
boulders; it was like running in place. After tussling with
this landscape for an hour or two, I was limp and sweating, pinching my cramped legs. The sun had gone so low
that I knew I would be finding my way home by moonlight
in any case, and I could see into the cirque, which was
big and symmetrical and presented a view of sheer bar-
barism; everywhere were these cruel boat-sized boulders.

Giving up and descending to the goats' draw again, I
had a drink from the stream and bathed before climbing
farther downward. The grass was green, sweet-smelling,
and I felt safely close to life after that sea of dead boulders. I knew I would never be physically younger or in finer
country; even then the wilderness was singing its swan
song. I had no other challenges in mind, and though very

tired, I liked looking up at the routes where I'd climbed. The trio of goats had not returned, but I could see their wintering cave and the cleft in the rocks where the spring was. Curiously, the bighorn ram had not left; he had only withdrawn upward, shifting away from the outcroppings to an open sweep of space where every avenue of escape was available. He was lying on a carpet of grass and, lonely pirate that he was, had his head turned in my direction.

It was from this same wash that looking up, I spotted the animal I took to be a mountain lion. He was skulking among some outcroppings at a point lower on the mountainside than the ledges where the ram originally had been. A pair of hawks or eagles were swooping at him by turns, as if he were close to a nest. The slant between us was steep, but the light of evening was still more than adequate. I did not really see the wonderful tail—that special medallion—nor was he particularly big for a lion. He was gloriously catlike and slinky, however, and so indifferent to the swooping birds as to seem oblivious of them. There are plenty of creatures he wasn't: he wasn't a marmot, a goat or other grass-eater, a badger, a wolf or coyote or fisher. He *may* have been a big bobcat or a wolverine, although he looked ideally lion-colored. He had a cat's strong collarbone structure for hitting, powerful haunches for vaulting, and the almost mystically small head mountain lions possess, with the gooseberry eyes. Anyway, I believed him to be a mountain lion, and standing quietly I watched him as he inspected in leisurely fashion the ledge that he was on and the one under him savory with every trace of goat—frosty-colored with the white hairs they'd shed. The sight was so dramatic that it seemed to be happening close to me, though in fact he and the hawks or eagles, whatever they were, were miniaturized by distance.

If I'd kept motionless, eventually I could have seen whether he had the proper tail, but such scientific questions had no weight next to my need to essay some kind of communication with him. It had been exactly the same when I'd watched the two wolves playing together a couple of days before. They were above me, absorbed in their game of noses-and-paws. I had recognized that I might never witness such a scene again, yet I couldn't hold myself in. Instead of talking and raising my arm to them, as I had with the ram, I'd shuffled forward impetuously as if to say *Here I am!* Now, with the lion, I tried hard to dampen my impulse and restrained myself as long as I could. Then I stepped toward him, just barely squelching a cry in my throat but lifting my hand—as clumsy as anyone is who is trying to attract attention.

At that, of course, he swerved aside instantly and was gone. Even the two birds vanished. Foolish, triumphant and disappointed, I hiked on down into the lower forests, gargantuanly tangled, another life zone—not one which would exclude a lion but one where he would not be seen. I'd got my second wind and walked lightly and softly, letting the silvery darkness settle around me. The blowdowns were as black as whales; my feet sank in the moss. Clearly this was as crowded a day as I would ever have, and I knew my real problem would not be to make myself

believed but rather to make myself understood at all, simply in reporting the story, and that I must at least keep
the memory straight for myself. I was so happy that I was
unerring in distinguishing the deer trails going my way.
The forest's night beauty was supreme in its promise, and
I didn't hurry.

SPLENDID,
WITH
TRUMPETS

Splendid with trumpets, the circus is back. It is important that this be announced because, for example, Tito Gaona, who is considered the greatest trapezist in history, is performing, as well as Gunther Gebel-Williams, who is downright sublime—the best animal trainer that America has seen within my span of memory, at least. Gebel-Williams is a sort of a Felix Krull —a creature of joy—and at the same time a conquering Alexander. He is supreme in the circus world for the sweep of his talents, but more than simply being versatile, he is inspired, performs with a sixth or a seventh sense, and a generation from now will still be the measure of how good another man is.

Tigers are a gorgeous culmination, fine-edged, private virtuosos, highly honed. The decoration of their coats prefigures their dramatic moods—the black spells and red-yellow blasts of sound. Elephants are the wise-heads of the animal world, beasts that by rights ought to survive us all. So if you have a child who likes animals and dreams

69

of living close to them, or likes grace and heroics, you must take him to see Gebel-Williams. Forty years from now, if there are still circuses, he'll go to one and will say with a smile, yes, that fellow is certainly good enough, but he can't match what *Gebel-Williams* used to do. And you— if you buy tickets early for Nureyev and Marcel Marceau, you must watch Gebel-Williams. In show business, he is the very best.

There are also some lions, exercised with much fustian by Wolfgang Holzmair. La Toria performs her quaint, severe "loop-swings." Pio Nock clowns on the high wire with his family ensemble, voicing the terror that the rest of us feel, and a man called Doval walks up there alone, intimate with the air itself, to a fluttering, unnerving roll of the drums. Twenty years ago I took a dim view of acts like Doval's. Harold Alzana was the wire-walker then, and I felt that many in the audience were hoping he was going to fall. I was in my teens and I supposed that I (and Alzana) need never die. Actually, the artifice of the circus operates in such a way that it may be the last place left where somebody can teeter on the brink of death and the crowd *won't* yell "Jump." Somehow they find that his triumph encompasses them.

A Spaniard, Gran Picaso, plays five-star Frisbee with one hand and juggles ping-pong balls using only the currents of his hot breath. Gheorghe Ionel burlesques with four Rumanian brown bears. A bonbon-type Pole named Nowaka does stripper kicks on a tight wire. Lou Jacobs carries a shoe in a gilded birdcage and whistles its songs. The clowns have sharpened their traditional routines, and

fizz dolefully across the rings, seeming to fill the hippodrome—though, as always, the biggest laughs come not
from the complicated skits they have worked out but just
when they drop their poor pants. There are speedy new
clowns, new colors, new gags. A baby outwits its nurse; a
rabbit gets the better of a mean hunter. "Teddy Trom-
bone" is played for the clowns, who hassle the band by
blowing a rusty mellophone. But they step back when the
chimps scramble past. Chimps hate clowns, thinking that
they're making fun of them with those weird faces, and
elephants dislike the clowns' dogs and are likely to do away
with one of them with a swipe of the trunk. The band-
leader is pursy-mouthed from puckering to blow for these
many years, but the ringmaster is a bluff roast-beef show-
man with lots of voice and teeth. He is loud-looking, like
the drummers whom country girls used to be warned of.

The band is a clock. Solemnly the horses clop into position, a marching army. Two girls spin by their teeth,
carillons rejoice, and the cheers of the house have an
underpinning of tubas. The men give a gladiator's salute—
we who are about to die—but fortunately they don't.
"Hoopla!" says the Bulgarian gymnast Silagi, landing
safely. "Hiiii!" says La Toria as she finishes one hundred
and seventy of her swings by one wrist—which may be a
record and is hundred more than she was doing last year.

Backstage, the big fellow who wears the Gargantua suit
stands resting in the bottom half of the costume with his
arm thrown fraternally around its top. Elena Ben Said is
kissing her pigeons and rubbing their feathers with her
soft throat. In the sour-smelling tunnels under the seats,

71

some of the ballet girls are getting goosed; there is a good deal of foreplay, hoots from the dressing room. Some of them are professional showgirls from Florida; others the elfin, disciplined troupers who speak with an accent and perform derring-do. I remember the thirst of watching them sunning in swimsuits between shows, or tripping in sandals to lunch, as part of the summer's heat and thirst. They straighten their bodices, touching their toes in the rosin tray. They have pink bodies and accented eyes; the men have sharp night owls' faces and a foxy look.

Long nets are in evidence under all the high-wire acts because Isabella Nock fell from her trapeze bar two weeks ago. Her heels slipped when she was trying to catch herself by them, and the lumbering fat roustabout whom you see standing underneath her bravely caught her as she fell, tumbling over, spraining his ankle. That's why he limps. The girls pose on high poles and wires with stony faces while the music plays sadly and gravely; then on the ground again they beam like the rising sun, walking out waving, with a bride's wedding smile. Offstage, a dwarf clown mimics exactly the dancing motions of another dwarf who is in the ring, thumbing his nose at him. The lion trainer trips up an Indian chief. The chimps scream as they are stuffed in their cages. There's a continual ruffle of noise from the crowd, a shrill rush of joy as the elephants come on—a low bridge for the elephant girls. Gebel-Williams crosses the tops of his elephants' backs like a hobo traversing freight cars. (Elephants' heads should be a phrenologist's delight—all knobby configurations—though they are chinless.)

The clowns serve for continuity in the show, observing

everything that goes on along with the crowd. During the "specs" and "animal walks" they swarm through the procession of wagons, myth figures and women in body stockings, and like kooks in a madhouse, carom off one another: gung-ho, salacious dwarfs who gallop; chalk-cheeked, misguided eightballs; and the various plaster animals (sometimes the soreheads are assigned to wear these get-ups so that the children don't have to see them). Jokes flower, water is squirted, and bombs go off. The youngest clown —a new runaway from home—is chased around the hippodrome track by a luminous skeleton wired to his back, and instead of the gag of the overfull auto, a "computer" grinds out additional clowns. Young fellows like Mike Bourbon, prancing in whiteface, and Doug Ashton, tough, zany, in minimal makeup, beating his way through the show, mix with Swede Johnson, an old rodeo clown in a seedy cop's jacket, and the Janus Brothers, two midgets in ruffles, whose egos are a running sore. Midgets seldom seem as happy as dwarfs. Built like babies, they are treated badly, being so miniaturized. Dwarfs are larger and, unlike midgets, are not proportioned the same way that other people are. Though their heads and trunks are almost normal in size, their legs and arms are warped, and somehow they capitalize on being misshapen and out of their deformity invent a style. The opposite of cute, they run all the more—they run everywhere, flailing their arms. Rugged, blasphemous-looking characters with a formidable stride, almost a charge, they scamper along peering up skirts, chuckling, cocking their heads at any man, as if to say *The bigger you are . . .*

In the march-around everybody turns out; the girls and

the elephants pass and repass, both the essence of the circus. Gebel-Williams vaults up onto the backs of his beasts as if up palace stairs. The band plays a cidery march. "Watch the stilts! Watch the stilts!" shouts the performance director, Bob Dover. He sorts through the dozen parade displays to set them in order, acting as traffic cop. He's comparatively young and looks like John Cassavetes, sloping and boyish, except that his eyes are devoid of expression. A shy, benign, sorrowful man, he ran away from home as a boy and came under the wing of the late Pat Valdo, then dean of the circus. It was probably not altogether a comfortable wing to be under, but as his successor he is coming into his own at last, married to a dancing girl, and hustling stray patrons out of danger, waving to the men at the spotlights when they are missing the action.

The teeterboard tumblers are proper martinets. The jugglers put ninepins and hoops in the air. Ponies and sulkies wheel round and round. The aerialists throw mirror-shadows of themselves on the ceiling and walls. The elephants rush in and out again. With clodhopper feet like big cannon shells and cracked- mud hides, squinting like Moby Dick going underwater, they run as if to the rescue. The horses also enter and leave the hippodrome at terrific speed—keyed up, of course, by their handlers. The man who is holding the lead pair will swing between them with his feet off the ground, and sometimes when there aren't enough hands to rustle them all, whole herds rush by on their own for the exit.

Once in the Madison Square Garden on 51st Street,

I saw Marilyn Monroe nearly trampled. She was on the animal ramp with a bunch of photographers, being escorted to pose for pictures in the basement. Still a flibberty lovely, she was in the process of divorcing DiMaggio, and was strolling in the center of a mob of assorted nightblossoms and plug-uglies, with her cosmetician just in front of her, touching her up, and a hairdresser following her closely, tweaking the curls on her neck. Suddenly the ramp shook with hooves, and about twenty liberty horses came tearing down at a gallop, with only two youngsters attending them. They had guyed them up for a Cossack trip and now were trying to brake them. The photogs and the rest of us fled to the side like good city cowards, leaving Marilyn squarely a target, but providentially a circus straw boss happened to be in the group—a tent foreman in a big hat, who here in New York had nothing to do. Just as the horses arrived, he flung himself across the ramp at Marilyn and knocked her breath out against the far wall. When she finally got down to the basement, she didn't fare very much better. The photographers pressed her so hard that she was backed almost against the tigers' cage without knowing it. Several of them roared at her from a distance of less than a yard and reduced her to tears. But still she was willing. After her people had fixed up her makeup she climbed on an elephant, but felt such vertigo when the elephant dipped that one of her breasts fell out of her dress. The cameramen lowered their instruments because the pictures weren't usable.

This year the most beautiful girl in the circus is Sarah

Chapman. She appears in the aerial ballet, then on an elephant and on a trapeze, while her husband, a wonderfully fussy, fastidious clown, a veteran hero who once suffered a forty-foot fall himself, stands underneath. Though as a star her abilities are not much above mediocre, her hair is a feathery, jet-black brush set off by her white skin, her arms are as round as a dancer's, and her smile has a special symmetry. She reminds me of an aerialist I once had a crush on. That lady divorced the scion of a high-wire family to marry the circus veterinarian—in the circus world a distinct step down. She performed alone after that, doing a classic cloud swing while standing on her head. She was often around the horse tents with her husband or playing with the baby leopards, looking lovely indeed with her hair tied back in a puff on her neck because of the heat, wearing frilly blouses, her teeth and features uneven and sweet, although she could smile in the limelight like an athlete. The vet was a popular man, their marriage was good, and I was a youngster agog, of course, not insinuating. Four years ago she died, leaving him mourning. He is still in charge of the horses, a civilized white-haired man with glasses perching on a sun-blistered nose. He goes fishing when the circus is out in the country, knowing from many years past where to go in every state, and late in the afternoon he will reminisce in the office wagon about the quarterhorse stallions that he used to buy from the King Ranch in Texas when he was building Ringling Bros.' herd. A horse act is like a typewriter, he says, cued the same way all over the world.

Doc Henderson, Lloyd Morgan, Trolle Rhodin and Tuffy Genders are some of the core of old-timers who operate the show. It is costumed prismatically, as usual, and is slick and light-footed—in fact, too light-footed. It has been staged at a tap-tap-tap tempo that allows little time for us to absorb the incredible, and leaves us instead with some aridly tune-filled stretches that disjoint and demean the traditional center of gravity of a circus. The march band has become a dance band, all saxes, minor-ironic. On opening night, the flyer Tito Gaona had an accident while doing a triple, apparently from hurrying— he hit the catcher's swing and nearly broke his leg. He went ahead with another triple nevertheless, blindfolded, but some of the other acts are really not very good, no replacement at all for Rogana, Fatini and Zachini, who have left Ringling Bros. within the past year. Even Doval, who is flashy and polished on the high wire, seems to take himself and his feats for granted after a lifetime at them, overstressing what's hard but faking fake falls perfunctorily. Harold Alzana, who began life as a coal miner, never let his act go stale in that way.

If the show has thinned slightly from last year's in the pursuit of freshness and songfests, however, the Broadway minds who conceive and guide it are at fault, not the performers. More and more toy animals are parading— penguins, kangaroos, pythons—but fewer real ones. An incongruous hayride-hoedown motif slows the show down, and then a dangerous racing haste is expected of the stars when at last their turn comes to perform.

A toy-manufacturing conglomerate, Mattel, Inc., is

acquiring Ringling Bros. and Barnum & Bailey, although its present stockholders only bought it from John Ringling North three years ago. (Their profit is said to be 600 percent.) This further depersonalization is probably bad news. We must hope that the performers, whose splendor and daring we can scarcely glimpse from our distant seats, will be decently dealt with by their new owners. The servitude in which circus people dwell is a deeper one than that of ballplayers, for instance. Their lives hang in the balance, they are paid rather little, they do not garner much publicity, and apart from a handful of struggling "mud" circuses, in this country there is only one organization that they can work for. They deserve better.

FRED KING

ON THE

ALLAGASH

One of the arguments used by the logging industry in opposing proposals that a few wilderness areas be set aside is that there is no real wilderness left in the Northeast, anyway, or east of the Mississippi, or in any mountain range in the West that may be discussed—no tract of forest that hasn't already been logged, no river drainage that hasn't been dammed. It's all gone now, say the lumbermen complacently. But it's all that we have, the conservationists insist, and so the battle is joined.

On the Allagash watershed in northern Maine, woods that have been logged over three or four times, a compromise was struck. The lumbermen gave up very little of their land, and yet the first of the nation's officially "wild" rivers was brought under state control—conveyed, in effect, to the canoeists. Because of where it is and because the acreage involved is small (24,000 acres in government hands, versus 1.1 million, for example, in the Boundary Waters Canoe Area of Minnesota), the Allagash

Wilderness Waterway has quickly come under recreational pressure, perhaps representing the managerial
dilemmas other areas will soon face. I wanted to see what
it was like, and—most unfashionably in this democratic
age—hired a guide so that I could use my paddle as a
writing table part of the time and, being a novice, not
bother with questions of navigation.

Fred King was talking about bush pilots in the motel
at Shin Pond, where we met. He said there were old
pilots and bold pilots, but he knew of one who was both
old and bold. This man would fly out a sick fisherman at
night in a little plane with no instruments, by moonlight
alone. Fred King keeps track of these things. He's fifty-
eight, looks forty-five, has short hair which is bluish gray,
round glasses, a boyish doggy grin, a face deeply cut by
grinning and a mouth big enough to grin with. It's a
pleasing face; his body is straight and quick like a chipmunk's and he has an immediate laugh, provocatively
loud, and likes to stop still when on the move and sound
off on the matter at hand, then impulsively move forward
again, seeming never to walk if he can run. At home in
Augusta he keeps a jug of Allagash water to mix with his
drinks, and doesn't much like December because of the
short days; "I'd sell December awfully cheap." Until he
became too controversial for the local talk show, he would
go on TV in December, in his red guide's shirt, and kill
the long evenings that way.

It's only been in the past ten years that Fred has canoed.
His father died when he was young, and though he had
started in college with the idea of graduating as an

engineer, he quit and went off for two years to the woods, wintering in a cabin he built for himself six days distant by team and wagon from the community of Ashland, Maine. He was trying to trap—this was in the middle of the Depression—but went about it wrong. The right-headed way to learn how to trap would have been to pair up with an older fellow and learn from him, he says. Instead he had a full-time job just surviving, and during the first winter had to reinforce his roof with material hauled on a toboggan from an abandoned shanty several miles away.

He still likes to be by himself. His ideas sound as if they had been worked out in isolation in the woods and perhaps spoken first in a loud voice all alone. He has a tight shipshape cabin on Chemquassabamticook Lake where he goes in midwinter and works on improvements, hauling now with a snowmobile. He's got to break trail for the snowmobile on snowshoes—it's not like the ads—but he loves the rigor of the winter woods, cooks for himself and sleeps fitfully, listening to the radio and waiting for his mouse trap to snap. The mice he feeds to the gorbies—Canada jays—outside.

Fred worked on highway crews and during World War II was a shipyard pipe-fitter in Portland, but has been self-employed ever since. He would buy a piece of land and build a house on it, doing all the work, then "find somebody fool enough to buy." By fifty he tired of that, not so much because it was strenuous as because he wanted to go back to his original vision of himself. Though not an exceptional woodsman, he's taken the trouble to learn some of the historical lore, and particularly to latch onto a few of the vanishing old rivermen and listen and learn from them, trying modestly to carry on some of the traditions in their name. He also has a kind of guffawing admiration of wealth: more successful men who have blasted a steadier ascent in the world he calls "roosters." "Quite a rooster," he'll say of a fellow who wears nifty clothes nowadays, and will boisterously recite a ditty he learned in school:

> "Dear Lord, in the battle that goes on through life,
> I ask but a field that is fair. . .
> A chance that is equal to all in the strife,
> And the courage to do and to dare.
> And if I should win, let it be by the code,
> With my faith and my honor held high,
> And if I should lose, let me stand by the road
>   and cheer as the winner goes by."

Another old chestnut of his is, "So late we get smart, so soon we get old."

The Allagash flows north for ninety-some miles. Its headwaters connect several lakes, and were tampered with in the 1840's by loggers who were competing to float the logs south to the Penobscot and down to Bangor instead of north on the Allagash to Canada by way of the St. John River. The tampering has since been set straight, and now a parking lot has been laid out beside the Great Northern Paper Company's bridge at Chamberlain Lake, a two and a half-hour drive from the nearest town. Fifty-four hundred people were waterborne on the Allagash in

1970, a number that's rising 15 percent a year and is concentrated in the two warmest months, so that the state authorities know that soon they will have to institute a system of advance reservations. The campgrounds, however, are tactfully dispersed, and though logging is going on within four hundred feet of the water, a screen of trees, deceptive but pristine-looking, has been left, like the false fronting of a movie-set street.

We put in at Chamberlain on July 17th in a brisk splashing wind, our old-fashioned cedar canoes contrasting with the light aluminum canoes more modernist types were using—the Sierra Club fellows with their families and dogs who fill up his stage set and offend Fred King's sense of what's wild. The vacationers who employ King like his big tents and good steaks on ice and the canned provisions and sauces he brings, though they're not sure they're roughing it properly. The chic way to travel requires carrying thin packets of freeze-dried food, and not much of it, and feather-light sleeping equipment such as backpacking mountaineers have more reason to want— a line that Fred doesn't swallow at all. In the first place, the men he admires, "Moosetowners" who are now in their eighties, used to earn their living poling thirty-foot bateaux up the Allagash loaded with tons of supplies. The measure of manhood was not roughing it on dehydrated foods but hefting a great big load on a portage and living well. Also, the Maine woodsman usually respected the rich as people who had won their spurs in another world, and did not expect them to prove themselves in the woods with feats of do-it-yourself, but were perfectly willing to

cater to the "sports" a bit for good pay. Fred says the
Sierra Club characters (most of them "lefties"), with
their "tin," "bang-bang" canoes, look like internees as they
stand in a row waiting for reconstituted soup to be ladled
into the tin bowls they hold. Instead of enjoying a meal,
they study their maps as if they were eating them.

We sports in his party probably weren't up to the role.
Sports lately are "pilgrims," he says laughingly, "groping
for something." They believe, as he does too, that even
in its protected status the Allagash River is being altered
irrevocably, and so they have rushed to experience it
before the herds finish it off. But his customers admire the
conservationists and disdain the lumbermen who controlled the region until now, while he admires the lumbermen and has little use for the Johnny-come-lately conservationists. They think that a rainy day on a canoe trip
is a disaster and therefore to be wet and uncomfortable
on a rainy day is natural, whereas he thinks that rain is
natural and that to be wet and uncomfortable on a rainy
day is unnecessary and unnatural.

We had sun, the trees thrashed in the wind and the
surface rippled in shark's-teeth patterns as we went up
the lake, until we turned close to the western shore. There
were mud beaches every quarter-mile. Chamberlain
is an expansive lake, with salmon and togue, and is
potentially dangerous when the wind rises. As we crossed
toward Lock Dam the waves ruffled up to the gunwhale.
King said that a canoeman's basic instrument was his pole,
not his paddle (referring again to the old-timers), so that
this deep-water stuff was an uneasy business for them.
We were using an outboard motor, however. I was a

passenger in the bow, his other customers, a Long Island couple, being towed in the second canoe.

The lock tender himself was a summer visitor, a white-haired salesman with an ulcer whose wife wrote children's books. He gave us a couple of minutes of lively water to get us started down the two miles of river that flows into Eagle Lake. Its pitch for a moment looked steep, brimming around us, and we could see varicolored streaks, as lurid as tropical fish, on the rocks underneath us where canoes had scraped. King gave a lesson in snubbing downstream with a pole, the bow being loaded heavily and the steering done by holding the canoe's stern in position, letting the current work on the bow. We saw a muskrat, a loon, and beaver-work in the winding channels, and then emerged on a wide, even prettier lake, the shoreline more indented than Chamberlain's, with moosier swards by the water and a hillier setting, with plenty of leafy hardwoods high up and behind. Terns, ducks, two loons, and an osprey flew over, and we had a fresh breeze at our tail. The loons whinnied in clarinet tones. At Pillsbury Island a boys' camp was in possession, with a great many canoes. We were using the motor all the way, intending to put twenty miles behind us, because in these public playgrounds one must travel out of phase with the particular contingent of enthusiasts who happened to start down the chute the same day, yet not catch up with the parties who set out previously.

We ran into waves tipped with whitecaps, the wind shifting into a headwind, and a navy-blue curtain lowered in front of us. The murky curtain turned purple, the water turned black and the wind hard and strong—the waves coming in gusts, the canoe shipping water—as we met the storm. It was a smothering front, and passing beyond it, we were soaked by a pellety rain, but found some protection in the lee of Farm Island, then in a narrows, where we tied up at Priest's Camp. In the drumbeating rain as, laughing, we threw up our tents, Fred pretended we'd almost drowned to make it more dramatic for us. He said that when he first began guiding he'd been scared he might do something wrong and had gone to an old-timer for advice: "Just take lots of eggs and jam, Fred."

We were sharing the site with a middle-aged Boston couple, the man equipped with muttonchops and a mustache like an English eccentric, and two local Maine fishermen who, trusting in the fact that it was mid-July, had neglected to bring a tent. Fred probably would have lent the Boston people some scraps of canvas, but he left the Maine men to sleep in discomfort under their canoe because they ought to have known better. My own companions were from Oyster Bay, the husband, Jim, once a Marine first lieutenant, now a market-research chieftain, well-heeled, revisiting his memories of sleeping on the ground in the Pacific theater thirty years ago, which he'd promised himself that he never would do again. He had four kids at home, a narrow head, a large jaw and a pouchy face that looked as if he had laughed at his boss's jokes about five thousand times too often, a face that looked as if maybe he had been served up one of his kids at a business lunch once and had gone ahead and eaten it anyway. But he was smoothly bright and intelligent, what is called an omnivorous reader, slept lightly, and was skillful and pleasant and easy with people. His wife, Audrey, whom I liked better, wore a tously blond wig over long black hair that she thought was "too oily," had a touching squint, a good heart and dental trouble. She was soft-natured, vaguely appealing, more loving than loved, a hard struggler; she loyally tramped after her husband in all his nerve-testing undertakings—climbing to fire towers, and so on—and was never allowed to be tired or scared. On Long Island, she said, she ran with him around the high-school track every morning at six o'clock, although she hated it. After twenty-eight years of marriage the word "dear" sounded sad when he said it, but they'd brought along nine days' worth of mixed martinis in plastic bottles, as well as a dose of the anti-Semitism which is sometimes an ingredient of stories around the camp fire. Fred partook too.

Next morning we went to look at a relict tramway which had hauled saw logs in the first years of this century, and a railroad spur used for pulpwood later on, both constructed in order to get the logs from this lake into a different drainage that would carry them south. During the 1920's as many as five thousand men worked here. Beans were cooked all night in holes in the ground; the hogs that went on the table along with the beans were kept on Hog Island. Farm Island was for pasturing the oxen, but half of it was never cleared and is still black spruce. Black spruce and white, and sedges and cattails, cover this industrial blur where "Dynamite" Murphy, the dynamiter, and other famous figures once worked. Now a mother duck was running on the water with flapping wings, teaching her babies to fly. I'm such a child of the times that although half of my ancestors were lumbermen in the West, when talking to a proud lumberman of today I all but blush for him as he recounts his exploits, so King and I didn't always see eye to eye at the railroad site.

We circled the lake, slipping into each estuary and up Soper Brook, then up Snare Brook. Dozens of ducks; fish nests down through the water, scooped in the gravel. A great blue heron flew up. A dragonfly chased by a king-bird got away by dodging close to our bow. The brooks were silty but the wetland grasses were a tender light-green. After a half-mile or so the alder growth would close in and beaver cuttings would block the brook, and where we had to stop we'd see moose tracks. When we walked, Fred was quick, and with his small intelligent face looked like a professor afield, though his right arm is beginning to go bad on him—too much holding a chain saw. In the black-fly season he sometimes sews his socks to his pants to protect his ankles, and leaves them on for four or five days, he said.

We admired clusters of magnificent white pine left by the spruce and fir loggers of recent times. The original booty up here was pine. Some trees were a hundred and fifty feet high, seven feet thick at the butt, and wanted for naval masts. Before chopping such a whopper, the loggers would throw a nearby spruce against it, climb to the top of the spruce and so reach the climbable branches of the pine, from which they could see for ten miles across a great spread of spruce forest to other "veins" of pine.

We stayed at Priest's Camp a second evening, enjoying a rainbow. A boys' outing party arrived, and there was a special avidity in the way King and Jim and Audrey watched them set up their camp: *these* boys weren't smoking pot. Rain fell hard most of the night, until a clearing shower came just at dawn. Then trilling loons and King's cry, "Wake up, wake up, up with the butter-cups!" I imagined him as the "cookee" around a logging camp in the old days whose light weight kept him from competing in physical feats with some of the men but who bubbled with jokes whenever they broke off work for a meal. He said, though, that he hadn't developed much interest in people until his late forties, having been con-cerned before then with excavations, machinery and physics.

We always started earlier than anyone else, just as we seized the best campgrounds and pushed past the trippers at every point, but the advantage of this for observing game was lost, either because of the outboard motor or else King's loud anecdotes echoing on the water. At such times, before the sun rose, when for an hour we had the Allagash to ourselves, he exasperated me and I was sorry I'd come with a guide, but of course from his standpoint this silence-on-the-waters was more Sierra Club nonsense. The old-timers moved through frontier America hollering as loud as could be, unless they were hunting—cutting the silence with hoots, dispelling some of the loneliness of the woods and warning the panthers and bears away.

To this day, in parts of Alaska where there are grizzlies a prospector will put a stone in a tin can inside his pack, so that he walks with a constant *clink-clank*.

In the passage from Eagle to Churchill lakes we saw mergansers, scaups, herons, gulls, and an osprey again. Baby ducks fled in front of us like fish flipping along the surface to dodge a deep shark, the mother among them flittering strongly to set the example. A logging bridge crossed above us; we saw an otter underneath. The shores displayed "cat spruce" (white spruce), sleek and bristly, beaver houses, cedars and drowned-looking alder-covered beaches leading to a fir point where the Indians used to camp to escape the flies. On Churchill, with the sun a silvery band on the water, we caught up with a swimming cow moose midway across. Her body was invisible; her head was like a blunt boat, the ears the housing, and her hairy neck hump nearly underwater. It was a groping blind-looking head, sightless as a whale's, a feeling and suffering-looking head, the nose so huge and vulnerable that other undiscovered senses might have been contained inside. Two terns were diving on her with creaky cries. Her ears lay back as her big pumping legs hurled her ashore, and she swerved to look at us, first over one shoulder, then over the other.

Churchill is a rangy lake, the shore opening and narrowing, with a mountain skyline. Heron Lake, formerly a holding pen for the logs, leads on to Churchill Depot dam. The ranger there, whose name is Clyde Speed, talked about the moose that he sees, and we toured the outdoor museum of log sleds, water sleds, old bateaux,

Lombard tractors, Watson wagons, and looked into the boarding house, and engine and blacksmith shops, all defunct. Lombard steam log-haulers preceded the internal-combustion engine in the woods for a decade or two around World War I. Each of them could do the work of sixty horses, a blue flame issuing like a blowtorch from the exhaust pipe on a cold night. They were precursors of the tank and farm tractor because they ran on a cater-pillar tread. In 1938 Fred King had walked to this spot to explore; he loved its tall tamaracks and big pines and gave us a chance to poke about. In places like this he always announced that he was only a "fake woodsman," and that although occasionally he spoke for some of the old fellows who couldn't go on TV themselves and spout off, if we wanted to meet the real thing we'd have to go farther afield.

The Chase Rips, the one risky spot in ninety-two miles, began here. Fred had been casual in speaking of it, once suggesting that Jim perhaps might want to practice a bit with his pole in Soper Brook, but now as we lugged our craft down below the dam (paying Clyde Speed to truck the duffels around) he began to hum nervously. We watched other voyagers as their canoes first entered the current like the little cars at a carnival being gripped by the cogs of a loop-the-loop.

I had an easy time in Fred's bow. Often he takes old people through these rapids who can give him no help, who are getting their final look at the outdoors. But Jim and Audrey, suddenly realizing they hadn't practiced enough in Soper Brook, were on their own, Jim cautiously trying to get the feel of the pole, hanging himself up against the bank several times. King, who had drifted ahead almost too far to shout, yelled at him to stand up and move more toward the middle of the canoe. "Stand up! You don't fight Joe Louis sitting down. Get on your hind legs!" He'd stripped to the waist. A moosefly bit him, and he laughed and said, "They'll bite a chunk out of you and fly up on a branch and sit there right in front of you eating the chunk."

The river before us fell off, abrupt as the end of a table; all of a sudden it didn't appear to be there. Then, curling up like a hairdo, it fluffed around us, high at the prow, as we slid down into the rapids themselves. The noisy water was popping in points, peaks and tufts, blotting out all other sights and sounds. We could have been surrounded by other canoes and not noticed them. This was the first pitch, full of rocks, several hundred yards long. The second was shorter but "downhilly," the many rips sticking up as if to chum with us, as the water curled and crabbed around. Riffles, bumps, a wild backdrop of trees. Jim was way back in the first pitch still but beginning to grab hold of the river's hand now. "Good boy!" King shouted to him, a regular educator, jittery on his behalf. "We'll make you an honorary Moosetowner. I ain't got the authority, but I can recommend you." Everywhere on the river there was midmorning light and a hiss as of thousands of snakes, the water backing up recalcitrantly into cowls. Jim's canoe came stumbling, angling along like a cub, edging to the bank, but he jumped out at every juncture to wade and push, as a canoeman should. We all took a breather together against some shore rocks to eat raisins and talk.

The third pitch was energetic with knobby rocks sticking up like bad luck itself, every one striped with canoe-belly paint. King has broken canoes here—a rock square-on at 45 degrees will do it, plunging through the bottom. A friend of his tried out a plexiglass design here but gave his bowman heart failure, the rocks skinning by just an inch or two under his feet. A canoe should go where the water goes. "Where's the water?" a canoeman asks himself in the rapids when perplexed. Then, camping alone at supper, all the company he has is the bugs in his cup.

Poling is like snowshoeing and paddling like skiing, and we were able to paddle for a little while. We passed several parties who were "frogging" (walking) their way down the channel, leading their canoes, having become discouraged from tipping over so much. The river was gala with rocks, a hustling hubbub. King's craft snuggled in like an invited guest—but, no, a big jar. We skidded and sidled by the tough spots. Fred said not to try to signal to Jim or he'd misunderstand, and it would distract him. Soon he did tip and swamp, the canoe underwater. "Not too bad being in the river, just lots of water and rocks," Fred said, jumping in too to help hold and right their canoe and recover the gear that was floating downriver. Now that their string of conquests had broken, the two of them fell out again twice in quick succession, but learned to leap when they felt themselves going so that at least the canoe didn't sink. "Once they get wet they'll get wet again." Watching, Fred sang with tension.

After having covered a mile and a half (it seemed much more), we stopped at a place called Big Eddy to dry out and have lunch underneath an old cedar, the water purling like Hiawatha's. When other people passed, we'd hear their piping shouts for a moment, but both the river and the dramatic forest—blue firs and black spruces—made them mirages.

We pushed on, the Allagash partying along, popping with rocks but forty yards wide, leaving plenty of current, till it tipped down steeply again and we slid at the edge of whole thievish mobs of rocks that nattered away, feeling their tug, zipping by Harrow Brook. There were scraps of canoes that had wrecked and washed down, becoming wedged in the rocks; some had been drawn up on the bank where they covered small piles of firewood, because a great many people had crawled ashore and spent time recuperating here. Jim and Audrey fell overboard twice more, though the river wasn't as severe. First he lost his balance; the next time she did. He was strong and uncomplaining but heavy and had lost his confidence, and Fred gradually formed the opinion that he was awkward and that over-education had spoiled him. Fred stopped really rooting for him, though continuing to mutter encouragement—whether or not Jim and his wife were able to hear. Being as safe as a sack of peas in Fred's bow, I felt guilty for having it all so easy and knew that I would have looked worse.

We enjoyed peaceful minutes of drifting too, with the bottom brown mud, just a few round white rocks dotted about, and the banks grassy, cedars leaning over the water, and white-collared birds darting close to our heads. Then for three hundred yards the river would turn feisty, roaring, tergiversating, as busy as rush hour, each rock having its say. We twisted through new rips and rapids, eluding sweepers, seeing the trout jump, and dragonflies in a mating clinch; jays called in the trees. The clouds were lovely, if we took time to glance upward. There were still-water sloughs, and gulls on the mud-banks, and parakeet cries from the bear-jungle. Then a swift chute, dark choppy water, on into a wide, luxurious pool. Buzzing birds in the woods, occasional pines, more shaggy cedar, big pairs of spruce, a heron flying high with folded neck, a gangly flying loon, some green grassy islands. A winter wren sang. Then again the water crawled with ripples, with stream birds flying up, the water slanting alive with bubbles over a gravel bar.

After these last corrugations a wide boggy low-slung valley interrupted the forest, and there were red-winged blackbirds, bitterns, and other signs of slower water. We saw a speck of a bird diving on an eagle or osprey, harassing it for several minutes; hummingbirds and robins do this. The Allagash is thought to be visited by three or four eagles.

The bogs gave way to Umsaskis Lake, which after the rapids seemed placid and big, with bumpy timbered hills all around. We rested our backs, using the outboard. Fred said that in the years following the invention of outboards the Moosetowners kept trying them out and discovering that they could pole upstream faster than a motor could go, so the older men never did bother adopting them.

We'd covered twenty miles, and camped on July 20th in the Thoroughfare leading from Umsaskis into Long Lake. The Oyster Bay couple were telling about their trip down the Colorado River and I was talking about other rivers I'd seen, when I realized that we were making poor Fred jealous; he wanted our attention fixed on the Allagash. They talked about their vacation in Japan too, where Jim wouldn't take his shoes off. "We beat the sons of bitches, so there's no reason why we should take our shoes off."

It was warm and the frogs on the Thoroughfare started croaking at 8 P.M. As I stood listening, the local ranger, making a last swing past, stopped to find out if everything was all right. He said that people in trouble generally just stand on the bank looking out, don't wave or shout. Sometimes he wonders how long they'd stand there if he didn't come over—two days, three days?—before they began to wave and yell.

Fred keeps a jeep at Umsaskis. The next day he drove us forty miles across International Paper Company roads to Chemquassabamticook Lake, where we boated to his cabin. The spot is close to Canada, and during Prohibition a good deal of booze was hauled to Fred's lake, where the canoemen took over and carried it via the waterways to Moosehead Lake and other resorts farther south. We passed some cabins of the era with double-split roofs: cedar shakes overlying a layer of earth, covering an inner roof composed of spruce poles.

Fred's maternal grandfather went to California for the Gold Rush, sold mining timbers there and brought back fifty thousand dollars in gold. Gone now, Fred laughs, with a backward jerk of his head as if he were swinging an ax. His cabin is at what sixty years ago was One Eye Michaud's logging camp; and he's found the "greenhouse" (root cellar), the old beanhole, lined with rocks, with charcoal at the bottom, the outline of the bunkhouse, and that of a trapping cabin which must have predated Michaud. In his own cabin, built of peeled logs that he rolled up on skids to the height of the eaves, he has a hundred-year-old pair of caribou-hide snowshoes, and other antiques; even a scrap from a cedar tree where he cut some life-saving kindling one snowy night when he was caught on the lake by a bitter headwind and had to sit out the storm on the shore. He got under a spruce with the biggest fire he could scrape together and thought of all the things he'd done wrong in his life. Later he came back and cut that particular spruce for his new ridgepole, dragging it home on a sled made from two fenders.

His curtain rods are old setting poles; his clothesline is tied between saplings skinned by the beavers. He had a potato garden to tend, and we went out to see the stump of a virgin pine with the marks of the broad-ax that cut it still visible and a forty-year-old birch tree growing on top. We saw two barred owls calling each other, and a woodpecker drinking down ants on a stump, and moose and deer prints on the sandy beach, among the debris of mussel shells the gulls had dropped. In the winter it's so cold that the wings of the ravens flying overhead seem to squeak like an ungreased hinge. One Eye Michaud is said to have wanted to maintain his reputation as a hard man, and so, out here in winter weather, a four-day walk from the nearest town, he might fire somebody and then, leaning into the kitchen, announce, "Don't give this man any food!" It kept up appearances, and the fellow's knapsack was immediately filled.

Fred used to sneak up here years ago, even building himself a squatter's shack on a ridge of rock maple and yellow birch, since logged. The logging roads now extend everywhere, if one looks down from the air, like tributaries that join the main arteries leading to Canada and the pulp mills. We visited a fire warden named Leslie Caron with a round wrinkled face such as befits a man born in the puckerbrush, who as a boy had carried the mail by dogsled. He said the weather forecasters "must have read last year's almanac," and that he would retire and "be a free nigger" next year. Fred told about catching a six-pound lake trout and taking it up to the watchman in the fire tower on Ross Mountain as a present, assuming he'd catch another on the following day. He didn't, and as soon as the fellow climbed back to his tower, his dog got hold of the fish and ate it. Now the spotting is done by airplanes. Caron in a jeep chases out to where they are circling and tells them where he is in relation to them, because they can't see him through the cover of trees. Then they tell him where the fire is in relation to him.

In the morning the sunrise was golden through the thick trees. A soupy mist covered the lake, which smoked like a hot spring. Two connubial loons floated side by side, then dived together. The water was as dark as blueberry jelly. We drove back to the Allagash and got under way toward Long Lake again. There we encountered some Explorer Scouts, the vanguard of a program which will scatter ten thousand boys every summer through northern Maine; also a private boys' camp, forty-four kids in twenty canoes.

Fred said there are three kinds of bears in Maine: black bears, maybe a few brown bears, and *Jalberts*. Sam Jalbert was born on a rock in the Allagash, and when he was three days old he fell off and has been in the river ever since. He poled upriver so much he grew arms as thick as his neck, and hands as wide as a shovel. He raised a family of ten kids and had to kill a lot of deer out of season to do it. Used to take sports down the Chase Rapids too. Once he stood on his hands in the stern and steered by tipping and balancing his body. The Jalberts helped dig the channels and build the dams, and this twenty miles we were doing today was Jalbert country, where they logged and had their landings. The logs couldn't simply be set on the river ice or they would be lost in the frenzy of spring break-up; they were kept at strategic points along the bank, then rolled in when the river began to relent but before it lowered.

Chemquassabamticook Stream came in from the west through a moosey flat—Fred has poled up there to his lake from the Allagash, taking all day. We saw a swimming beaver and three otter, two of which ran up on the bank like muddy rascals. Here at Harvey Pond is an old farm clearing, once a freight depot during the towboat era, before that a place where people stopped for vegetables as far back as 1820, along the so-called California Road, a wilderness path which headed west. The original Harvey was a squaw man with a long white beard and twelve kids who married and settled here, liking the warmth and bustle after a lonely life.

An osprey and some splendid ducks flew overhead. There was a last dam, with lilies and water weeds and fish jumping. A channel was maintained by the towboaters for the rest of the way to the St. John, and we sought this out where there were rapids. A couple of horses would drag upstream a boat sixty feet long and ten feet wide (One Eye tried one seventy-two feet long). Barrels of pork and beef weighing three hundred pounds were placed in the bow, barrels of flour behind them, and buckets of lard and blueberries alongside the tiny cabin in the stern. Coasting back, the horses got a free ride.

We passed bits of islands covered with driftpiles, saw a doe and a fawn, a sheldrake with seven ducklings, a squirrel swimming the river, its tail like a rudder. A heron flew up and stood for a minute atop a fir tree. The river curved gently in a stretch sweet as honey, softening its watery sounds so that we could hear the white-throated sparrows. After tilting again with a few rocks we entered a dead water which lasted for an hour's paddling, birds warbling all around, the water smooth, black and waxed. Tying the canoes together, we drifted as a raft, eating Fig Newtons, and hearing chain saws. Sweeney Brook, Whittaker Brook and Jalbert Brook joined the current. Fred told the story of a guide on the St. John who used to drift along with a gallon of booze at his side. When he and his sports approached a serious rapids and they shouted across to him from their canoe over the roar of the water to ask how to deal with it, he would raise his tin cup and tell them, "I'll drink to that."

While Fred's "brain was in neutral" we hit some rocks, then met more brief rustling rips, rollicking through the Long Soo Rapids for a mile or so, through lovely still country. Only the water popped, a confabulation of rocks, with sandbars and other complexities and many dead elms and ashes that the ice had girdled in the crush of the spring. Fred sometimes picks fiddlehead ferns for his supper here. Entering Round Pond, we paddled to his favorite campground, and baked some bread, cut up chub for trout bait, and watched the ravens harassing the squirrels. Jim fished a springhole while I went to see Willard Jalbert, the Old Guide, as he likes to call himself, having become a bit of an institution. His description of fighting rearing bears with a double-bitt ax sounded as if he'd been looking at *Field and Stream* covers, but last fall at eighty-three he had shot a deer, and still could wend his way through the rapids with an outboard full-throttle, or hold his canoe where he wanted it with his pole while casting with his free hand. He once rode a log over the fourteen-foot drop of the Long Lake Dam, and used to play tricks on the ospreys, throwing out chub for them —a fish that is the butt of many river jokes—attached by a line to a log. "Everybody for himself and God for us all," he would call, going into the rips. But it has all somehow ossified now that the wilderness is gone.

At dusk we went for a joyride on the windy water. A

thin-lipped bright sunset, a loon's giddy titter like a police whistle with water in it. Rain with thunder during the night.

From before sunrise, hard logging was going on at Round Pond, all by Canadian labor, the logs being trucked to St. Pamphile. The truth is the Yankee big-timber-logger has been a myth for several decades, and old-timers like the Jalberts disguise their dismay at the fall-off in gumption among young Americans by grumbling that the hunting is tailing off because these Canadian woodsmen must be shooting the deer, tucking their carcasses among the logs and smuggling them out of the country.

We got started at 6 A.M., a sailing hawk peering down at us. A mist almost the color of snow lay between the lines of trees, so that although the weather was warm it was a wintry scene. In the Round Pond Rips a couple of ducks babbled in the thick of the fun, the water reverberating around them. Next, the Musquacook Rips and islands. King's echoing voice in the quietness irritated me exceedingly because this was not *my* sixtieth trip, but as he spoke of his "walking stick," which was his pole, and his "rain shirt," his poncho, exclaiming resoundingly, "Bubbles mean troubles," I had to remember that this was real history he was reliving, that he was a link with the boisterous rivermen whose intent was to knock down the forests and let the light in.

A buckskin-colored deer exploded with springy bounds. We saw a merganser family, a ridge scalped by a tornado. In a dead water we looked down and saw grasses growing on the bottom, while a whole populace of insects bounced in the air. The sun streamed through the morning vapors in warm yellow combinations on the west bank, but on the east the view was still snowy-looking. The black-growth forest humped into low hills. We floated past grassy islands, then sibilant stretches, the water combing through the rocks, turning the big ones yellow with reflected light and leaving a platter of calm downstream of each. There's a disastrous-sounding crunch when a canoe hits a rock and the floor lifts under one's feet, but the sound is worse than the results. We passed an old shack with a sod roof, now burgeoning with raspberries, and saw Savage Brook debouch through its delta, and Five Finger Brook. The water itself looked like running gravel, and we passed several old cabins that used to belong to characters like Sporty Jack (so called because of a birthmark he sported), and the Cunliffe Depot, the abandoned headquarters of a logging boss who rivaled Michaud. Michaud's hay farm was two miles below, now devoid of buildings but spacious after so many miles of woods. Then beaches and finally a slough called Finlay Bogan, where we saw kingfishers, fish jumping, islands foliaged with willows and silver maples, ice-scarred. It became a still, rainy day with some occasional neighborly thunder. We ran by a few gentle rapids and shoals, seeing huge waterlogged stumps that were shaped like moose. The river here was a dream—rustling, windy, wild-looking and lush—chipper with birds, overhung with sweepers, dense with slow channels forking between the islands. It was beautiful and remote. The pioneers chose inter-vale land such as this whenever they could because the river had already partially cleared it for them and laid down topsoil in which the natural wild grasses had seeded, so that their stock could browse.

At the approach to Allagash Falls the water grew deep, the bottom rocky and the forest black. Fred began to hum as we entered the rips that led to the lip, and we squeezed over to the east bank and camped in the crook of land where the portage begins. The water is churned butter-yellow as it goes over, and it spouts off the rocks below like the wake of a ship. I swam in the bombast below the falls, in deep potholes where the water was warm. It's a fat, plentiful falls, not notably high; once some daredevils went over in a bateau and survived. Looking down from above at the charade of destruction, suddenly I missed my wife. It was so lonely watching the water go over and smash that the mosquitoes began to seem friends. Fred, who was turning ornery now that the responsibilities of the trip were nearing an end, shouted from the supper fire, "Beavertail sandwiches" (Spam).

In scratchy places the channel generally stuck close to the outside bank. We'd try to go where the water went but not where it was making a fuss. Below the falls the Allagash achieved its maturity. It was plump, and the birds were dashes of white overhead, singing from every side. In a dead water, a large tributary, Big Brook, flowed in. Then McGargle Rocks, two short rapids with a pool between. We saw various map-eater parties in bang-bang canoes. Between McGargle and Twin Brooks is a nondescript stand of fifth-growth white birch and knobby pulpwood, not showing the logging industry at its best. As usual, Fred's voice scared off the moose in front of us; once we saw a stream of fresh pee on the gravel where one had fled.

The Twin Brooks enter the Allagash directly opposite each other in the midst of a rapids. There was a roar, and the channel was first on the left and then crossed over while we hopped about in the swells. "'I'm lost!' the Cap'n shouted," Fred yelled in the fastest turbulence amid the rocks, before we slid into a pool where a seagull sat. We'd covered eight miles in two hours.

The water got moving again. The government-owned wild area ends at Twin Brooks, and soon we saw log trucks alongside the bank, and a ramshackle structure, the Allagash Inn, at Eliza Hole. The Allagash Inn was One Eye Michaud's jumping-off point on the river, where he kept his successive wives. Two of the four were mail-order floozies who decamped with his assets, but when he was old and pitifully sick and poor, the first of them came back and nursed him.

One expects to arrive at some signs of civilization at the mouth of a river. Ahead we could see the ridge carved by the St. John. The Allagash makes an S-turn to delay joining it, through Casey Rapids. We saw two last deer, smelled a skunk, an animal that prefers a civilized habitat, and heard new bird calls—field and song sparrows, bobolinks, meadowlarks. Crows had replaced the wilderness ravens.

Then the jukebox of the Allagash Pool Hall. Allagash proper is a sad shantytown, a sleeping shell of the Moosetowners' settlement, with everyone drawing food stamps now, but there are canoes on the lawns. It's ragged, not even quite right for potato country, backed smack up against New Brunswick. The old-timers, lame with arthritis after so many years of exposure to rain and cold, when often they slept in the snow next to a small fire, have become supersensitive to the cold. They find it torturing, tack up insulation everywhere, or pray for the money to winter in Florida.

I had a butterscotch sundae and a strawberry milkshake. Fred King departed like a boy let out of school: no more entertaining or catering to us, no more wincing at the bumps delivered to his canoes. He would drive south until he got tired and sleep by the side of the road. Our vehicles had been brought around from Chamberlain Lake, but Jim and Audrey's new Chrysler had not weathered the trip well. The two of us left them changing a tire, putting gas into the empty tank from a one-gallon can and reminding each other that no minor mishap should spoil such a fine trip.

THE
ASSASSINATION
IMPULSE

Most of us take a slightly more condoning view when the topic of assassination relates to a public figure we dislike. In the news photographs from the South after John Kennedy died there were many smiles. Some people laughed or grinned, some clapped; it must have been the same with Lincoln, even McKinley. And if, let's say, Spiro Agnew, upon unexpectedly attaining the Presidency, died violently, we know how many muffled whews would greet the news, not least in humanities, history, and religion departments in universities nearly everywhere. Though there would be some crocodile tears and public faces of solemnity, reminders that the most elementary principles of order by which a republic should maintain itself were being destroyed, there would also be plenty of comment to the effect that if it boiled down to a choice between disasters, Mr. Agnew in the greatest office of responsibility was a worse danger to the nation and its Constitution than the humiliation of another assassination. People would even claim that the real travesty of due process pre-dated his killing to his appointment as Vice-President. After a chat of a few minutes with Mr. Nixon, who'd sensed "a strength" in him, all our destinies had wound up in his hands.

Nevertheless, nobody advocates assassinating chiefs of state nowadays, not even those of hostile states; it's a Pandora's box. When I see the President in person, I'm sure I'm not the only man who wonders whether a madman may not run out of the crowd, red-dog through his bodyguards and stab him right in front of my eyes. The tense cluster of armed agents surrounding him are employed to think about nothing else. His visits in New York are ceremonial—he makes history elsewhere—and so the only history that might be made here on the street would be unscheduled and tragic. Yet one does rather expect to see some history made; furthermore, one of the last forceful taboos still operating forbids killing public officials—a taboo stronger, more emotional now, than even patricide. Imagine facing a court for having killed *the President!* How much easier to have only killed your friend, your wife? Even Jack Ruby, an assassin's assassin, became instantly and by association a kind of universal pariah, beyond thinking about except as someone who for the rest of his life ought to "make baskets," as a good friend put it to me. How would Sirhan Sirhan do in a prison yard? Probably not at all well. Prisoners, too, want to feel that they retain a social link, and from the killing of a President—or candidate—the spiral down to general, demoralized disintegration for everyone might quicken irretrievably, until nobody would be safe and the new power figures who arose would simply withdraw behind glassy barriers.

So this crime is not manslaughter, it is crime against the populace, and consequently the taboo has survived since the days of regicide. Perhaps its very survival focuses extra attention upon the possibility. Indeed, even to let the thought slip through one's mind and pass one's lips is an offense. You can be overheard in a bar or restaurant telling an acquaintance that you have an urge to shoot your business partner or sleep with your mother, and as long as it doesn't sound like an outright plotting session no one will call the cops; nor would much come of it, in any case. But mention the unmentionable—that sometimes you experience the impulse to murder your President— and whether you were smiling or not, you won't merely be put under surveillance, you may wind up in a federal prison, and it will be a hasty process getting you there. The very *thought* violates the law. A hallucinatory postcard sent from New Leipzig, North Dakota, to Pennsylvania Avenue can cause the sender to be imprisoned for up to five years.

During a seedy phase of life in my early thirties I used to attract the notice of bank guards. When I reached the teller's window after waiting in line, I'd find a guard or two poised next to me, although they'd turn their backs and pretend to be looking the other way. My look of haste and unkempt agitation brought them on, but I used to speculate about the shattering change my life would undergo if, on a crazy impulse, I handed the girl a deposit slip scribbled with the words: "Give me whatever you have."

My first contact with the Presidency was as a college student of Archibald MacLeish. A one-time Brain-Truster,

he had a few photographs of Roosevelt and other memen-
tos around, but the most apparent mark on him, it seemed
to me, was his efficiency at organizing his time, his tight-
lipped impatience with a defective telephone, and his
masterly ease with people. He was generous to his students, and these quaint mannerisms may have been acquired at other junctures of his life, but later I was to see
my father assume this same sort of whirlwind style after
conferring with John Foster Dulles, and to notice it in two
publishing-house editors who went to the White House or
the ranch at Johnson City to edit Presidential memoirs.
Power energizes the onlooker as well as the man who actually possesses the power, and if in some way a fellow
becomes a sidekick of the President, whether as a full-
fledged Brain-Truster or as a man Friday, he too is likely
to wrap on that bold and ruthless look of business-first.

When, however, a person *not* an aide or adviser stumbles within hailing distance of the Presence, if this particular individual—who, after all, gets just as flushed and
vitalized—isn't inclined to beam and scrape the way the
great majority of us do, then instead he may feel a rakish
urgency to sound the old raspberry and sock the President
on the button with this swift surge of energy. There are
the two of them: one who for no necessarily very good
reason, after an enormous expenditure of decades of fierce
ambition and inner violence, makes history with practically every sneeze and one of them who doesn't.

The President often seems more remote alive than he
would dead. We needn't fear him, dead: needn't wonder
whether he's been seeing *Patton* again or revisiting irra-

tional, vindictive crannies in his mind which have made their existence known before and which in a crisis might bring the curtain down for millions of us. Besides, no man is so patronizable as a dead man. Death is the equalizer, and with what cozy grief we congregate to watch the funeral caisson roll. He is a tabloid centerfold; snugly we mourn.

I happen to be familiar with dead people because I was in charge of a morgue in the Army. Tending the bodies, I gradually shed the unease which I'd brought to the job. They were wheeled down from the hospital wards after having been prepared by the nurses, and my first task was to untie all of the tidy tapes and strings, open up the hooded areas, and free the arms and legs. After the doctor had autopsied them, civilian undertakers came, black men for blacks, white men for whites. The white men arrived in pairs, one for each end of the stretcher, but the black undertakers, unable to afford a helper, materialized alone and pushed the stretcher out the door at a steep angle like a wheelbarrow.

Death has a flat smell, like a heavy gas, that seems to nullify many of the indignities the dead are subject to. As far as I could judge, these corpses lay comfortably at rest, maybe more comfortably than a sleeper does, with the relaxation that other people go to class to learn, and wearing modest but authentic-looking smiles. The smiles did not seem simply a position the mouth had slacked into. Although the man's death might have involved much pain or even strangulation, apparently just at the end, as if he'd sighted something, he'd *smiled*. This fascinated me.

Sometimes an accident victim would not have had a chance to rid himself entirely of his expression of surprise at what was happening to him, but even suicides, I discovered, were smiling as they died. In their case, it was generally with irony, like the expression of a man who has just frantically chased a bus for blocks, run and run and at last jumped aboard, and then, standing in the aisle, panting and fumbling for his change, begins to wonder wryly why in the name of heaven he was in such a hurry.

Dead men, like old men, learn something and win small victories. Of course, to have become accustomed to dead bodies does not mean that one could murder; the murderer deals with the living. Anyway, I've seldom fantasized about killing a President—less often than about harming my own beloved baby (that other unbreakable taboo) when she was helpless and tiny, crying frettingly at night. But would I *grieve* if somebody shot Agnew, for example—wooden nickel, wooden Indian that he is? Doubtless his family loves him, but I don't in the least. Himself a violent man, like Nixon, a cruncher, hating people's guts, full of the killer instinct, he'd be more likely to dance on an opponent's grave than I, despite my fantasies.

It is always the powerless who are required to be peaceful. Men who have attained power by shoving aside every rival, who have access to every microphone in the country and command armed forces beyond counting, astonishing much of the world with their tactics—chemical warfare, saturation bombing—cry shame at political gatherings if someone interrupts them with a shout. This, they say, is

112

"violence"; violence is anathema. Every success story in government used to make the pilgrimage to South Vietnam and pose toughly for the photographers with hands on hips looking at humbled prisoners or touring scenes of carnage. On all sides there is the din of violence; it is the protesters alone who must remain mild.

I do not advocate violence, because it is the road to murder, and what interests me about murder is only that the potential exists in us. Murderers, too, are distressed to find that it exists in them and are particularly surprised when they find out that while the act was certainly final for the victim, for themselves it was habit-forming. In British Columbia I've heard stories from the age of riverboats and itinerant horsemen of mysterious fugitives from the western U.S. They built cabins along the watercourses, cleared ground for a garden, fished, hunted and trapped, constructing a lookout to watch for trouble coming from downriver, perhaps, and even if no real facts about their pasts ever caught up with them, they became known as killers all over again simply because they killed. Murderers have extraordinary tempers, and in the give-and-take with frontier neighbors, in meeting travelers on the trails, sooner or later somebody was sure to rub the fellow the wrong way. He might contrive to obfuscate the clues, but once again he would be labeled as a killer by all his neighbors, and two or three years later probably still another poor clunk would disappear after an argument with him.

One of these stories differed from the rest. The renegade was not the usual sneaky, venomous runt but a tall, manly cowboy, more typical of western movies than of the West. Though shadowed by rumors, he was intelligent and able, and had been making himself useful around the town of Fort St. James in the few months since he'd arrived. Along with a crony he was working at a sawmill while investigating the opportunities for homesteading. He liked the great long lakes and wild hundred-mile stretches of forest with goldfields here and there, and hoped to stay. Then abruptly one evening he quarreled with another drifter in the bar in town. He didn't shoot the man, though he trembled, holding himself back, as if verging upon an illness. Instead, all his dangerous energy was concentrated on getting out of the bar, exploding curses, catching his string of packhorses, weaving as he chased them, and saddling up. He didn't want to be a gunman at all—that was part of the past that he had tried to leave behind back in the States. Breathing fast, trying to subdue his temper, he hollered for his traveling friend to hurry. This is the last the old-timers of Fort St. James remember of him—seized as if with epilepsy but looking tall, effectual and deadly up on his horse, calling for his friend, bristling, crackling with energy, intent on eating up the minutes until he'd left town and couldn't shoot the other guy. Such a lonesome, brilliant figure; what place could he find to settle down in where the same thing wouldn't happen again?

Once when I was walking in Central Park I saw Lyndon Johnson being helicoptered out of Manhattan during a period when he had reason to fear being shot. He had been routed to the helicopter from the Waldorf through the park itself, away from roofs, and the idea of an assassin was so imbued in everybody's mind that though I wished to boo, I felt the tautness and was afraid. When several people started clapping, the Secret Service men fanned out. Nobody in the entourage looked happy. The President, edgy, dyspeptic, was feeling in his pockets, perhaps for Tums; reddened by the wind, he stopped to wave at the small crowd. He seemed so American that at that ferocious moment in the decade I hated him, but so American that obviously he was like me—like us all.

Eisenhower was the President whom I was bodily in a position to harm. He was not a man I ever hated, but the issues of assassination involve a person's office more than his personality or what he advocates. Had he not been pinned so still and presented to me as a sharp irritant to the taboo against assaulting him, the thought would never have occurred to me. (Oddly enough, in retrospect the episode makes me fonder of him.)

It was late October 1952. He wasn't yet President, but clearly was about to win against Adlai Stevenson. Journeying by train from New Hampshire, he'd spoken first in the textile towns of Lowell and Lawrence in Massachusetts where half the labor force was out of work, and then addressed a hundred thousand people on Boston Common, his largest crowd so far. Pounding "Godless communism," he'd said he was "a no-deal candidate" and called for "leadership morally and spiritually strong." Al Smith's daughter had announced her support for Ike, "a Happy Warrior," and in her honor everyone had sung "The Sidewalks of New York." Henry Cabot Lodge, trying for re-election against John Kennedy's Senate bid, was with Ike; as was Christian Herter, Republican candidate for governor, later to be Secretary of State; and Senator Leverett Saltonstall; and William Knowland, Republican leader in the Senate. They were heading for a circuit of other Massachusetts manufacturing towns, but when their motorcade entered Harvard Square an estimated twenty thousand students and Cambridge residents interdicted this plan. A nightmare photo in the next day's *Times* pictured the candidate standing in glaring sunlight in an open car, sporting a ghastly grin, packed round by a tumultuous mob, his arms spread wide for sacrifice.

It still was part of the election process that a candidate must entrust himself with a light and open heart to the good will of vast crowds of his countrymen. For them, this turbulent procedure was the essential ritual among the other slapstick, sweaty scenes of nomination and candidacy. Television electioneering was too slick; if the people were going to confide their fortunes to one man he must entrust himself to them. Also, everybody recognized that this exhausting press of eye to eye and flesh to flesh across the nation educated a man to the realities as no other schooling possibly could, and at the same time might bring to the surface any out-of-the-ordinary kinks he had.

The incident involving Ike may have helped speed the end of this species of folksiness. I remember the state troopers, frantic, marooned in the crowd, hauling at their capsized motorcycles. The press bus was stalled in the crush a couple of hundred yards ahead, and none of the chauffeurs or prominent family groups included in the motorcade could think of what to do. Eisenhower smiled in order not to seem fearful, waving until his arms were limp, while people jumped to catch his hands and perhaps try to pull him over. This was the so-called Silent Generation, but student generations are not really so monolithic. All of us were roaring now, the blue bloods up on their club balconies and the rest in a disruptive mass, exulting in their power. The feeling was neither pro nor con, though some of the newspapers later tried to claim that the emotion had only been enthusiasm for Eisenhower. No, we were just *rioting*, as students do, and two Secret Service bodyguards and the city police were turning black and purple. Henry Cabot Lodge, Leverett Saltonstall, Christian Herter, with cane and limp, and Senate Minority Leader Knowland had moved to the front bumper of Eisenhower's car, where they were swinging roundhouse blows at the closest students as best they could. Waxen above the mob, Ike grinned and waved, his naturally red coloring sinking to yellow. Though he had my sympathy, this delirious scene masquerading as mere mischief went on so long that it became unsettling. Since we were flirting with the taboo, my way of passing the time was to see really how easy an assassination would be. Five times I squeezed myself up to within stabbing range of the candidate, then, having attained the position, let myself be pushed back to the sidewalk again by the pressure of the crowd. Five times a different fellow in my shoes might easily have killed him.

John Kennedy was campaigning through the Lower East Side on the one occasion when I saw him. Still boyish like his younger brother, he wasn't yet invested with the presidential manner. Joking, leaning toward his young advisers in the front of the car, he radiated supple glamour but not power, and looked as though he might have enjoyed getting out and joining a student riot himself.

I saw De Gaulle in 1962, who of all contemporaries was perhaps the ideal figure for assassination. He was winding down the war in Algeria, besieged at home by paramilitary murderers but also venerated by them, a leader already possessing such luster in history that a few sparkles would have illumined his assassin too. King Olav of Norway was on a state visit, and De Gaulle stubbornly insisted that he and Olav were going to ride the length of the Boulevard St. Germain to get from one place to another—no helicoptering, no unceremonious skulking through side streets. All night the police made harried preparations, and bright and early the crowds were out for this courageous gauntlet-run. It was a good deal riskier than any of Lyndon Johnson's adventures, though, as with Johnson, most citizens gladly cheered their leader when he appeared.

These Frenchmen, too, were confronted with the regicide taboo. Great man that he was, would someone knock him off? The authorities played mouse and cat. Nobody knew whether De Gaulle would use an open car, and whenever a vehicle full of inspecting officers scooted by on a trial run the people at street level peered into it; a gunman with buck fever high in a building might have blasted away. It was the trick of which-shell-is-the-pea-under, because after the last inspection, when troops and policemen, posted every five yards, were all alert, two or three limousines sped by in military sequence, and only by some animal sense did the crowd know that they shouldn't disperse. Still they waited; nothing had drawn fire. Unexpectedly, another covered limousine darted down the boulevard unaccompanied by security cars, as though to catch an assassin by surprise. The driver's foot was jittery on the accelerator, as if anticipating rifle shots. In the back seat were two big men, and next to the driver a deferential-looking assistant had turned to speak to them.

Still the police scanned the rooftops, and the crowd waited for the moment which they'd know was the real thing. Five minutes, ten. We heard sirens and a fleet of motorcycles coming from the Quai d'Orsay. Though these weren't lagging, they weren't scurrying like rabbits, either, in the manner of the earlier limousines. There was a steady, majestic tempo, the gait of kings. I admired De Gaulle, and more important, this wasn't my country, so I was at peace; but beside me a man crouched in anguish, eaten up with nerves, twitching, glancing over his shoulder, groping under his jacket as if for a concealed holster, exactly like a regicide. The motorcade reached us behind a V of motorcycle cops, and in an open touring car sat two imposing men, turned toward each other in conversation, one dressed in Norway's blue uniform, the other in the brown of France. There was no gunfire—though the fellow alongside me seemed in an agony—and they passed on.

Many people in the crowd were sighing and murmuring, uncertain now whether or not they'd seen their president, because at least this last appearance had had an aura of his grandeur and style. But before anybody left, there were new wailing sirens, accompanied by the clatter of horse hooves and the deep rumbling of a motorcade. This time the momentum was most convincing—maybe the horse hooves did it—and the figures, when they reached us, were straight as well as tall. Sublimely at his ease, De Gaulle was turned toward us, of course, not facing inward. The king may have been a little less comfortable, being a tourist in this crisis, but after all he was a king. And Charles De Gaulle, a king by natural selection, the greatest Frenchman of the century, gazed at his fellow citizens with that calmness which bespoke everything. One wondered whether he had even known about the ignoble charade that his security staff had staged moments before. A month later I was to see Pope John, a mesmerizing man, offering a leadership of love. De Gaulle's was not of love but of serenity, and a reverberating cheer went up from all of us. All except for my neighbor. As stealthy as a killer, he unholstered his gun. I wondered if I ought to grab him (knowing that I wouldn't dare), but then he spun around, looking only overhead at the windows and roofs.

IN THE
TOILS OF
THE LAW

Lately people seem to want to pigeonhole themselves ("I'm 'into' this," "I'm 'into' that"), and the anciently universal experiences like getting married or having a child, like voting or jury duty, acquire a kind of poignancy. We hardly believe that our vote will count, we wonder whether the world will wind up uninhabitable for the child, but still we do vote with a rueful fervor and look at new babies with undimmed tenderness, because who knows what will become of these old humane responsibilities? Sadism, homosexuality and other inversions that represent despair for the race of man may be the wave of the future, the wise way to survive.

Jury duty. Here one sits listening to evidence: thumbs up for a witness or thumbs down. It's unexpectedly moving; everybody tries so hard to be fair. For their two weeks of service people really try to be better than themselves. In Manhattan eighteen hundred are called each week from the voters' rolls, a third of whom show up and qualify. Later this third is divided into three groups of two hundred, one for the State Supreme Court of New York County, one for the Criminal Court, and one for the Civil Court. At Civil Court, 111 Centre Street, right across from the Tombs, there are jury rooms on the third and eleventh floors, and every Monday a new pool goes to one or the other. The building is relatively modern, the chairs upholstered as in an airport lounge, and the two hundred people sit facing forward like a school of fish until the roll is called. It's like waiting six or seven hours a day for an unscheduled flight to leave. They read and watch the clock, go to the drinking fountain, strike up a conversation, dictate business letters into the pay telephones. When I served, one man in a booth was shouting, "I'll knock your teeth down your throat! I don't want to hear, I don't want to know!"

Women are exempt from jury duty if they wish to be because of their sensibilities, their menstrual delicacy, and the care that they must give their babies, so usually not many serve. Instead there are lots of retired men and institutional employees from banks, the Post Office or the Transit Authority whose bosses won't miss them, as well as people at loose ends who welcome the change. But some look extremely busy, rushing back to the office when given a chance or sitting at the tables at the front of the room, trying to keep up with their work. They'll write payroll checks, glancing to see if you notice how important they are, or pore over statistical charts or contact sheets with a magnifying glass, if they are in public relations or advertising. Once in a while a clerk emerges to rotate a lottery box and draw the names of jurors, who go into one of the challenge rooms—six jurors, six alternates—to be interviewed by the plaintiff's and defendant's lawyers. Unless the damages asked are large, in civil cases the jury has six members, only five of whom must agree on a decision, and since no one is going to be sentenced to jail, the evidence for a decision need merely seem preponderant, not "beyond a reasonable doubt."

The legal fiction is maintained that the man or woman you see as defendant is actually going to have to pay, but the defense attorneys are generally insurance lawyers from a regular battery which each big company keeps at the courthouse to handle these matters, or from the legal corps of the City of New York, Con Edison, Hertz Rent A Car, or whoever. If so, they act interchangeably and you may see a different face in court than you saw in the challenge room, and still another during the judge's charge. During my stint most cases I heard about went back four or five years, and the knottiest problem for either side was producing witnesses who were still willing to testify. In negligence cases, so many of which involve automobiles, there are several reasons why the insurers haven't settled earlier. They've waited for the plaintiff to lose hope or greed, and to see what cards each contestant will finally hold in his hands when the five years have passed. More significantly, it's a financial matter. The straight-arrow companies that do right by a sufferer and promptly pay him off lose the use as capital of that three thousand dollars or so meanwhile—multiplied perhaps eighty thousand times, for all the similar cases they have.

Selecting a jury is the last little battle of nerves between the two sides. By now the opposing attorneys know who will testify and have obtained pretrial depositions; this completes the hand each of them holds. Generally they think they know what will happen, so to save time and costs they settle the case either before the hearing starts or out of the jury's earshot during the hearing with the judge's help. Seeing a good sober jury waiting to hear them attempt to justify a bad case greases the wheels.

In the challenge room, though, the momentum of confrontation goes on. With a crowded court calendar, the judge in these civil cases is not present, as a rule. It's a small room, and there's an opportunity for the lawyers to be folksy or emotional in ways not permitted them later on. For example, in asking the jurors repeatedly if they will "be able to convert pain and suffering into dollars and cents" the plaintiff's attorney is preparing the ground for his more closely supervised presentation in court. By asking them if they own any stock in an insurance company he can get across the intelligence, which is otherwise *verboten,* that not the humble "defendant" but some corporation is going to have to pay the tab. His opponent will object if he tells too many jokes and wins too many friends, but both seek not so much a sympathetic jury as a jury that is free of nuts and grudge-holders, a jury dependably ready to give everybody "his day in court"—a phrase one hears over and over. The questioning we were subjected to was so polite as to be almost apologetic, however, because of the danger of unwittingly offending any of the jurors who remained. Having to size up a series of strangers, on the basis of some monosyllabic answers

124

and each fellow's face, profession and address, was hard work for these lawyers. Everybody was on his best behavior, the jurors too, because the procedure so much resembled a job interview, and no one wanted to be considered less than fair-minded, unfit to participate in the case; there was a vague sense of shame about being excused.

The six alternates sat listening. The lawyers could look at them and draw any conclusions they wished, but they could neither question them until a sitting juror had been challenged, nor know in advance which one of the alternates would be substituted first. Each person was asked about his work, about any honest bias or special knowledge he might have concerning cases of the same kind, or any lawsuits he himself might have been involved in at one time. Some questions were probably partly designed to educate us in the disciplines of objectivity, lest we think it was all too easy, and one or two lawyers actually made an effort to educate us in the majesty of the law, since, as they said, the judges sometimes are "dingbats" and don't. We were told there should be no opprobrium attached to being excused, that we must not simply assume a perfect impartiality in ourselves but should help them to examine us. Jailhouse advocates, or Spartan types who might secretly believe that the injured party should swallow his misfortune and grin and bear a stroke of bad luck, were to be avoided, of course, along with the mingy, the flippant, the grieved and the wronged, as well as men who might want to redistribute the wealth of the world by finding for the plaintiff, or who might not limit their deliberations to the facts of the case, accepting the judge's interpretation of the law as law. We were told that our common sense and experience of life was what was wanted to sift out the likelihood of the testimony we heard.

Most dismissals were caused just by a lawyer's hunch— or figuring the percentages as baseball managers do. After the first day's waiting in the airport lounge, there wasn't anybody who didn't want to get on a case; even listening as an alternate in the challenge room was a relief. I dressed in a suit and tie and shined my shoes. I'd been afraid that when I said I was a novelist no lawyer would have me, on the theory that novelists favor the underdog. On the contrary, I was accepted every time; apparently a novelist was considered ideal, having no allegiances at all, no expertise, no professional link to the workaday world. I stutter and had supposed that this too might disqualify me—I saw homosexuals disqualified whenever their mannerisms gave them away—but, no, although to me a stutter in its way is as suspicious an ailment as homosexuality or alcoholism, these lawyers did not think it so. What they seemed to want was simply a balanced group, because when a jury gets down to arguing there's no telling where its leadership will arise. The rich man from Sutton Place whom the plaintiff's lawyer almost dismissed, fearing he'd favor the powers that be, may turn out to be a fighting liberal whose idea of what constitutes proper damages is much higher than what the machinist who sits next to him has in mind. In one case I heard about, a woman was clonked by a Christmas tree in a department store and the juror whose salary was lowest suggested an award of fifty dollars, and the man who earned the most, fifty thousand dollars (they rounded it off to fifteen hundred dollars). These were the kind of cases Sancho Panza did so well on when he was governor of Isle Barataria, and as I was questioned about my prejudices, and solemnly looking into each lawyer's eyes, shook my head—murmuring, No, I had no prejudices—all the time my true unreliable quirkiness filled my head. All I could do was resolve to try to be fair.

By the third day, we'd struck up shipboard friendships. There was a babbling camaraderie in the jury pool, and for lunch we plunged into that old, eclipsed, ethnic New York near City Hall—Chinese roast ducks hanging in the butcher's windows on Mulberry Street next door to an Italian store selling religious candles. We ate at Cucina Luna and Giambone's. Eating at Ping Ching's, we saw whole pigs, blanched white, delivered at the door. We watched an Oriental funeral with Madame Nhu the director waving the limousines on. The deceased's picture, heaped with flowers, was in the lead car, and all his beautiful daughters wept with faces disordered and long black hair streaming down. One of the Italian bands which plays on feast days was mourning over a single refrain—two trumpets, a clarinet, a mellophone and a drum.

As an alternate I sat in on the arguments for a rent-a-car crash case, with four lawyers, each of whom liked to hear himself talk, representing the different parties. The theme was that we were New Yorkers and therefore streetwise and no fools. The senior fellow seemed to think that all his years of trying these penny-ante negligence affairs had made him very good indeed, whereas my impression was that the reason he was still trying them was because he was rather bad. The same afternoon I got on a jury to hear the case of a cleaning woman, sixty-four, who had slipped on the floor of a Harlem ballroom in 1967 and broken her ankle. She claimed the floor was overwaxed. She'd obviously been passed from hand to hand within the firm that had taken her case and had wound up with an attractive young man who was here cutting his teeth. What I liked about her was her abusive manner, which expected no justice and made no distinction at all between her own lawyer and that of the ballroom owner, though she was confused by the fact that the judge was black. He was from the Supreme Court, assigned to help cut through this backlog, had a clerk with an Afro, and was exceedingly brisk and effective.

The porter who had waxed the floor testified—a man of good will, long since at another job. The ballroom owner had operated the hall for more than thirty years, and his face was fastidious, Jewish, sensitive, sad, like that of a concertgoer who is not unduly pleased with his life. He testified, and it was not *his* fault. Nevertheless the lady had hurt her ankle and been out of pocket and out of work. It was a wedding reception, and she'd just stepped forward, saying, "Here comes the bride!"

The proceedings were interrupted while motions were heard in another case, and we sat alone in a jury room, trading reading material, obeying the injunction not to discuss the case, until after several hours we were called back and thanked by the judge. "They also serve who stand and wait." He said that our presence next door as a deliberative body, passive though we were, had pressured a settlement. It was for seven hundred and fifty dollars, a low figure to me (the court attendant told me that there had been a legal flaw in the plaintiff's case), but some of the other jurors thought she'd deserved no money; they were trying to be fair to the ballroom man. Almost always that's what the disputes boiled down to: one juror trying to be fair to one person, another to another.

On Friday of my first week I got on a jury to hear the plight of a woman who had been standing at the front of a bus and had been thrown forward and injured when she stooped to pick up some change that had spilled from her purse. The bus company's lawyer was a ruddy, jovial sort. "Anybody here have a bone to pick with our New York City buses?" We laughed and said, no, we were capable of sending her away without any award if she couldn't prove negligence. Nevertheless, he settled with her attorney immediately after we left the challenge room. (These attorneys did not necessarily run to type. There was a Transit Authority man who shouted like William Kunstler; five times the judge had an officer make him sit down, and once threatened to have the chap bound to his chair.)

I was an alternate for another car crash. With cases in progress all over the building, the jury pool had thinned out, so that no sooner were we dropped back into it than our names were called again. Even one noteworthy white-haired fellow who was wearing a red velvet jump suit, a dragon-colored coat and a dangling gold talisman had some experiences to talk about. I was tabbed for a panel that was to hear from a soft-looking, tired, blond widow of fifty-seven who, while walking home at night five years before from the shop where she worked, had tripped into an excavation only six inches deep but ten feet long and three feet wide. She claimed that the twists and bumps of this had kept her in pain and out of work for five months. She seemed natural and truthful on the witness stand, yet her testimony was so brief and flat that one needed to bear in mind how much time had passed. As we'd first filed into the courtroom she had watched us with the ironic gravity that a person inevitably would feel who has waited five years for a hearing and now sees the cast of characters who will decide her case. This was a woeful low point of her life, but the memory of how badly she'd felt was stale.

The four attorneys on the case were straightforward youngsters getting their training here. The woman's was properly aggressive; Con Edison's asked humorously if we had ever quarreled with Con Edison over a bill; the city's, who was an idealist with shoulder-length hair, asked with another laugh if we disliked New York; and the realty company's, whether we fought with our landlords. Of course, fair-minded folk that we were, we told them no. They pointed out that just as the code of the law provides that a lone woman, fifty-seven, earning a hundred dollars a week, must receive the same consideration in court as a great city, so must the city be granted an equal measure of justice as that lone woman was.

Our panel included a bank guard, a lady loan officer, a

young black Sing Sing guard, a pale, slim middle-aged executive from Coca-Cola, a hale fellow who sold package tours for an airline and looked like the Great Gildersleeve, and me. If her attorney had successfully eliminated Spartans from the jury, we'd surely award her something; the question was how much. I wondered about the five months. No bones broken—let's say, being rather generous, maybe two months of rest. But couldn't the remainder be one of those dead-still intermissions that each of us must stop and take once or twice in a life, not from any single blow but from the accumulating knocks and scabby disappointments that pile up, the harshness of winning a living, and the rest of it—for which the government in its blundering wisdom already makes some provision through unemployment insurance?

But there were no arguments. The judge had allowed the woman to testify about her injuries on the condition that her physician appear. When, the next day, he didn't, a mistrial was declared.

Lunches, walks in the Civic Center. I was reviewing two books and finding I could concentrate on them in the midst of the hubbub better than I might have under easier circumstances at home.

My ticket was drawn for another case. A woman carrying a year-old child had been knocked down (or said she had) by a parked car that suddenly backed up. Her attorney was a fighting machine, a fighting bantam—put him in a room and he would fight. His face in its heavy head flushed dark; one could see him as a child having temper tantrums. Combative as he was, however, when he wasn't raging he exuded geniality—genuinely wanted to be liked. Warm and *hot,* warm and *hot;* he whispered forensically. He was another of those veteran attorneys working for a contingency fee and sure that by now he knew a great deal about human nature and how to manipulate it, although in fact there was clearly some disastrous flaw in his judgment of people that he would never discover. Call him Fein (not his name).

His adversary—a word that Fein used with a smile, introducing Mr. Lahey (not *his* name)—was a man who disliked fighting. A ruined, short-nosed Irish drinker with a big seedy body, a bloated face, he held his hands tight to his chest or pushed them down hard on the table to keep them from shaking. He could no longer look anybody in the eye, not even the jury, and instead cast his gaze toward heaven when he made his summation, which, since his glasses magnified his pupils, was distressing. Besides feeling for him, I had the impression that he had not been a bad advocate in the beginning. As it was, he scarcely spoke in the challenge room, only shook his head when he wished to object to the other man's tactics. "You object?" Fein asked. Lahey nodded. Fein seemed fond of him, nevertheless, with that affection compulsive gladiators have for opponents who furnish the chance for a tussle, though his face lost its winning smile and flushed pugnaciously whenever he looked from us to him.

Lahey, who really seemed to know a little bit more law, so that even his minimal, unhappy, purely defensive efforts had some effect, did not return this friendship. Even asking us questions was burdensome to him. Here in the challenge room where the judge wouldn't intervene, Fein was going on and on, unimpeded, about the suffering of this mother and her tiny child. "But we don't want sympathy!" he said. "No," Lahey snickered. "You just want cash." Flushing plum-red, Fein told us that Lahey wasn't the insurance company's regular representative but just an "off-counsel."

Fein challenged a director of CIT, one of the nation's corporate giants, who may have been the richest man in the whole jury pool, exercised another hunch or two, then got around to asking about insurance stocks. Two of us, an IBM employee and myself, put up our hands as holders of bits of ITT, a conglomerate which has insurance interests. Lahey, silently shaking his head, objected to everyone being cast off the jury whose connection to the industry was as slender as that. They went upstairs to ask the judge. The judge ruled for Lahey, apparently, and told them that now only one of us could be challenged on peremptory grounds, so that Fein had to choose. The IBM man wore a rep tie and had hair that was as black and neat as his shoes. I wanted to stay on the jury, so I laid on my lap the books I was reviewing, which had identifying labels on them from the *Times*, figuring that if he was choosing between IBM and the *Times*, a plaintiff's attorney would pick the *Times*. That's what he did, looking sheepishly at me and stressing with some sense of theater that I must be fair enough to ignore the resentment which a juror is likely to feel toward a lawyer who wants him off the jury—not he but his client was the injured party.

So our group consisted of me; a round-faced black bus-driver; a well-dressed real-estate man who was carrying the *Wall Street Journal* and reading a skiing magazine; a brogue-speaking retired bank teller, who said that he had started out at the bank sweeping the floor and worked his way up; a cabdriver, formerly a bartender, who looked like the map of New York, had lived all over it and was a philosopher; and the headwaiter on the milk run at a hotel.

The court attendant who took us in tow was chuckling because he'd fixed the judge's wagon at lunch. The judge had sent him out for a sandwich and coffee, and in order to teach him not to do it again, he'd brought back two sandwiches, the wrong kind, instead of one, and no cream in the coffee. He was a limping old campaigner. The judge was an adequate little man who often stood up when he spoke, as lawyers do. His mode with the jury was like that of an optometrist explaining something to a customer. He was a stickler but always polite to the other participants too, though his job seemed to have lost much of its interest for him. Basically, no doubt, he was an impatient man, but by sixty had mastered this by hedging himself in with the precision of his job, by cramming his face with exaggeratedly pleasant expressions instead of scowling, and by whispering instructions as quietly as possible when he wanted to shout.

The plaintiff, being cross-examined about events that had occurred two years ago, screwed up her face and squinted determinedly, making a decided distinction between the lawyer who was working for her and the lawyer opposed.

She was West Indian, dark, in her early thirties, not so much pretty as sensuous-looking, with an odalisque's walk and a thick coif of hair. Her baby, three years old now, was snoring softly on a bench. She compressed her lips with the force of her concentration after each answer she gave. Like the defendant, who was a private security guard, light-skinned, lean as a knife, wearing his pistol and handcuffs right in court, she had probably been coached. Both of them bumbled in testifying, however, and since the six of us on the jury turned out to be divided evenly about whom to believe, we kept reverting to those bungles, three of us excusing hers as signs of her sincerity, and three excusing his and criticizing hers.

She said that in crossing a street empty of traffic she had walked behind his parked car, which lurched back abruptly, knocking her screaming to the sidewalk and throwing the child out of her arms. She said she'd gone to the doctor seventeen times for her contusions and for medication, massages and heat treatment of her shoulders and neck, and had taken the baby ten times. But she'd had no x-rays and had walked directly home to her other children, not going to the hospital for emergency treatment first. Her main mistake was to tell us she hadn't heard the car's engine and "would have" if it had been running. How could she have been hit if the motor wasn't running? There goes her case right there, said the jurors who were afraid the insurance company was being bilked. They had that sentence of testimony reread to us later in the jury room.

The man said that while it was true that he was sitting

135

in his car, he hadn't started it; the car had never moved. The first thing he knew, out of the blue, this lady rapped on his door claiming she was bleeding and that he had backed into her; maybe she'd tripped on the curb. *His* blunder, which struck me as less a matter of verbiage than of veracity, was to give conflicting accounts of the distance he was from the nearest parked car. The avenue stretched downhill, and at first he said that if he'd wanted to move he had plenty of room just to coast away from where he was without backing up. Then it turned out that there was a car right in front of him. He was not a licensed driver, had only a learner's permit and was driving without the chaperon required by law. When the woman knocked on his door to claim that he had hit her (she said he'd hastily climbed out of his car as soon as she screamed), he gave her his name and address, offered to take her to the hospital, and then went across the street to find, as a witness, the girlfriend he'd been visiting; but they'd since broken up and she was not in court.

At one point Fein managed to inform us that Lahey had been afraid that the defendant himself wouldn't put in an appearance; instead, his client's doctor was absent. For this reason, though he had been asking ten thousand dollars damages each for the mother and child, he felt it best to reduce the child's to four thousand dollars. In addition, he was asking a thousand dollars for the husband's loss of "consortium and services," which he gave us to understand meant sexual intercourse. In his charge the judge enlarged this to include "fellowship." The stenographer, a mannered young man with a Roman haircut, had forgotten to come back after lunch and had to be summoned. The charge was a conscientious one, however, no longer mouthed as if we on the jury were U.N. visitors. I'd come to like both Fein and the judge—Fein as a next-door neighbor whose barbecue smoke one would share, along with his pride in his kids and his delight in friendship that bridged disagreements. He tried to fix our eyes to his as he summed up, speaking hoarsely as though the trial had been going on for weeks, letting his voice sink and rise.

Then we were alone. We settled around the long table designed for a jury of twelve, in postures elaborately casual, as if we expected to battle the way movie juries do. The man who had been reading the skiing magazine had dressed in loafers and chinos and a sport jacket today, and in educated accents he took the lead. He said the woman hadn't organized her thoughts or her case properly; otherwise she wouldn't have made the mistake of saying that the car which supposedly hit her wasn't running. And if your case isn't organized properly you don't deserve to win it. He had property on Long Island and in Vermont, and the insurance premiums were too high. Also, why didn't the street fill with witnesses if she had screamed?

The peppy teller, an endearing individual, didn't like the idea of paying out money on the unsubstantiated word of a woman who didn't have enough sense to get x-rays. Also, he regarded the driver's gun and handcuffs as a sort of character reference, because in his own line of work such licensed guards were trustworthy. Being nearly contemporaries, he and the cabbie had been at home with each other all along, trading jokes during every recess, he in an Abbey Theatre brogue and the cabbie in the accents of the Lower East Side. But like me, though we didn't come straight out and say so, the cabbie was leery of the pistol and cuffs. He had once lived in East New York, where the accident occurred—just as he'd lived in every other known neighborhood—and he explained to the man in chinos that this was a tough neighborhood and didn't fill up with witnesses just because a girl screamed.

The teller suggested that the girl had been jaywalking. The cabbie and I stressed that the defendant was driving illegally, didn't know how to drive in the first place, and that apart from his driving abilities we had difficulty believing him—was it really likely that this woman had stumbled on the curb, skinned herself, and simply looked around for somebody in a parked car to sue? If this character saw he was being set up like that, why hadn't he called the police? But we want justice here, said the teller. One-to-one testimony was no proof, and he doubted her. I said that nobody was going to jail, or even have to pay a fine; this was a civil case in which the evidence, or our impression of it, need only be "preponderant."

The busdriver, who was wary—alone with these five white men—and had already heard some jokes about "witch doctors," referring to the woman's medical proclivities, had postponed giving his views. Now, nervously, speaking fast, he edged into a position of sympathy with her and raised an interesting question: why, if he hadn't hit her, would this tough guy with his pistol and cuffs meekly hand over his name, address and learner's permit to a woman who without reason tapped on his window for the plain purpose of victimizing him in a fraud?

Having waited all of us out, the headwaiter now said heatedly that he didn't trust any woman, that he "just used them and discarded them." He made a tossing motion, like throwing toilet paper into a john. His allies were a little taken aback, and I said (since I was providing the heat on our side) that if he had told that to the lawyers downstairs he wouldn't even be a member of the jury. He was a stiff, large, unusual man, a German, who pinned his ears tight to his head with the temple pieces of his glasses. In the challenge room he'd seemed like something of a caricature, talking about driving "only in Germany" when asked if he could drive, and about how as a European he always accepted authority when asked if he would abide by the judge's charge; "in Germany it's not like here, you know."

We were released at five because the judge had a dental appointment. At ten the next morning, we greeted each other and found ourselves still lined up three to three. Just as the cabbie philosopher was best at arguing with the teller, I was more effective with the man in chinos, being the same age and from a background that he considered comparable to his own. He put his *Time* and *Wall Street Journal* on the table and I countered with my *New York Times* review books. In accents I remembered from prep school he complained about the amount Fein would receive from any settlement we gave the woman, but I brought in how much insurance lawyers were paid in a state like New York which lacks no-fault insurance.

We all recapitulated our reasoning, their side being fair to the driver, believing his version and dismissing his slips as honest ones; ours doing the same for the lady. As time

139

passed, however, our side turned out to be more solidly aligned. For one thing, our sympathies were at least partly engaged; we had the confidence and expertise of two professional drivers operating; and then the headwaiter began to lapse into what might best be described as psychodrama. He told us that the reason he never believed any woman was that one had once accused him of indecent exposure—"showing his peeno"—and thereupon he began to imitate masturbation in a vigorous way. He also stood up and paced, though there was no room for pacing, and showed us the placement of his hernia scar, the injury having occurred while he was waiting on a governor's party of eight, with heavy silver service, and had tried to carry the entire main course on one tray, to spread it out all at once in grand fashion.

Other people also spoke personally. The busdriver, who was still wary of the rest of us, especially since both the plaintiff and defendant were Negroes, mentioned times when fakers on the street had tried to stage incidents so as to sue him, making it plain that this story did not strike him as of that kind. On the Lower East Side the cabbie had once hit a girl on roller skates while hurrying home for services on Rosh Hashanah. The retired teller had ten grandchildren, he wanted us to know (the cabbie had six), and was not an unfeeling man—which nobody had thought. He was a dear; he simply was not used to giving out money so freely. The fellow in the chinos told us about a friend of his who had driven down Park Avenue drunk one night and hit three policemen. Although he was insured for five hundred thousand dollars, the jury awarded them $1.3 million and he was bankrupted.

All of us, who might not have spent five minutes actually helping the woman at the scene if we had been witnesses, were invested with the law's solemnity and were spending what added up to five hours in these deliberations. But the night's sleep had made my friend the skier more amenable. Breaking the solidarity of his side, he offered to let the woman have one thousand dollars, not because he believed her but as a compromise. I'd suggested two thousand dollars for her and one thousand dollars for the child, the cabbie had said two thousand dollars and five hundred dollars, and the busdriver fifteen hundred dollars and five hundred. I said that if there had been any independent medical evidence we'd probably be asking for more, and that if we had wanted to bargain we could have walked in suggesting a figure double what we were ready to settle for. After all, her lawyer had first asked for ten times what we had in mind.

Now the cabbie really came into his own. In luckier days he had managed a taxi company which owned four hundred and fifty cabs, and in his soothing manner he began to recount the details of a dozen, two dozen, three dozen accident cases out of the countless assortment he'd dealt with, pointing out that the standard out-of-court settlement was five or six times the doctor's bills, declaring that he was convinced an accident had occurred, and that the learner-driver, scared because he was driving illegally, had begun by lying in his report to the police and so was lying still. With the broad, hospitable benignity of the old melting pot, for an hour or more he kept quietly filling in every silence with authentic street stories about New York accidents, making it all seem less exceptional to us, bringing it into perspective as a business risk for the companies involved. For every three cabs in a fleet, he said, a hundred dollars a week in insurance money was set aside to pay claims like this. In counterpoint, and maybe almost as effective in reducing the resistance of the other side, the headwaiter in his violinist's suit was striding along one wall of the narrow room doing unaccompanied cadenzas in a hollow voice of a sort that might have been interesting to scientists on the other side of one-way glass. It was an interior monologue, not without pathos. No, he wouldn't give any woman such an award.

Being a good fellow, the man relaxing in chinos agreed to come up to two thousand dollars if we who were above would come down. We did on condition that the teller would not require us to go lower. He was the foreman, by chance—the foreman is the man assigned to Seat No. 1— and remained wholeheartedly against any money at all being paid out. We recognized that in a practical sense we were a five-man, not a six-man jury, and that unanimity would be required. The man in chinos observed sarcastically that the baby didn't need money for candy and should no more receive a payment than the husband who claimed he hadn't been able to screw his wife for a couple of weeks. But I said that the baby had bled like anyone else, that you didn't have to be of voting age to suffer (the judge had refused to allow Fein to suggest "psychic scars"). I said that my first memory was of a train wreck, but didn't add that the memory seemed rather a happy one, because we were debating now, trying to score points, not even pretending to listen to each other judiciously.

Though the woman had spoken with the accent of the British West Indies, the cabbie explained her fluffs in testimony by going so far as to claim she was an immigrant new to the English language. He kept on with that legendary, big-hearted, big-city talk about every man getting a break, about generosity, a New York open to the masses of an older world. It was an unequal contest. By bringing in his six grandchildren he got the teller started again on his ten, and by and by the teller gave in, first to the extent of one thousand dollars, then one thousand five hundred, then two thousand. He was so exasperated that he wanted to give half of it to the child just to spite the mother, and I, still resenting Fein's attempt to dismiss me from the jury—as Fein had suspected I would—thought that this sounded like a good idea because the cabbie had told us lawyers got less of a cut from money which was awarded to minors. The man in chinos shrugged and went along, so we'd reached our decision: a thousand dollars to the woman, a thousand to the child. We patted each other, brothers after the struggle.

"No!" said the headwaiter firmly in court when we were polled, not so ready to knuckle under as I'd imagined.

The last day or two, the jury pool swelled again to the initial crowd of two hundred, and people chatted in tête-à-têtes. When a new case was called nobody except the postmen and Transit Authority employees wanted to take the chance of being chosen for it and perhaps held over. One man told the lawyers that frankly he was sick and tired of hearing about auto accidents. I raised my hand and said I owned some ITT shares and would thus

143

be biased in favor of the insurance company. The court clerks sallied forth from their inner sanctum to tell us about their six-week vacations. There was a sense of satisfaction and repletion at having seen some action and done some service. I had watched bits of trials from the spectators' section in the past, strolling out after half an hour if my interest flagged, but this was different.

On Friday I got home with a stamped receipt for ten days' work at twelve dollars a day, and found in my mail a stringent official warning that I must appear at New York's County Courthouse to explain why I hadn't shown up when called for jury duty and why contempt proceedings should not therefore be instituted against me. My answering note was lusciously righteous.

TWO

CLOWNS

Clowning is the one pro-
fession in the circus which has no limits on what can be
done, and where youth and physique don't count for
much. A man may start late in it or may operate in the
realm of hallucination if he wants. Usually clowns take a
role which is close to the earth—a plowman-pieman-tinker
type, a barefoot sprite whose sex is uncertain because he's
infantile. They're overly tall or small or in some way
out of it—innocent and light of heart, yet stuck with some
disfigurement which is an extension of what the rest of
us are supposed to want: a nose with "character," for instance, or tously hair and a fair skin. But these possibilities
ample for the average rather passive though contentious
fellow who makes clowning his career, are trivial detail in
the persona of the few great clowns. After apprenticing
in paleface as a simpleton for a few years, with a thick,
giddy, up-arching, imprinted smile, such men will gradually start to draw a more scored and complicated personality with the greasepaint, developing a darker role.

145

Otto Griebling,* who is the best American clown, wears
a rag heap that has grown so shapeless as to seem moun-
tainous. His nose, instead of bulbous, is bent and decomposing in a face the color of a frying pan. His resentful
stare, eaten up with grievances, is as calculating as a
monkey's. He plays a bum whose universe has been so
mutilated and circumscribed that all he knows is that he's
free to sit where he is sitting or walk where he is going to
walk, and any impulse we may feel to try and cheer him
up is itself cause for outrage, not worth even a bitter laugh.
He hasn't lost so much that he isn't afraid of further blows,
but as he shuffles along with a notebook, compiling a
blacklist, marking people in the audience down, all his
grudges blaze in his face. Like a sore-footed janitor (he's
seventy-four), he climbs into the crowd to put the heat
on selected guests—begins perversely dusting their chairs,
falling in love at close quarters, gazing at some squirming
miss with his whole soul, leaning closer still, until, in-
explicably furious, he slaps her with his cleaning cloth—
she may try kissing him but it won't work. Now that in
actual life his vocal cords have been removed, Griebling
has inaugurated a "broadcast," too. Wearing a headset and
a microphone, he follows the rest of the clowns, whispering a commentary on their fate, on each mishap. His role
is madder, more paranoid and ruined, than Emmett Kelly's
famous tramp was; less lachrymose, it fits the times. With
faded baggage tickets pinned to his cloak, he tries to
powder his scorched face, looks for old enemies in the

* Otto Griebling died in New York City, April 19, 1972.

crowd. Obviously long past attempting to cope, he simply wants revenge; yet he's so small-time that instead of being fearful we laugh at him.

Added to Griebling's troubles is the same seething irritant that seems to bother all clowns. Nobody likes these ovations which are bestowed on the man in the center ring. Suddenly he loses patience, grabs three tin plates, clacks them together and insists that the audience hail *him*. He juggles perfunctorily, since what he's interested in is not the juggling but the applause, and signals with his hands for a real crescendo. Setting two sides of the arena against each other, he works them up almost to the level the trapeze troupe achieved. But he isn't a bit satisfied. It never quite reaches the imagined pitch. Besides, it is too late for consolation now—too much of his life already has gone by!

Pio Nock is the Swiss master clown. He's old enough to have a daughter who romps on the single trapeze, dangling her yellow hair, wriggling from side to side, looking like butterfat in the strong lights. Nock confronted big cats and the flying trapeze when he was young and now is a high-wire clown, although he does some conventional clowning as well. He plays a sort of country cousin, a man floundering past the prime of life with nothing to show for it except his scars, not even an ironic viewpoint or the pleasure of vindictiveness. Where Griebling stands in baffled fury, past tears or shouting, torn between petulance and outraged astonishment, Nock is a man who doesn't look for root causes, doesn't even suspect that he has enemies or that the odds might be stacked against him.

From every misfortune he simply goes on trying to learn. And for this characterization he doesn't rely much on greasepaint or costumes; instead, he makes queer hollow hoots, like the sounds in a birdhouse. As a trademark they have the advantage over costumes that the kids also can imitate them. They troop out of the auditorium parroting him.

Whenever Nock's country bumpkin gets slapped around, he's always willing to forgive the prankster if only the fellow will teach him how to do that particular trick so that Nock will never be slapped around quite the same way again. Of course, during the show we discover that there are more pranks on the earth than Nock will ever become proof against. We learn that life has limited its gifts to him to these few satisfactions—after the fact. After all, if the world appears upside down it must only be because he is standing on his head. Punishment follows each blunder; yet when he sees a nice girl—his daughter—up on the high wire, he decides that he wants to make an endeavor at that also. At first the ringmaster stops him, but escaping the ringmaster's grasp, he climbs a rope ladder and in pantomime is instructed by her in the rudiments of wire-walking, cheeping eagerly at every lesson learned. The next thing he knows, he is out on the wire, terrified, alone, all the tips forgotten, whistling if he can. Whistling in the dark, a man in a jam, he teeters, steps on his own feet, gaining experience by trial and error, keeping his courage up with those strange hoots, which seem to epitomize how absurdly fragile life is, how often we see a tragedy in the making, as well as its end. The band plays music representing the wry look we wear while watching a stranger's funeral procession pass.

Nock stumbles on the wire and slips to his knees; wobbling, he looks downward, giving an unforgettable peep of fear. He's a short man with long legs and one of those wedgelike noses that even without makeup poke out starkly. His hoot is really like a sigh distilled— the sigh that draws on one's own resources as being the only source from which to draw. A man in the wrong place, again he jerks and nearly falls, giving his peep of mortality, and casts all his hopes just on the process of being methodical, doing what he's been taught as if by rote, which is what most of us do when we are in over our heads. But now he discovers he's learning! His obtuseness has shielded him from the danger a little, and suddenly he finds that he is getting the knack. He lets out a tombstone-chiseler's hoot. Now comes the moment when he can enjoy himself after having learned a particular dodge.

Pio Nock and Otto Griebling are great stars, and the image they leave in my head is so accessible that I don't miss them after the circus moves on. In the case of those performers who do mere heroics the memory does not survive as vividly.

JANE
STREET'S
SAMURAI

God knows, the people in the housing project across town where five people have been murdered in a single year need a force of private police to protect them, their nightmare being compounded by the fact that several of the murdered were elderly and helpless, and any who were not had the dead-end impregnability of the corridors of a modern building to contend with. Much better the old tenements with hall toilets to duck into, fire escapes, back ways and front ways, and cracked entry doors that a push might splinter.

We on Jane Street now have a set of private condottieri patrolling, however, and I'm not glad. I'm especially sorry if this means that other streets in the Village will follow our lead. Armed men frighten me. I'm accustomed to putting my trust in my own eyes and experience and the variety of gaits that I have, culminating in a sprint. I'm used to the police riding in cars, and judge the shapes of night figures accordingly, so I'm apprehensive of anybody who looks unduly tough or like a soldier of fortune. It's not as if these particular soldiers of fortune, holding clubs (so impressive and stern, like the sergeants who taught me to use a bayonet in the Army, and more police-like in appearance than most bona fide policemen are), will signal an end to the presence of the other ones— those who work for themselves and are not paid by us. All it means is that there are going to be a lot more armed men on the street, and that walking in this walking-neighborhood of ours will involve more quandaries and challenges than it does right now. My own instinct is that things are not quite bad enough in the Village to justify hiring clubs. Far better the confederation of whistle owners on Bank-Bethune Streets than a collection of small warlord armies proliferating (though why nobody ever blows "Wolf!" on his police whistle I don't know).

Jane Street is a short street and has two high apartment buildings with lots of contributors who have chipped in, so it can afford to pioneer. I live in one of these buildings, and a man and a woman from the Committee came to me, but I said no. I said that if I lived in a rent-controlled apartment instead of the sky being the limit and my paying for a doorman, as I do, I might sign up with them in order to prevent my plug-in equipment from being stolen. I said they were asking the tenants to assess themselves extra rent to hire doormen for the street itself. This might sound reasonable, except that the trouble was they were not in fact hiring doormen for the street but condottieri and samurai, who would introduce new atmospherics of violence into the neighborhood,

151

abridge ancient freedoms, make walking distinctly more tense and less pleasant, and life more jungly and fraught with complexity and sights which we attempt to avert our eyes from.

I don't mind a few stew-bums sitting on the sidewalk; I may be a stew-bum myself one day. I like to saunter, and much prefer sidestepping them to the glare of suspicion I'd get from the hired outriders on, say, Horatio Street, where I'm not known, for walking so slowly. This ambience will spread. These private armies will be featured in real-estate ads. Many people like weapons around; last year they were shouting, "Off the pigs!" Myself, I prefer a few bums.

I am a middle-aged man with a long memory, and so although, for example, like many other liberals I am no longer a member of CORE but give my tithe to the Nature Conservancy instead, nevertheless I do have residual memories. I don't yet find that life is short, and for good reason, from many memorable sights and experiences I have had here in New York City as well as elsewhere, I do not like to see billy clubs and police uniforms on every street corner. Our despair should not have reached such a point. If, by and by, it does, then let the police be public servants, not private armies of condottieri.

ON THE
QUESTION OF
DOGS

The idea has gotten abroad in New York that nobody in a metropolis should keep a dog. There is a lot of shitting on dogs going on. "Children before dogs," and so on, as if most of the dog-owners didn't have children as well and as if children didn't love and profit from dogs. My daughter weighs half as much as our dog, stands shorter than he does, and in the absence of woods and a farmyard to wander around, learns a good deal about where her roots in the world are from him, learns about her own wellsprings of love and the initiative of love, because of course he's a different proposition from us and her affections as they encounter his are different—discovers that there are bigger things than herself in the world besides us.

He's a large country dog (both images that set the sort of person who objects to dogs to gnawing his elbows and toes), and during the winters he doesn't spend in the city is curled up asleep in his polar-bear coat in deep Vermont snow like a husky. He was middle-aged before he first smelled a stone building or went for a drive in a car. (He smelled a river that we were riding by and jumped right out of the window like a puppy to go for a swim, not realizing that we were traveling fast.) The city is a smorgasbord of new smells, but the cranks say it's mean of us to deprive him of that winter spent vegetating in the snow. What they fear most in a dog—these amateur sanitary engineers who would chop themselves off at the knees if it would free them entirely from their origins on the land—is that he actually may be an honest-to-goodness *animal,* and not some kind of substitute human being and therefore fair game for them, comprehensible to them. They hate the fact that milk comes from the udders of cows and that grapefruit juice is mostly water which has been down percolating in the soil.

Admittedly, we live near the lower Manhattan waterfront, with its *Gold Star Mother* ferryboat, where the addicts line up for a methadone fix, its House of Detention, and many truck parks, gritty dead lots, and the West Side Highway and a derelict railroad spur running above. Find the right spot and what is a little uric acid there? But if our site is less citified than some, as a group we make up for that by the size of our dogs: hundred-pounders on occasion, Airedales, shepherds, Great Danes, Great Pyrenees, Afghans, Saint Bernards, Salukis, big wolfish chows, Malemutes, Newfoundlands, collies like mine. We are up with the sun, cold but alive to the morning because of the company we keep, smelling the sharp west wind, and much happier-looking than those other outlaws of the city who keep cars and are looking for some place to park. We are out kite-flying, if you want to know, our eyes fixed away on a reality as big and old as the sky. We have tugging on the end of our string the friendly spirit of *Canis,* fifteen thousand years removed from the Near Eastern wolf, fifteen million years removed from the fox, thirty million years distant from the ancestral bear-racoon, forty million or fifty million years removed from ancestral weasels and cats, and from our own line by sixty million to seventy million years, perhaps. The dog family is thought to have originated in North America, dispersed, then come back. And here it is, with poundingly cheerful feet, kiting across the street, sniffing out traces of life. If after all this time the world of life is grinding to an end, it won't be by the agency of dogs. Nor will they give up the ghost without a final leap of the feet and grin of their pointy teeth. Even set down in this ultimate slag heap on the waterfront, if they can't find any life, then, nose to the ground, wagging their tails, they seek out the wastes of life.

The pennyworth psychology of the day would have it that keeping pets is a way of avoiding the mainstream concerns—of putting one's tenderness in a jewelbox, so to speak—a premise that, like any other, can be illustrated if you pick your cases carefully enough, because there are certainly some fanciers who confine their affections to a fish tank. My own impression is that a commoner, deeper motive than escapism is the wish to broaden one's base, to find the fish in oneself. Another fascination, especially with small wild creatures hemmed into a terrarium or cage, is seeing how they cope, and helping them cope. Every man is an experimenter and every experimenter is a small boy, but in this day and age the observer's promptings are not generally cruel; it seems quite crucial to us to know how they *do* function and cope.

No matter how sensibly their needs have been anticipated, however, I wind up pitying wild animals and want them released. But where released? They are pushed face to face with us wherever they survive. Even in the effort to help them survive there are absurd misplays. Recently an entrepreneur somehow gathered together two hundred specimens of a South American sidenecked turtle which is on the list of endangered species and flew them to California, where he hoped to capitalize on their rarity. Instead they were identified and seized by federal officials. So the federal men confiscated the shipment of turtles to teach him a lesson. What did they do then—fly them back? No, killed them.

There's an excellent pet store on 14th Street called Fang and Claw, Aldo Passera, proprietor, where I go to look over the field. Burmese and Ceylonese pythons cost $150 or so, button quail are $25 apiece, sungazar lizards $30. Hornbills and stump-tailed macaques are for sale. The prettiest beast Passera has is an emerald tree boa for $125, and the biggest a regal python of seventeen feet, at $44 a foot. If I went in for wildlife, what I'd buy for my house to represent what has gone before and paralleled us and diverged from us and just stood still would be a common iguana, I think. An iguana as green as a tree, with a stillness about it, but undaunted, tall, gallant in posture, with a mouthful of teeth and a face like that of a god's palace guard, carved by the millennia as if by the workings of water and wind on a grim cliff, only more so. More sculpted than sculpture, an iguana's face is really a great double take, reacting maybe to what was going on in the room forty-five minutes ago and maybe to what was happening during the Triassic Age. It's a face like a trumpet blast, practically a caricature of fortitude, and so it's a face to come home to, a face to get a grip on, I should think. If I wanted a wild animal, it would be that.

But I go for the intelligence and good will and good spirits of my dog instead. He is my fish, my macaque, my iguana, and more.

MARRIAGE,
FAME, POWER,
SUCCESS

Marriage is taken to be a sign of health even if the marriage is bad just by the fact that the person can sustain its rigors for the sake of appearance and in order to be a good Joe while juggling the other tough aspects of living as well. On the other hand, if a marriage is good, it's life with a blue ribbon around it; there's nothing quite like it, it's Biblically rich, it's riding first-class. This is a month when my marriage is not breaking up, and the days are delicious and pleasant indeed—much kissing, much talking of leaving each other (a subject not mentioned when leaving is really in mind), much seeking new twists for our teasing, each calling the other a monster with teeth clenched in love. No question about it, it's happiness—I carry my child like a mahout on my shoulders for miles. Marriage is the high road, foursquare, a public endorsement, a framework within which a good many things begin to look plausible which otherwise might be dubious indeed.

And success—ah! I remember watching with astonish-

ment my father's confusion as he fumbled to straighten his
tie when unexpectedly we met a higher official of his
corporation in the dining room at Lake Placid, where we
were skiing. Yet some years later, I remember being actually short of breath, and losing control of the muscles of
the throat which keep saliva from running down into the
windpipe, in the presence of a famous writer. I could
hardly breathe; I panted as softly as I could and choked
on my spit; my voice changed pitch. The fellow himself
might be drunk and miserable, but I was giddy with a
sense of spiritual prosperity just being close to him, and
this not with one famous author but with several over a
decade or more. With wet eyes I followed the celebrated
in other fields too—Don Budge, Spencer Tracy—seeing
how they reddened with well-being when recognized. It
"went to their heads."

Success in my father's realm didn't mean getting in the
papers but living well—big lawns, old houses, fine clothes
and trips. When he went into the hospital for an operation, he dressed as if for a meeting of the board, that being
one way he knew to communicate that he was a man of
importance and that any mistake that killed him would
cause inquiries. Success also meant clubs: both funny
clubs and power-base clubs. There was a luncheon club
he belonged to in Paris which had no dues but which required a man to get up on his hind legs once a year and
tell a good story. If nobody laughed, his membership was
rescinded. Another funny club, in London, was nominally
for yachting but mostly existed for its newsletter and its
cubbyhole rooms overlooking the Thames. Clubs had

their place in *Who's Who*, but some were a serious matter, like the country club where a man played golf and the sailing club where he boated. In the grueling week's schedule these respites, if they didn't perhaps prolong life, certainly made it possible to keep up the pace. Then there was the club down in Washington where one could entertain at lunch and be counted when there on business, and the club or clubs in New York—first just the club of one's college, then a larger circle—which were really a central bastion in the practice of one's profession, almost indispensable.

Being admitted to practice before the Supreme Court, a ceremony within the legal fraternity which had no practical significance for a backstage attorney like my father, was another clublike ritual. One's old law professor, Felix Frankfurter, might nod from the bench. And there were the guest memberships. A friend coming east from San Francisco could enjoy the courtesies of my father's club during his visit, and out there my father would enjoy the conveniences of his. When he was convalescing, still very ill, and couldn't travel more than a handful of blocks, he was living on Park Avenue at 35th Street. His club was on Fifth Avenue, at 54th Street, however, and so it wasn't a question of reciprocal membership in San Francisco then, but at the men's club on Park Avenue at 38th. That favor, done for him by an old friend, seemed a great boon.

When I was in college, hoping to make a splash eventually, somebody suggested that the way to plan for it would be for me to sit home and write the books, which we'd have to assume would be good, and, impersonating me, he would go out night-clubbing and to parties and pat hands with Leonard Lyons and sock Frank Sinatra. Whatever one thought of Hemingway, success as a writer at that time involved being famous like him. Steinbeck, Saroyan, even down to some of the lowly *New Yorker* crew, had satellite images as to how they dealt with their fame. A checkered employment history, a few pals in the underworld, a feeling for animals, kindness to barmen, boldness with friends, marital irregularity, steadfastness in enmity, sacrosanct writing hours and yet quick pick-up-and-go: these were the clues.

Now we have no Hemingways, even in regard to the handling of fame. Nabokov is too wordy and foppish in interviews, Malamud too squirrelly, Cheever and Algren too private and wounded. Mailer has trained up his fame as carefully as a tomato plant, and Bellow is too vulner-able, too much Everyman (once I was with him during a break in rehearsals for one of his plays, and as the beauti-ful girls in the cast called to him in husky, whispery voices from the door of the delicatessen across the street, it seemed that whether or not he was going to end up going off with one, he was considering doing so with the same guilt and trepidation *I* would have felt).

Mailer does come closest to the role, as he himself used to remind us. For a while, writing little, during the loony period of his life, he seemed like the fellow who had sug-gested that he could do the night-clubbing if only some-body else would write the books. What especially aroused one's sympathy was his incongruous shortness, like a fire-

161

plug, and his crazy, wretched air at parties, most people looking askance at him and giggling cruelly into each other's ears, "There's the madman who stabbed his wife." Well, not all the talent was flung to the winds, and the gap between the man who sits at home writing the books and the man out drumming up printer's ink has shrunk rather than widened, so that his hopes for himself, once seemingly crashed to earth, are still arguable.

With Mailer we have some embodiment of the physical Hemingway concept of fame: the bull-roar voice at a P.E.N. party rocking and silencing the bathtub sailors like a ninth wave; the visiting fireman whom graduate students say they stand next to and surreptitiously match drink for drink to find out what his liquor consumption feels like. William vanden Heuvel edges up to Mailer proffering a paw that's hanging down limp at right angles, like a ritual of submission almost too good to be true, and he is a papa to women, a veritable fertility figure whom my own wife dreamt about when pregnant—he gave her the sound, paternal advice not to get tired, since tiredness in the woman breaks up more marriages than all of the other disenchantments combined. The last glimpse I had of Mailer, he and a slick chick were leaving the Harvard Club on a brisk November evening on their way to eat. He suggested to her, "Let's run," and they did, Mailer doing very creditably—one of those representations of a sprint in which the legs do not step out very far, moving quickly but conserving strength by a very short stride. It was a sprint by which he demonstrated to the girl and himself that he still could run without in any way forcing a test of how fast.

Most Mailer tests are bona fide, but always writing or marital or financial challenges, never physical, and so they are not unlike the tangles that other writers set for themselves. For the old Hemingway physical foolishness and amplitude one must look to a few sideline figures, such as George Plimpton. To be sure, Plimpton has neither the Hemingway physique nor the pugnacity; on the contrary, his commitment is specifically to lose (how sad he would be if he ever won!). But he has staked out for himself challenges of immense physicality, honoring boxers and trapezists far more directly than any of Mailer's protestations do, honoring Hemingway too. Maybe ultimately the man he sets out to do obeisance before is not these temporal champions but the old writing master himself.

Generosity is another Hemingway attribute to fame that one must look to Plimpton for. Probably Hemingway was not very generous at all, no more than Mailer, both being too competitive—nice guys finish last, and all that—generous to women and waiters only. But the physical bulk, the Mosaic beard, the Papa pose, with the passing of time, make us suppose that Hemingway, basking in fame, should have been a generous man. Instead it's the skinny Plimpton who is generous—Plimpton and another New York writer, Pete Hamill, who may be the most generous of all and deserves mention particularly here in connection with Hemingway fame because it is Hamill who, locally, almost alone is maintaining that celebrative function Hemingway valued so much: recording the midnight feasts that he has with movie stars, con artists, revolutionaries, cornermen, the good meals and drinking bouts, the good men who live here in town. Hamill, of course, is proudly provincial, as

Hemingway wasn't, and wouldn't know the first thing to do if invited out into the woods on a fishing trip—wouldn't want to know. But the celebration of the good things that come with success is there.

This sensuous sense of the enjoyment of fame has been scattered and lost. Success for my father was lawns, clubs, trips, a Colonial house and other things that at least were fun to have. But is what writers want so much fun to have? Nowadays they tend to look for investments, to take a block of RCA stock in lieu of an advance, or they are looking at real estate. The clean handling of fame is what's asked for—not too much clowning with Eugene McCarthy, a low profile, a civilized private life well enclaved within the mysteries of the craft. One thinks of the admirably elusive Updike and Roth.

None of my friends who have had movie sales have enjoyed what appeared on the screen, but the big sales of a book itself bring plenty of pleasure. Seeing it displayed, seeing it read—the more readers the better—by the hundreds of thousands in paperback. One wants it on newsstands and in college libraries—this more than fame, like wishing good things for one's children. Just as acting is not really a board and two mummers, but must be vivified by an audience, so writers yearn to reach loads of people and only want to block out the grotesqueries of fan mail, the career calculations, as tainting the dream. I can easily place limits on how much money I'd care to make, how much fame would satiate me if the world were my oyster, but to wonder how many readers I'd like to have . . . None captive, certainly, but millions who opened a book of mine and found something for them—millions! How large would that ideal audience be? Like James Michener's? Johnny Carson's? When the world achieves a population of fifteen billion people, would one want them for an audience, just before they all die? Though we are beginning to sicken of past concepts of growth, artists may never cease longing for a big audience.

Power, now, has that changed? Power has nearly brought the world down around our ears; yet side by side with the revulsion there is love of it still. My Irish friends come back from touring the battlefronts of Londonderry with blood in their eyes—more delight and exultancy than tragedy, really, not like when they flew back from Vietnam. They think it's 1936 and the war in Spain. The Italians embrace the Mafia for their own, and one remembers how every Jewish intellectual who could flag down a cab flew to Israel after the Six-Day War (a lady I knew slept on the desert floor with a tank commander), while here in New York the kids jammed into automobiles and sped through the streets waving Israeli flags and pounding their fists on the doors of the cars, all in the triumph of victory—this after the horrors of World War II.

We have blood in our bones. Power, fame and success, we want them. One's beginnings are humble. Some years ago I sold an idea to *The New Yorker* for twenty-five dollars (a friend wrote it up), and the *Reader's Digest* bought four words out of a book of mine for fifteen dollars. Then three years ago I first heard breathlessness over the phone. A girl called, after I'd published a short story about alligators. "Would you come and talk to our herpetology club?" she asked, her voice trembling.

I go to the *Village Voice* and talk to my friend there,

Ross Wetzsteon. The *Voice* is a child of its times and
subject to as many criticisms. Nevertheless it has about it
the excitement, the variety and fervor, the many personalities, even the brilliance being nurtured, that one reads
of in literary memoirs about *The Nation, New Republic*
and so on in their heydays. He and I are old friends and
are probably in our busiest years—busy to distraction—
and whatever finally comes to us in the way of success, it
is great fun.

WOMEN
AFLAME

I've learned one new thing
about women I didn't always know: that although there's
immensely more difference between individuals than between the sexes even in caricature, still I *am* afraid of some
women, quite a number of them, whom even to pass the
time of day with at a party or at the grocery store seems
wearying, fruitless and dangerous in a way different from
the unpleasantness of being with a difficult man. I'd
thought I'd lost my original boyhood uneasiness with them
and would never again be scared. Instead, the main defense I have against their formidability is my own, which
is of that standard brand any man can adopt for himself
if he wants—the cranky, Old Guard, untrammeled man.
No more untrammeled than they are, but untrammeled
enough. In part, being untrammeled means making a lot
of the fact that there is plenty to life besides what is provided by the opposite sex. Homosexuals have this quality
in a funny way, as long as their own sex life isn't too important to them. Lately they sometimes seem to be the

only people who laugh. Footloose, with nothing to lose, they've taken over the role of the stage tramp of earlier years, who felt free to laugh at a world that he had no stake in.

Sex itself is less necessary to me now, yet at the same time seems much more sticky and unmanageable to contemplate, looking at these heavy-faced, large-looking women I meet and thinking of doing or asking physical favors of them. The first sexual intercourse I saw that I paid much attention to was between leopards, so instead of a nice forsaken unforsaken tenor-voiced groan at orgasm time I used to conjure up what might be interpreted as a snarling sound back in the cavities behind my nose, and once we two youngsters were aligned on the same track the act seemed as simple as that. These darts of ecstasy every two or three days (what do we get, four thousand of them, by hook or by crook, in a lifetime?) were as plain a proof as any to me of the existence of God—not that he gave us this pleasure, but that it was a pleasure so obvious in purpose. We monkeyed with it, with our condoms, pills, abortions, as we monkey with every other condition of life, but there it was, proof of a kind.

What impresses me now as proof is the incredible, helpless intensity of love one directs to one's child, and to nobody else's, an intensity verging on pain, yet not to be severed, overriding every other emotion except possibly self-love. When I pick up my daughter at school I see women en masse. This is a world they have to themselves, and it's rather awesome, seeing them with new babies slung across their chests, as well as the children they've come to pick up. I don't denigrate their good looks just because they've borne children, but seeing them on their own ground, sometimes I find them huge, humpy, re-doubtable, not so musical-voiced or pretty—it depends upon what I've been hearing or reading elsewhere. In elevators I also meet them at close quarters, busy about their careers in the world, which are now—rightly so—to be indistinguishable from ours, just as their bodies are becoming indistinguishable—this not only because of the Women's Liberation Movement, which is subject to back-lash adjustments, after all, and can be improved, but because of the older, somewhat parallel and equally momentous slide toward the death of sex. Sex now as relieving oneself, a meal or a wine to be casually budgeted for, or else (the high sign to pard over there) getting one's ashes hauled. This development, strangely enough, will play straight into the hands of the Old Guard, untram-meled man, because the very secret of his ability to keep going has been just such an attitude.

Once in a while some of the shock troops of Women's Lib come into the bar which I patronize. With chagrined, friendly grins they make reference to their need to avert complexion troubles and various other legendary ailments said to be induced by a prolonged absence from men. Men as a nerve coolant, an antihistamine. "Me Tarzan, me babymaker!" I say, however, being married, and don't go off with them.

One of a father's duties is to make his daughter ticklish, maybe the first aperture for all later sex. And yet how silly a little duty it is: shall we say oppressive? What would his new duties be, to efface himself? To be human, the answer might come (though what is more human than an Old Guard father?). I don't say I have a better answer, and I'm not against change. Unisex, or sexes that have simply been "castled," as in chess, so that the one which stood on the right now stands on the left, are not terrifying concepts to me. When I'm in one frame of mind they may be distasteful, but in another they're not. We're in for worse changes than that. Nor does the bitterness offend me. Bitterness is supposed to be an outlaw emotion, but why should it be? No matter what may have happened, it is unacceptable to show bitterness; only sadness, disappointment or humility are okay. I don't agree to this. I'm full of bitterness, find whole weeks of my life bitter weeks, and I'm rather in luck, so if these burly women in their movement for liberation choose to be bitter, that's all right with me.

But some of us will be unrehabilitated. Hard-bitten, rough-handed, we'll live on as curios, not to be messed with but smiled at and bypassed. I like living alone when necessary. Living alone on the beach or on a mountainside, one soon gets used to getting by on food smeared with Hellman's mayonnaise and one's memories at night. Getting past the evenings, one has lovely days.

I exaggerate. My wife and I are ridden with the same problems that would have threatened to prevail over our marriage ten or fifteen years ago. She is old-fashioned also—by no means one of these inane housewives who can watch a husband come home bruised from a ten-hour job and set the poor creature to cooking supper in retaliation

170

for her own inability to find a job. She has a career; we make a practical, unvindictive division of tasks, and whatever becomes of us, our problems are old. When I run into a woman whom I've loved in the past, I feel no fear of her, either; the same absolute trust wells up.

It is the dykiness, the Amazon hoots, the bodies so proud of being husky that disturb me, and the fall-out on innocent parties who turn into blinkered, dispirited, self-pitying frumps. Perhaps I speak selfishly. You can't cook an omelet without breaking eggs, the cadre will say. I know that we need more, not fewer, disruptions, and we're going to get disruptions fast and furiously anyway that will put Women's Liberation into a class with the struggle for a fair property tax. I expect continual disruptions all the rest of my life. At some point the air will turn orange with the cries of the starving, for instance. Even the oceans will prove no barrier, the noise of those dying cries crossing the thousands of miles as an anguished hum. What do we know of disruption to compare with that? And just as I expect worse disruptions of many kinds, I expect to keep on protesting against them, angry or suffering because of them. That's part of being alive. But must we split into two camps while awaiting these events—the stocky, Hun-faced, "liberated" souls (I think of the physical person of Bella Abzug, whom I like better in the newspapers than when I see her in person, kissing her way down a row of newspapermen), and then, standing off to one side, a smaller band of gaunter, hard-bitten, "untrammeled" men?

THE
NEW ENGLAND
WILDERNESS

1

Like California and New York, Maine is really two states, not north versus south or city versus rural but long coast and big woods. The dangerous ocean and huge boreal woods gave it distinction from the beginning. It was a colony of Massachusetts Bay, a place for the poor and adventurous to go, with strong arms and weak heads, the raffish, the skeptics, the fortune seekers, the drinkers, the people whom Puritanism didn't suit or didn't want. Flying parties of Frenchmen and Indians fought early arrivals, but by 1790 there were a hundred thousand white settlers on the scene and scarcely six hundred Indians left, out of perhaps an original twenty thousand.

In 1820 Maine got into the Union as part of the Missouri Compromise, bribing Massachusetts to release it in exchange for half the proceeds of the sale of all its unoccupied lands. This quick orgy of speculation (a Mr. Bingham from Philadelphia bought two million acres for twelve and a half cents apiece) froze the patterns of settlement much as they were at the time. The population remained concentrated near the coast, and the large timber companies formed from these nineteenth-century holdings still continue to own two-thirds of Maine. Half the state, or ten million acres, is set aside as the Forestry District and has been kept uninhabited to this day, a circumstance as cruel economically as it is strange, because for decades now all of the logging in Maine has been done by contract labor commuting from Canada, where much of the wood goes to be sawn.

The contrast of absentee wealth and resident poverty, along with the fact that a kind of miniature frontier was preserved, have made for a special buccaneering spirit which is characteristic of Maine. These woodsmen who couldn't own land, who could only be squatters, developed a talent for poaching both game and logs, for boasting and legend-building and physical feats to compare with Mike Fink's on the Mississippi and what was going on in the cow and gold camps and Bunyan country out West. Indeed, it was claimed that Paul Bunyan came from Maine, and returned there nailed up in two empty molasses hogsheads for burial. It was said of the Allagash rivermen that they were so "catty" they could throw a bar of soap into a pitch of white water (if they had any soap) and scramble across on the bubbles. Some of the fellows left the scars of their cleats in the ceiling of every bar they entered by jumping and turning a somersault. The boots of a river driver who drowned were hung in a tree on the bank where the body was found. They all went to work at dawn, ate four or five meals a day to keep going and, since their provisions were beans, held farting contests at night and then spat tobacco juice on the stove to kill the germs. Eight snowy months brought three hundred to four hundred dollars to loaf on during the summer.

Maine is contradictory and big and brash for New England, not as ironic as Vermont or New Hampshire, nor as disenchanted with the American dream. Hiram Maxim, inventor of the modern machine gun, was born in Maine, as well as such people as Winslow Homer and Edna St. Vincent Millay; and there has been plenty of chance for freebootery. By 1840 there were a half-million people on hand and 1,381 sawmills with a yearly cut of 225 million board feet, a figure that rose to 640 million board feet in twenty years and to 785 million board feet by 1899. Though he made such a point about not going West, Thoreau did tramp off to Maine whenever Concord got claustrophobic for him, and thrilled to it—died speaking of its moose and red Indians.

The Abnaki, people-of-the-dawn, had seen the sun rise on the American continent every morning. They were an Algonquian nation befriended by the French, the first North American Indians to accept Christianity. They had fought the Mohawks across the White Mountains and had witnessed the explorations of the Cabot family, Verrazano, Champlain, Henry Hudson and Captain John Smith. In 1569 three English sailors marooned by Sir John Hawkins in the Gulf of Mexico met up with them in the course of walking to Nova Scotia. The first French colony was established on the Maine coast in 1604, the first English colony three years later, though both were abandoned

174

almost immediately. Then in 1617 a smallpox epidemic wiped out whole Abnaki villages, leaving no one alive to bury the dead. In 1628 a group of Pilgrims from Plymouth set up a trading post at what is now Augusta on the Kennebec River and made such a profit that they paid off their debts to the Merchant Adventurers of London with Abnaki furs. The French encouraged the Indians to fight the English-Americans, but because bounties of up to a hundred pounds apiece were paid for Indian scalps by either side, the soldiers often killed their allies in order to collect. After the French had finally been defeated and New France ceded to Britain in 1763, the Americans incited the surviving Abnaki to fight on their side in the Revolution.

In the original wilderness the Abnaki lived peacefully and rhythmically enough. In the spring they caught alewives, shad and salmon and planted their gardens. During June they moved to the seashore after porpoises and seals and seabird eggs and nestlings; also clams and lobsters, which they dried for winter use. Early in the fall they returned to the riverbank villages to harvest the planted corn and squash and to gather berries and nuts. When the temperature fell and it got cold enough for meat to keep, the men set off on long hunting trips, chasing moose and caribou till they mired in the snow, or trapping deep-forest furs like marten and fisher. Before the spring break-up they trapped beaver and otter, and afterwards muskrat, until the rivers were clear and the fish runs began again and a new cycle started. A moose's heart was as big as a cannonball; the tongue cooked with cranberries was de-

175

licious. One of Thoreau's friends ate turtle, trout, moose-meat and beaver in a single day on a summer expedition.

I came to Augusta in April 1971 to find out how much was left of New England's wilderness and what was in store for it. The people I'd corresponded with had made it plain that there was very little left, if any, and since that little ought not to be publicized they weren't eager to help me find it—the mountains I climbed ought at least to be unnamed mountains. I defined wilderness as a place where one should carry a compass and wouldn't meet other people; where one would be alone willy-nilly and couldn't beg off from the experience by hailing a ride from a passing log truck if supper was spoiled or the weather soured. I was surprised and disappointed to learn that there was no such thing any more, though from a personal standpoint I did find enough pockets of wild country to be less discouraged—I'd know where to go in the woods, if nobody else did. With seventy million people living within driving distance of the north woods for a long weekend, no place is inaccessible. Sixty thousand people a year climb Mount Monadnock in New Hampshire. Two hundred and fifty thousand climb or ride to the top of Mount Washington.

Of course the worst slopes of the Presidentials are always there for those who think wind and cold and the danger of falling and killing oneself are wilderness—wilderness to them being nine feet of slickrock, "the ecstasy of insignificance," as a climber at the Appalachian Mountain Club put it. Yet by September the paths had been so

176

overhiked that the Trail Crew were talking about how much the mountains must like the hard, cleansing fall rains and wondering why the land didn't just get up and walk away. Huge loads of sewage and trash from the huts up on top were being helicoptered out; the trails had been worn into root-studded ruts; rare timber-line vegetation had been trampled to death; and the campgrounds down in the woods were almost disaster areas, not because people selfishly litter but because there are so many of them. All the manuals of the past taught a whimsical pioneer lore that was more appropriate to the frontier solitudes— like camping at random where the heart pleases, cutting a fresh, fragrant bed of balsam boughs, digging a drainage ditch around one's tent, digging a firepit and cutting wood for it. Now people should pack in Coleman stoves and fuel instead—"Carry in, carry out," "Leave nothing but footprints"—and apply for what in the West is called a Wilderness Permit.

At the Maine Department of Fish and Game I talked with the man in charge of planning in the windowless office he shares with Civil Defense. Though his excitement about his computer was dizzying, it seemed unsecured. He told me a box and a half of shotgun shells is shot off for every duck killed, but seemed to know very little about ducks themselves. The publications of the department are sumptuous, but the warren of green cubicles reminded me of a Gogol novel—all these government clerks modestly shuffling papers, overlooked by enlarged photographs of the lagomorphs and the mustelids on whose lives their work had little bearing. At their meetings a faculty-club pettiness was apparent, and they regularly change the names of their Refuges to honor retiring colleagues. Most Fish and Game offices are satrapies, and Maine's is no exception—self-funded by license fees so that the legislature has no handle on it. Salaries are low, nonetheless. The pay scale for biologists in New Hampshire, for instance, goes from seven thousand dollars to a top of eleven thousand dollars for the chief himself.

One hopes that at least the departments won't do any harm. At the time of my visit Maine's was campaigning to open a limited season on moose, which not long ago were nearly gone from the state and had not been hunted extensively since 1921. The herd had finally grown to fifteen thousand, but this rush to hunt them struck many people as foolishness, since it publicly declared them surplus when, as it was, five hundred a year were being poached. (Wildlife managers tend to regard as "waste" any animal that lives to a ripe old age without being part of a "harvest.") The state legislature voted the proposal down, whereupon Fish and Game, in its pique, canceled the one study of moose life and habitat it had going, inadequate though that was (budgeted for four thousand dollars, out of the department's annual three million dollars). The explanation was that this marvelous great wilderness animal, descended from a beached whale, as the Indians say, wasn't "game."

I talked to Howard Spencer, the Chief of Game, a smooth, politic man, who was wearing a tie dappled with flying ducks. Back in 1954 he was gutting bears to look at their stomach contents, but in middle age he has taken to writing about waterfowl. He told me that teal, wood ducks, goldeneye and mergansers are doing all right, and Canada geese even better, but that black ducks, the most important species from a hunting standpoint, are on a downtrend, both in Maine and throughout the East, with a 55–65 percent annual mortality. Eagle and osprey reproduction has virtually stopped—no more than twenty grown eagles remain in the state. As for beavers, the season is juggled according to local conditions, the landowners sometimes objecting to them because they drown trees, while the fishermen and hunters root for them because they build ponds. Flying in and out, a pilot in Patten had trapped four hundred beavers that winter. Spencer said that two hundred thousand deer licenses are sold every year, that the deer kill is thirty-five thousand, and the bear kill from nine to twelve hundred. In 1957 a $25 bounty on bear was revoked, and since then they have been given a five-month closed season, a one-bear limit per hunter, and the cubs are protected.

The Chief of Inland Fisheries, Lyndon Bond, whom I spoke to next, is a sallow, reflective man—good company— who says that since most lakes in northern Maine are as infertile as battery water, phosphate or sewage pollution isn't yet much of a problem; indeed, its first effect would be to increase the fish food. His staff, he said, stocks 600,-000 brook trout fingerlings annually, 400,000 landlocked salmon, 300,000 Atlantic salmon, 230,000 lake trout, 100,-000 brown trout and 50,000 rainbow trout. These are all cold-water fish, requiring clean flowing water and more oxygen than such warm-water fish as pickerel, bass, horned pout and perch, which may be transplanted between weedy ponds but needn't be raised in a hatchery. Both brown trout, originally a European fish, and rainbows, which are Western, are hardier than brook trout, able to survive in marginal water. The browns, which grow to four or five pounds, are especially tough, but are unpopular with the go-go, impatient modern angler because, being such good survivors, they are cautious and difficult to catch.

With the standard fish there's no question of extinction—Maine alone has thirteen hatcheries—but only the problem of reclaiming the rivers and lakes. For a couple of centuries logs by the million have been tearing the spawning beds out of the streams, covering the beds that they missed with silt, while the bark turned the water acid. Then there's factory pollution, and the dams are the greatest impediment. Even at present, only one of three hundred sea salmon smolts put in the water will live enough of its life to make a real spawning run. But fishing is like motherhood in New England as an issue; what's more, these problems are rather easily solved. Little by little the log drives have been brought to an end, and sophisticated fish elevators and ladders, with "attraction water," are being installed at the big dams. Salmon, alewives and shad can withstand more pollution than people have thought. In the Connecticut River sea-running fish already can reach Turners Falls, Mass., and in another decade will be spawning in Vermont on the White River.

On the other hand, what's good for the fish may not be so good for the game. As the loggers have switched to hauling by road instead of letting the rivers do that chore for them, they've crosshatched the puckerbrush with roads; cumulatively up to 10 percent of the woods is becoming road.

I went to the University of Maine to talk to the state's deer-research leader, Fred Gilbert. He's first-rate, a Canadian three years out of graduate school. He has a heavy face, a massive broken nose, a level look, a muscular straightforward bulkiness, and is graying prematurely. Like most game men, he's thoroughly a predator and has to restrain a certain irritation in speaking of the camera-hunters and birdwatchers who get a free ride as things stand, having access to thousands of acres of wildlife lands purchased with hunters' fees. He says that the main tug of war in the outdoors is not between hunters and Audubon types, however, but between the vacationers and the natives. He doesn't look forward to the time when every well-paid electrician in the city wakes up to the fact that for about the price of a new car he can buy himself a woods cottage in Maine. Summer people hollow out a rural community to a shell of itself—empty four-fifths of the year—and to an ecologist they are much more destructive of habitat than the most reckless logging practices because they simply take the land out of circulation altogether. Like everyone else I was to talk to who was concerned with the subjects I was investigating, Gilbert believes the best solution is large-scale zoning designed to keep open land in the hands of the public, so that instead of thousands of cottagers, each hoarding his tiny parcel in a summer-suburb arrangement, everybody will have ac-

181

cess on an equal basis to recreational land, land of a size to provide a real contrast to life nearer the city.

In theory, Maine's unique system of private ownership of enormous chunks of the state might make this easier to achieve. Great Northern has 2.4 million acres, International Paper 1.1 million; the Seven Islands Land Company manages 1.7 million acres; Scott Paper Company owns perhaps 750,000; St. Regis and Georgia Pacific each have in excess of 500,000 acres; and the Dunn Heirs, the Huber Company and Brown Company own another 300,000 apiece. Public zoning might be made to stick more effectively when applied to these voteless corporations than to a multitude of private citizens—except that if citizens do well in the legislature, corporations do well behind the scenes. For example, a Nader group recently discovered that for forty years tax assessments on all these timberlands had been determined by the landowners' own surveying firm, the James W. Sewall Company of Oldtown, Maine. This caused quite a stir in the state. Another Nader group, in California, has proposed the radical notion that so basic a commodity as land should be subjected to the anti-trust laws if holdings exceed, say, fifteen thousand acres. Paradoxically, however, such anti-trust action and tougher taxation could hasten the end of what wilderness is left.

As we talked, Gilbert's students would bring in the slender pink jawbones of deer so that he could estimate their age by the wear and tear on the teeth. With his likably challenging manner and mind, he seemed a man at home with his job, his superiors and his career—one of the strong young centurions of science. For the spring his project was to examine fifteen hundred deer heads and one hundred moose heads for the presence of a meningeal thread worm, *Pneumostrongylus tenuis*. In the larval stage these organisms live in ground snails and slugs. On the average, five or six mature ones are found in the covering of the brain of a deer, doing little harm because both parasite and deer are native to the New World and so the deer have developed antibodies to prevent penetration. But moose and caribou did not immigrate across the Bering Strait until the recent Ice Age and hence are far more susceptible, caribou especially; the worms ravage their way right into the brain. At the time of first clearing and settlement in the Northeast they moved north with the deer population, shuttling back and forth from deer to snails. Consequently the caribou were decimated. Caribou are trusting herd animals of the deep mossy forest, vulnerable to a hunter, but even when a small protected band was reintroduced on Mount Katahdin in 1963, they soon died out. The density of deer, snails and *Pneumostrongylus* was too high for them. Higher concentrations of deer are needed to wipe out the moose, but moose never spread far into deer country. Interestingly enough, though whitetail deer have also fanned out from the East clear to the Pacific coast, this terrible parasite was stopped at the edge of the Great Plains by the absence of suitable hosts for its larvae, so that Western game animals were not infected.

Deer and moose both live on the buds and bark of deciduous trees during the northern winter, but moose, with their long legs and rugged constitutions, plow through the drifts, bowling the young trees over or reaching high up for a meal, requiring no shelter. By contrast, deer, with their dainty feet and light springy bodies, though they strip the same saplings for food, must huddle most of the time in deer yards in the midst of dense copses of fir and spruce to conserve their warmth and avoid bogging down in the snow. Their margin for survival is small, and they can only subsist at all where there are conifers to shelter under, as well as the broad-leaved trees which furnish their food. This means that by mapping the yards from the air and regulating logging practices in the locality, the game men will be able to control exactly where in the north woods deer can survive. Wherever it is determined they shouldn't be, *Pneumostrongylus* will be absent too, and the moose will prosper and multiply.

Thirty-six key yards in the Forestry District have been mapped so far. The emphasis still favors deer because they are revenue-producing and moose are not, but if it should shift—if moose come to be hunted—a queasy moment may arrive (no doubt after a poll of the hunters: my planner friend with the computer will want to do that) when the department changes its instructions to the loggers and condemns whole local populations of deer to a lingering death by exposure. Already the biologists decide what fish shall live in a great many ponds and lakes by killing off everything with a chemical agent and then starting from scratch with the particular trout desired and a forage fish for it to live on. (The terminology is that these ponds are "reclaimed." This trend towards formulating the precise mix of fish that are wanted in the water

184

and of animals that are wanted on land appeals so irresistibly to the tinkerer in man, and to bureaucracies in general, that it may be irreversible, even though it signals the end of good hunting and fishing. The woods, which already are classified in terms of whether the trees are commercially of interest or are "weed" species, will become a sort of game farm.

The leading wildlife biologists whom one reads—men like George Schaller, David Mech, Roger Payne—are suffused with the sadness inherent in their work, mourning beasts that are soon to vanish, and extending their tender regard to all the wild world. The perimeters within which their science can operate are shrinking as fast as their knowledge expands. My planner, on the other hand, had spoken enthusiastically about a research project for recruiting the likeliest sportsmen by age and income, getting them to buy licenses with a mailing campaign, and stocking the brooks nearest them on a put-and-take basis, brooks perhaps too polluted for fish to live in the rest of the year. In the same way pheasants are stocked in areas of prohibitive snowfall where they can't survive for long, but when the hunters nearby invest in bird dogs a misguided experiment becomes institutionalized. Of course, blue-chip staffers like Fred Gilbert don't approve, and in more closely settled states, such as Connecticut and Massachusetts, a move is afoot to give Fish and Game some responsibility for protecting the whole balance-wheel of natural life, thereby bringing in a new mentality. In Connecticut only 60 percent of departmental funding comes from license fees, and the department caters to other interests—providing bulletins directing bird watchers to the bird sanctuaries and marsh lands the state owns, and so on.

Everywhere land is the watchword, although, unfortunately, few people outside the profession yet realize this. Connecticut owns 150,000 acres of itself; Rhode Island, 50,000; Massachusetts, 240,000. New Hampshire owns only about 1 percent of its land but has the White Mountain National Forest for open space, 728,000 acres, occupying 12 percent of the state. The Green Mountain National Forest in Vermont is a third as large, having got a late start, but the state Forest Service picked up 120,000 acres in the bygone days when land was cheap, and by clever maneuvering the Fish and Game people have lately acquired about 80,000 more.

Gilbert mentioned the remarkable odyssey of the coyote eastward, a success story. One or two hundred now live in Maine, five or six hundred each in New Hampshire and Vermont. Big specimens have been shot in Cornwall, Connecticut, in western Rhode Island and in New Bedford, Mass. Besides being mercurially adaptable, coyotes are creatures of broken brushland and the edge of the forest, which is just what northern New England is becoming as the farms revert. Fisher are another bright spot in the gloom. Ingenuous, lush weasels of the old-growth woods, they were trapped almost to extinction by the time of the Depression, and yet have rolled back from the brink, changing their diet to fit man's backyard, booming and thriving until there is even some talk of bountying them. They eat tabbycats and mice and rats, and along with their present superfluity they've suffered an inevitable fall-off in reputation. The texts of the past ranked the fisher as the fastest animal in the woods, quicker than marten or squirrel, but now many biologists describe them as clumsy and slow. The truth seems to be that fisher, which are almost as big as otter, and peripatetic (but travel the ridges instead of along rivers and streams), are slow-moving when on the ground, and can even be run down by a man in a field, but are downright legendary once in a tree. A movie crew is said to have gone through two hundred red squirrels while trying to capture on film a fisher making a kill.

Gilbert agreed that salmon could be restored in our rivers wherever the public wishes them to be; the place to worry about them was in the overfished ocean and the cesspool-sinkholes of the littoral zone. He said the few eagles that have lived through the worst years of pesticides may gradually bring back the race because they've already suffered the effects biologically, whereas man won't feel the consequences to *him* for another quarter-century. Though his prognostications were gloomy, as any ecologist's tend to be, his vigor itself was rather cheering, and he told me he envied the canoe trip I planned later on—the ground was stored full of water for the summer ahead because the surface had not had time to freeze before the first heavy snows of the previous fall.

Still in Augusta, I went to see Frank Gramlich of the U.S. Fish and Wildlife Service and found him to be another breath of fresh air. Meeting a series of cloudy-faced state bureaucrats had discouraged me, but here was a federal free agent who took a wider view. With all Maine as his territory, Gramlich dispenses sympathy, netting, noise-making devices, scary balloons and hallucinatory chemical feeds to people pestered by blackbirds or gulls—airport officials, blueberry growers, radar-site commanders, and so forth. Sometimes he puts a raccoon to work on the problem. He also autopsies starlings to monitor the effects of the pesticides, fights orchard mice, and advises about "wildlife enhancement" on military reserves. He's blue-eyed, large in the face and meaty in build, a retired sergeant, irreverent, humorous, tolerant and self-deprecating on the telephone. I heard him talk to one naval officer who had a sea-gull problem, for instance, with that wonderful skill at euphemism and accommodation that sergeant majors display. Gulls were a considerable nuisance at the naval base but are a protected species as well, so Gramlich suggested holding a little close-order drill near the nesting site.

Herring and black-backed gulls, being scavengers, double in population every ten years and have never had it as good as they do alongside man. Much the same is true of the blackbird family—cowbirds, crows, grackles and others, including the raven, which ranges north of the Arctic Circle and was formerly a beleaguered wilderness bird but is staging a comeback, feeding at dumps and on winter-killed deer. One of Gramlich's hobbies is eagle-watching along Maine's big rivers; he thinks there may be as many as a hundred eagles living in the state, at least seasonally, and that a few young birds do appear every year. Thus, since eagles live up to thirty years, he expects to continue seeing them occasionally as long as he lives. One must stop one's car, park off the road, get out of the rush-rush mentality for a while, look up much farther, deeper and higher than one is accustomed to, but if you do this, in the course of an afternoon spent along a major valley like the Penobscot or the Kennebec, you will still see an eagle cruise by. He doubts they will outlive him, but in the meantime, very high and unknown to practically everyone, he told me, they are still there.

I went to the Maine Forest Service headquarters too, acquiring a prodigious armload of publications. The Information and Education man responsible for them was a barking, nasal, ironic chap with a big nose, and we sat in his office trying to discuss the weird situation of a state with 7.8 percent unemployment and half its land area uninhabited, logged by nonunionized, commuting Canadians, the wood milled in Canada, as well. But unemployment is only one of Maine's problems. For instance, during the last thirty years of the nineteenth century its population grew just by 10 percent, while the rest of the nation's increased 97 percent. In addition, the timber companies have their own devil to point to: the fact that in the industry's formative years a virtual maze of short-hauling, price-gouging railroads lay between their lands and the cities where the wood might have been put to good use; so they shipped it to Canada instead.

Because the Forest Service was created to watch out for and fight fires, much of its budget still derives from direct assessments the landowners pay, and there are tight ties between it and the paper industry. More than one disgusted conservationist told me that whereas in a fight the Fish and Game Department is generally as neutral as possible as long as its own power base isn't threatened, the Forest Service takes a position identical with of the industry and acts as its political instrument. Besides firefighting, its duties involve managing public campsites on paper-company lands, fighting the spruce budworm, sawfly, pine weevil, birch borer, gall aphid, beech scale and other villains, and advising farmers on how to upgrade their wood lots. It has no enforcement function because the state does not as yet regulate forestry practices. Though this is surely coming eventually, the several staunch men I interviewed will hate the day. As is traditional in Maine, going back to the heroic age of the river drives, they have a high regard for the stockholders whose woods they look out for. In a sense, woods heroes couldn't exist without rich men to serve. To *be* woods heroes they must be underpaid, and so it's a gruff but cooperative relationship—you fellows can be heroes if I can be rich. Strength and a gift for physical feats are also unequally bestowed, and daring men look down just as condescendingly as some of the rich do on those passers-by who are unendowed.

The phrase used constantly, "State of Maine," implies a state of mind, a stance and predicament, and landowners and woodsmen alike think of themselves as individualists. When land becomes merely government land and woodsmen part of the Civil Service, who can be a hero? In New Hampshire the members of the Appalachian Mountain

Club's Trail Crew earn thirty-eight dollars a week, and cruise and clear fifteen miles of trail in a day, moving at a jog. Shaggy, skinny, they scatter out and sleep on the ground even when they are back at headquarters for a day off. But the young men who parallel them on U.S. Forest service paths, and who are well paid—paid overtime on the rare occasions when they get out so far that a truck doesn't fetch them home to their beds for the night— dawdle along, working as the world does, with about as much delight.

When talking to division foresters for the State of Maine—men in charge of as much as five million acres— I've pointed at their wall maps and asked if there was anywhere they couldn't promptly get to by car. They said no, not entirely pleased, because though the fires don't get away from them as easily now, these are men near retirement who are glad to have spent their young years in woods large enough that an assignment like blazing a boundary line meant three weeks alone, and a hell of a fright if suddenly they did encounter another man (bears one could take in one's stride). Professionally, foresters are supposed to hate a wilderness, and the youngsters who have never known one think that they do. The downed trees are a tangle nobody can walk through, dead spars stand everywhere instead of going to the mill, and young saplings and poles are strangling each other for light so that none can grow well. The foresters say that just as carrots are thinned in a garden, so must trees be; in woods left as wilderness they'd have no work to do. But the older men saw the last cathedral groves of virgin yellow birch,

rock maple, red spruce and white pine that had been
left after the first cut-through—perhaps lost in a forest
too huge at the time, before airplanes were employed to
search every last acre out. Or they saw only the unforgettable butts, because the saying was that no man
who cut down a pine would live long enough to see the
stump rot to dust.

Such sights are not soon forgotten, even though the cry
now is for every forest to become a tree farm. Naturalists
dislike this new attitude, believing that a woods made
into a garden, each tract cropped in rotation, is no longer
a woods. Some animals, like the marten and Canada
lynx, and a fantastic bird called the pileated woodpecker—
spectacular-sized, with a crested red head, strong sweeping wingbeats and a flashing black-and-white plumage—
seem to be disappearing because they need a habitat
which includes a natural assortment of dead as well as
living trees. Contemporary forestry, whether practiced
on private or government lands, makes no allowance
for dead or even for mature trees, because those that
live beyond adolescence have stopped growing fast, and
just like every other living thing, have started to dete-
riorate inside. The ideal of most foresters is a one-crop
woods which is cut at an age corresponding to eighteen
in a human being. The variety of trees on a New England hillside—with fir and spruce going for newsprint
and toilet paper, yellow birch for dining-room furniture,
ash for tool handles, beech for clothespins and crating,
and maple for bowling pins—is not their idea of efficiency.
Of course, there are senior foresters locally who resist

the mow-'em-down theory, and the weight of tradition
and possible regulation waiting in the wings may prevent
drastic meddling with the flora of the region, but the
schism between forester and naturalist is a painful one.

So is that between naturalist and hunter. I have land
in northern Vermont which I make a point of not posting;
I've explored the drab mills where many of the hunters
work, and I might be out with a shotgun too if I were in
their shoes. But when they actually arrive, creeping with
pistols into the brush after the animals and birds which
give me such delight, I fret, twist, and run in and out of
the house, beside myself, as if my clothing were stuck full
of pins. And yet anybody who looks into the future recognizes that these bickerings between forester-naturalist-
hunter are a tiny matter compared to the sea change in
the affinities of Americans as they settle for good into a
suburban life style. All factions have reason to worry if
the broad majority of citizens lose that mysterious sense
of felicity and exuberance they once had in the presence
of natural grandeur—the feeling of having known it before, of being linked to it via thousands of centuries before
they were born—and simply stop caring.

This is happening now with the ocean, the wildest of
all spectacles. How many people make a sea crossing, or
care that they don't? Soon no one will care; the memories
will go. It's too expensive a proposition to preserve any
wilderness at all without lots of support at the polls, and
when you count all the parties, from the Audubon men to
the snowmobilers, and allow for the good-hearted city-
bound dreamers as well and the conservative idealists who

believe in a rugged outdoors on principle as part of the nation's birthright, even all of them together may not be enough. The most practical plea may be the final one, which has already emerged, that insists on the right of a minority to its pleasure—a pleasure in this case so deep-seated that it can be equated with religious freedom. But even this argument may not succeed.

I drove north to Millinocket, a town of 7,400 souls near Mount Katahdin which was built and is owned by the Great Northern Paper Company. The company was organized in 1899, when an engineer realized that the West Branch of the Penobscot here has a head of a hundred and ten feet of water, suitable for a mill. GN has a middling reputation among conservationists but apparently is quite retrogressive locally, opposing the restoration of a $50,000 cut in the school budget that spring, opposing a $1,500 efficiency study of the police force, or even the hiring of a clerk. According to the newspaper, even the chief's travel allowance was taken away, although he had been elected president of the Maine Police Chief's Association. It's a grubby, uncared-for town, and as Harry Kearney, the supervisor of Baxter State Park, said, there are no public-relations men on the scene. (A few months later in Bangor I stopped in to see John Maines, who is in charge for GN in Maine. It's a rough-diamond city, but Maines is a chubby-faced, indoor man, a sociable chuckler. He indicated that it was perhaps something of an embarrassment for the company to own an actual functioning town in this day and age, but owning 2.4 million acres—more than twice as much land as the White Mountain National Forest and Green Mountain National Forest combined—was grease for the wheels.)

Harry Kearney, who later in the year resigned and reportedly was working as a milkman, impressed me. Stubborn and cautious, a former game warden, he had been objecting to some of Great Northern's logging practices within the park, fighting the Fish and Game hierarchy too, and strictly enforcing the 560-person limit on camping inside the park at night, so that he had no lack of detractors. As a boy he'd camped and swum at Chimney Pond, a famous showpiece in a high basin just underneath Katahdin's main peak; now, revisiting the place, a heavily used campground, he felt disquieted but didn't know why. He was sitting on a familiar rock and eating his lunch, and gradually the memory crystallized. This rock had been one that they'd jumped to from shore and then dived into deep water, but now it was part of the shore and bordered by shallows. Plenty of erosion was evident in any case, so he sought to close the camping spot for a while and establish another. When I talked to him he thought he'd succeeded, but when I returned in July his successor, a young fellow named "Buzz," had reopened Chimney Pond to camping. "Erosion," Buzz told me, "is caused not by people but by nature."

Maybe feeling embattled himself, Kearney had spoken about Percival Baxter, who was the visionary responsible

195

for the park in the first place and who lived to be ninety
years old. His longevity was a great stroke of luck for
everybody because he kept on acquiring land right up until the end. Baxter was a cannery heir from the coast, a
lawyer and gentleman, a state legislator and two-term
governor of Maine. During his period in office (till 1925),
he tried hard to persuade the state to acquire its heirloom
mountain, Katahdin, and some of the surrounding heights
and lake country. He failed, but in 1930 he took the step
of purchasing 6,700 alpine acres himself and deeding them
to Maine. Then the wish expanded; he set himself a goal
of 100,000 acres, meeting with immediate resistance from
the landowners as soon as he'd acquired the barren high
slopes and tablelands and wanted real timber country.
Not a lumberman, he was from Portland, and in northern
Maine the whole idea of a public park seemed crazy, if
not subversive. But he was rich, influential, and he wan-
gled and nagged and kept at it and at it, agreeing almost
always to let the seller log every tract before it changed
hands. As early as 1937 he was thinking ahead far enough
to ban float planes from the lakes and to establish a sanc-
tuary for game. When he reached his first goal, he set out,
still in good health, to acquire a total of 200,000 acres, and
lived long enough to do so. The state had the grace to
accept his conditions and deeds, but often in my inter-
viewing I got indications that he was thought a bit of a
crank—at least in the back country—was joked about,
toyed with by the heads of the companies even when
finally they humored him and gave in, and went unap-
preciated in his own time.

196

The White Mountain National Forest began to expand from New Hampshire into Oxford County, Maine, but in 1951 the Maine legislature stopped it not far from the boundary with a prohibition rescinded only recently. So the next largest piece of Maine in the public domain is the Allagash Wilderness Waterway. The original concept of Conrad Wirth of the National Park Service in Washington had been that 782,000 acres of canoe wilderness be bought federally and preserved. This was whittled down, after much consultation and compromise, to 296,000 acres, centering on a ninety-mile corridor of the Allagash River, before the official proposal was issued in brochure form in 1961 by Secretary of the Interior Stewart Udall. The timber lobby in Maine then raised a hue and cry about confiscation in the state, but did not succeed in dissuading the federal authorities. By 1965 Maine was forced to come up with a counter proposal, which almost exactly halved that figure to 145,000 acres just by the expedient of leaving out nearly all tributary streams and lakes. Udall would not accept such a cut, and 200,000 was settled upon. Since Maine had insisted upon state control and the use of state money to purchase the land (aided by a matching grant), only 24,000 acres was actually bought, however. The rest of the announced acreage remains in paper-company hands and today is being logged within a few hundred feet of the water. The result is a narrow, vulnerable, straight-line "wilderness."

Superhighways tend to beeline people through the countryside, and Kearney told me he hoped that once people got traveling fast they'd shoot straight by Katahdin and the Allagash, clear to Labrador, their feet on the accelerator all the way.

In the West, Katahdin would look like a big bluff set on a watery plain. One climbs it today in the summer in three or four puffing hours, picnicking on top with thirty other people, so that the awe and savagery of the place which Thoreau captured on paper in 1846 will never again be experienced by anybody, even during the winter season. One can risk one's life in the jungly districts of a city too, after all; that does not make it what we call a wilderness, there being no jubilation of *discovery*. In March, the month before I came, the mountain had been climbed by four groups, and the park registered one hundred-and-eighteen "camper-days." As of April 141 inches of snow had fallen, and the drifts looked tired, grainy and soggy. Katahdin was hidden in clouds when I drove to the entrance of the park, where the snowplows stopped. A few hungry crows patrolled. If I was wondering about rigor, however, here was more rigor than I wanted in any New England winter. The fatigue, the mental ordeal, is what is really referred to when people ask if you have what it takes to withstand a northern winter, and so far I've lacked the confidence and have been a migrator, like most of the birds.

On the roads west to Greenville on Moosehead Lake the trucks carried tree-length logs. Even de-barking is done at the mill, though the old loggers did it by hand in the woods in the sap season, peeling the bark off the trees and leaving it intact in long slippery shells on the ground like a snake's shed skin. Greenville is an airy, summery village, a former outfitting point as well as a resort. A white-haired bush pilot of some renown named Dick Folsom who is located there lends it a bit of éclat, especially since he is native-born. I hung about his hangar, looking at maps. A marvelous concentration of light from the snow on the lake illuminated everything. The planes fly on skis until the first week of May, when Moosehead finally breaks up.

Folsom was as diagnostic as a doctor in suggesting what I ought to do in the woods later on. In manner he's quiet and intelligent, his long face enlightened by his handsome hair; he might as easily have an office on Park Avenue as wrestle with the winds, except that his age and seriousness give him a veteran's patina. Still, I had the feeling, as with most of the woodsmen I met and liked, that he had been limited by the absence of real contest and challenge and wasn't the same pilot he would have been in a better wilderness. Big swamps and deadwaters, old-growth trees, big complicated wildlife in a matrix of scarcely mapped mountains enhance the woodsman who must deal with them, but none of the professionals I would be talking to in the course of the coming months so much as slept out once a year any more. With their campers and cabins they were changing along with the country. Folsom's business, like that of the airlines, is with people who first ask themselves, Shall we drive or shall we fly?

He told me that the best canoe river is the St. John for the hundred and sixty miles from Fifth St. John Pond to Fort Kent. (The St. John flows on for nearly three hundred miles more to Bay of Fundy at last.) Forests hold water—"forests grow fish," the slogan goes—and much of this headwaters watershed lies in adjacent Quebec, which is heavily farmed compared with Maine, so that sometimes the river runs out of canoeing water, but it's Maine's pride and joy. For years Senators Edmund Muskie and Margaret Chase Smith have been trying to have the Corps of Engineers dam the upper St. John for public power. The Maine Natural Resources Council, the Sierra Club and so on have campaigned against this, with the support of the timber owners as well, but so far the only opposition effective enough to stall the idea has been the private power companies of southern New England—strange bedfellows—who have the swing votes in the U.S. House and don't want public power.

Folsom said hunting up here is tapering off lately, because so many of this generation of hunters are scared of the snow. They want enough to track with, but as they drive north they stop as soon as they find a few inches. Despite the leisure and mobility to make them gung-ho, they mostly road-hunt, get up later, and stay indoors if the weather is bitter. Some, indeed, never leave home, buying the licenses out of nostalgia, only to discover that their kids have been soured on hunting by Vietnam.

The mechanization of logging produces huge browsing areas for deer and moose—first the slash itself, then the suckers and shoots that sprout up. It was not until World War II that the chain saw replaced the ax in these woods. Now even a loader costs sixty thousand dollars, and modern business philosophy expects profits to rise 10 percent a year. There is a clash brewing between the selective-logging theories carefully nurtured over the years by the industry's aristocrats, such as the Seven Islands Land Company, which hopes to employ helicopters to lift the logs out to its trucks, thereby cushioning the remaining trees from damage, versus the economics of a complete clear-cut. Scott Paper, which is run from Philadelphia, is starting to clear-cut, and at the same time to divide up the southerly shores of Moosehead Lake, which it owns, into cottage lots.

I drove southwest along the Kennebec and Androscoggin drainages in lovely weather, with the sunshine seeming to lengthen, the temperature comfortably in the thirties, the snow on the ground beginning to shrink. Endless woods collared in snow, pretty red-and-white towns along the Sandy River, sugar pails hanging on the maple trees, some small sawmills. Being a little lonely, I looked forward to the creature comforts of a shower and steak.

You come upon New Hampshire's White Mountains suddenly and leave them just as abruptly; they are a brief, circumscribed range, ringed and bisected by highways. Because of the ease of access, six or seven hundred campers spend the night at a spot suitable for one hundred, and mountain shelters built for twelve people may have to accommodate fifty. In Pinkham Notch I met John Nutter and Ken Olson, both twenty-five, who manage the Appalachian Mountain Club's operations there. Their club had put in lots of rescue work on Mount Washington during the winter (nineteen rescues, three bodies). Mount

Washington is 6,288 feet high, an altitude which is climatically comparable to 10,000 feet or more in the West. Its run-off feeds the Saco, Connecticut and Androscoggin rivers, and its summit is at a confluence of conflicting air masses and has a morphology that brings about a "Bernoulli effect" in wind velocity, like a constriction in a pipe. Erosion has been modifying this, so that a wind speed of 140 mph is now extraordinary; the measured record of 231 mph was set back in 1934. Still, the winds do exceed hurricane force more than a hundred days in the year.

The mountain was first sighted from the Atlantic in 1605, first climbed in 1642 by a white man named Darby Field and two Indians. We don't know for sure that young Indians in their testing ventures alone hadn't climbed these significant peaks long before. Probably some did, but the conventional wisdom has been that since, like most primitive peoples and most frontiersmen, they found life richer and less spooky below (some of what seems a wilderness to us was a wilderness to them too), there were no exceptions among them, none who dared the gods.

Climbers naturally make of Mount Washington a darling. Almost seventy have died there, starting with Miss Lizzie Bourne. "Here in the twilight cold and gray/lifeless but beautiful she lay," says the sign on her cairn. Huntington Ravine is a proving ground for mountaineering groups going to the Alps and Himalayas; yet it is aswarm with tyros too, some of whom have outfitted themselves like Sir Edmund Hillary, only to get into perilous trouble because they forgot to bring a flashlight along, or have let their maps blow away. The mountain has also been personalized by the strange cadre of men who link their lives to the weather station on top, the TV tower, the cog railway and the "carriage road," preferring life in the clouds to life below.

At breakfast at the Pinkham Notch lodge you see that Appalachian Mountain Club members are a breed of queer ducks too—peppy, skinny fellows with curious genteel accents and middle-level jobs, and some crusty, nanny-like ladies. It's a civilized club of purposeful walkers with sensitive faces who roll out of their double-decker bunks at 6:30 A.M., when the night man strides through ringing a cowbell. It was founded in 1876, and except for the fact that it lobbied for the establishment of the national forest system in the beginning, has tended to stick to its knitting, concerned with the local mountains and furthering hiking in them. Lately, under pressure from some of its members, it has gone to court with a few amicus briefs as part of the new conservation movement. Even within the White Mountains it usually restricts its attention to government lands, however, not the large private holdings, and seeks to accomplish its ends by allying itself with the recreation-minded wing of the Forest Service rather than by adversary tactics.

The Green Mountain Club operates the same way in Vermont, though on a much smaller scale. But the Appalachian Mountain Club has gotten mired in the "hotel business," as some of the kids who work for it complain. The budget for the dormitory installation at Pinkham and the high huts and shelters is now $432,000 a year, and I was touched by how Olson and Nutter managed to invest all this—including "the Appies," as the kids call them, sitting at long boarding-school tables thumbing guide-books—with some of the air of a commune. The paradox is, says Nutter, that in order to save any sampling of wil-derness you must bring great numbers of people in, orga-nize a Four-Thousand-Footer Club with forty-six specified peaks to be climbed, and all the rest of it, so that each voter can see the landscape for himself.

Education—this was the note sounded everywhere, as in a losing battle. Many of the old countrymen I talked to could recognize twenty-five birds by color and song, while their children hardly knew four or five. Since tour-ism is an industry so destructive to wild land, Nutter and the others who minister to it from the side of the angels do so with misgivings. Apparently there are always going to be more snowmobilers than snowshoers, more people with motorboats than canoeists, more downhill skiers than cross-country enthusiasts, for whom the mountains need not be scalped.

The Appalachian Trail winds over Mount Washington, hitting the high spots on its way to Katahdin three hun-dred and fifteen miles away. In places it's in danger of being loved to death by day-hikers, but to walk the whole two thousand and twenty-five miles from Georgia to Maine is gigantically inspiriting, most of the people who have done it say. They soon rid themselves of much of the equipment they started with, walk a quota of miles each day but not at set hours, sleep and go, sleep and go, some-times by moonlight, eating honey, nuts, fruits, and suffer a tremendous reentry depression when it's all over. Nutter says that they don't stand out in the dining room at Pinkham Notch except for their beards, don't seem crazy or lonely, except that they talk so frequently about *each other,* having pored over the logbooks in every shelter. Sometimes a man will send a letter ahead to another fellow on the trail whom he's never seen, confiding to Nutter, "He's not going to make it." Branley Owen, of Knoxville, traversed the Appalachian Trail in an incredible seventy days just after his release from the paratroopers, which was an achievement right out of the bag of tricks of the real frontiersmen, though he was somewhat condescended to for it; it was thought by some hiking officials that he hadn't savored the countryside properly. In the old-fashioned wilderness, of course, trails took the easiest path, avoided scenic heights, and men traveled fast. One wishes today that if they are going to be purist, the hiking clubs would take their own admonition to "leave nothing but footprints" more seriously. They litter every knoll or saddle with the name of some deceased scoutmaster, never leaving a mile of path in silence and peace.

A boy in Gorham, New Hampshire, trapped three red and two gray foxes, six ermine, three mink, three raccoons and one muskrat this winter—for whatever the figures are worth. I met Harry Thompson, an Indian-looking, middle-aged trapper from Tamworth, in the office of one of the district rangers. He'd caught fifty fisher, each worth maybe thirty-five dollars, and at one point caught a muskrat and mink in the same trap under the ice in a stream—the mink must have overtaken the muskrat for a meal. He said trapping an otter (worth thirty-two dollars) is as difficult as trapping a snake because they so seldom put their feet down as they swim, weaving all the way. The trap must be set in a neck of the stream. The first month after hunting season is poor for him because the woods creatures are stuffed with shot meat. He saw his first bear of the spring on April 4th. Ranching, he told me, has brought the price of a twenty-dollar mink down to four or five dollars, and a five-foot, dollar-an-inch beaver is now below twenty-five dollars.

The district ranger, Verland Ohlson, has nine assistants to manage two hundred thousand acres. A hundred thousand have commercial timber on them, of which a thousand acres a year are logged. Land outside the National Forest is now three or four hundred dollars an acre, ten times as much as it cost a decade ago. He suggested that New England has become like California, full of refugees flocking for salvation. It's true enough, and New Englanders, who are precisely the people who *didn't* go to California, or even halfway, don't like this at all. Soon they start to think the enthusiasm is insincere as well as half-baked. They watch a city couple fall in love with a run-down farm, gush over it, rush back and forth, drawing up plans, then sell it the following year instead, doubling their money; this again and again. What sometimes is not understood is that the same couple may have married in a genuine fervor of infatuation but will shed one another shortly after abandoning the project of the old farm, that each will then take a high-powered new job, plunge into it with absolute earnestness, yet quit the next year.

I visited the headquarters of the National Forest in La-
conia, New Hampshire. Headquarters men generally serve
only a couple of years before being transferred; their eyes
are fixed on the regional office, and since the Forest Service regional office for New England is out in Milwaukee,
a good deal of management theory is brought East on the
basis of testing done in the Midwest. My man was lunky
and hearty, wearing white sideburns and the kind of
agreeable expression that is meant to indicate that everything said to him is mighty instructive. He'd worked in
Colorado and Michigan and found Easterners to be "more
conservation-minded." He agreed, though, that nationally
the Forest Service's priorities are slanted toward timber
harvesting rather than recreation, wildlife or watershed
protection (the best watershed being a wilderness). He
said the main reason was that ninety-five percent of the
Service's budget requests to the Congress for timber management are being filled, as opposed to only thirty-five
percent of its budgeting for these other concerns. The
White Mountain National Forest, though comparatively
small, is the fourth heaviest used of all—two million vis-
itor-days a year—with more money spent on search and
rescue than on fire control. The Presidential Range is over-
crowded, certainly, but at least there is some remoteness
in the Pilot Mountains, the Carter Range, on the East
Branch of the Pemigewasset, in Bean's Purchase, the Wild
River Valley, and in the Mahoosucs, a mountain group adjoining the Forest owned by the Brown Paper Company.
All these, he told me, are redoubts where one can be alone
for a day or two.

New Hampshire was one of the first thirteen states.

(Much of Vermont at the time of the Revolution was called the New Hampshire Grants, although it was claimed by New York as well.) Thus New Hampshire began its existence with a confidence lacking in both Maine and Vermont, which were chafing at duly constituted authority. It was close to Boston and the textile cities of Massachusetts, and it was wide in the south and narrow up north, so that it quickly gathered more population and industry than Vermont, which is about the same size but opposite in shape. Even out in the boondocks, New Hampshire was never as agricultural but was more loggers' country; statistically it's now one of the most industrialized states, has several factory cities and a large bedroom-suburb populace too in the towns bordering Massachusetts. It votes Democratic more often than Vermont, but has a quirky, deep-dyed conservative streak and still has no sales or income tax, so that fiscally it lives on the brink of absurdity and what farmers are left are forced off their land by the property tax. The State Assembly is the third largest legislative body in the world (four hundred members), and besides being unwieldy and erratic, is underpaid and meets only in alternate years. Since the members tend to be rich or retired, the system is self-perpetuating. One effect is, for instance, that the paper companies admit that New Hampshire tax policy on their wild lands is the kindest in New England. Another is that the Department of Fish and Game, with a license income about equal to Vermont's, has acquired only 5,500 acres for the public and has one hundred and eighty-five employees, whereas Vermont's department gets along very well with a hundred and twenty employees and has bought 80,000 acres with the money saved. If New Hampshire's men tried to buy land with an eye to the future, the legislature might figure they had more money than they knew what to do with and start taking some of it away.

What the woodland in New Hampshire *has* had going for it all these years is the solicitude of many influential Bostonians who were concerned about where they spent their summers. In the process, in 1911, they helped to create the funding authority for all Eastern national forests. Western forests came into being by a stroke of the pen because they had never passed into private hands, but in the East the land was already owned; as late as 1867 the State of New Hampshire sold 172,000 acres of the White Mountains to various speculators at fourteen and a half cents apiece. In order to salvage some, it became necessary to convince the lawmakers in Washington, D.C., that a serious pattern of mistakes had been made and, reversing the thinking that had prevailed, to have the government buy back land previously sold by the states, countering the arguments about socialism with an early statement of the public ethic of conservation in the United States.

In 1901 the Society for the Protection of New Hampshire Forests set up shop in Boston in an office on Joy Street next to the Appalachian Mountain Club's, with a directorate of good Bull Moose-type Republicans that interlocked with the AMC's. Its chief staffers have always been professional foresters who try to maintain a friendly relationship with the timber-company land managers, in-

209

stead of carrying on like the botanical equivalent of anti-vivisectionists. They do lobby, however, and organize buy-a-tree campaigns to acquire key parcels of scenery—Crawford and Franconia notches, and Sunapee, Kearsage and Monadnock mountains—passing these on to the state when the time is right. Paul Bofinger, the latest staffer, with offices in Concord nowadays, is thirty-seven. He's an abrasive, focused, contemporary sort who knows how to get on the phone and accomplish what he can. Seven or eight hundred thousand acres within the state are owned by the paper companies, and the problem is that if these companies are only a division of a conglomerate their own foresters are little better than inventory recorders in the decision-making that goes on in New York City and elsewhere. (Until recently, Brown Company, which holds the most land, was controlled by an Italian industrialist named Sindona; he was bought out by Gulf and Western.)

In business terms, sustained yield—the idea that forests should be logged carefully in order to grow up productive again—is, after all, a notion out of the Victorian era which said that one should never "dip into capital." The accelerative conglomerate managers of today aren't much interested in the situation their successor's successor will inherit in twenty or forty or eighty years. Moreover, they are perfectly aware that they are sitting on a gold mine of acreage that can soon be diced up for summer development instead of pulp-growing. People will insist upon a place to go in the summer, and both conservationists and developers begin from this assumption in their maneuvering. When specialized developers like Boise Cascade move

210

into the state, they skillfully create a whole new anti-regulation lobby where none ever existed before; joined with the paper companies, this combination triples the Society's difficulties with the legislature. Though naturally Bofinger has his allies also—the Parks Commissioner is a former AMC official—all summer long, smiling loggers kept telling me about his defeats.

I went to Boscawen, New Hampshire, and talked to Helenette Silver, New England's best wildlife biologist. Like Fred Gilbert in Maine, she's been assigned by her department to work mostly on deer, that being the cash crop. She lives in the 1760 house where her husband was born—once the town's poor farm, after New Hampshire towns ceased selling their poor at auctions, which was the original way of dealing with them. She's a woman of sixty with a rabbity face of vertical lines, straight hair pulled back, an anxious forehead but amused eyes. She is shaped like a darning egg, is a self-made biologist with a vaguely literary air—like a secret writer—and during World War II was employed as an engineer by the Signal Corps at Fort Monmouth, New Jersey.

We sat at a long antique worktable in her library, which is stacked with books, and talked first about coyotes, because in a monograph published in 1969 she had proved at last that the "coydog" reported from the Adirondacks and northern New England for the past thirty years is not a hybrid but a true-breeding variant of the Western coyote. Over six years, she and her husband observed a litter of five dug out of a den in Croyden and fifty of their descendants. Indeed, what had first attracted me to her was an illustration in that monograph showing her hunkered down next to the pen, looking very much like the pictures one used to see of the New Hampshire housewife who wrote *Peyton Place*, but with her mouth open and her eyes closed, howling, while the coyote beside her happily joined in. Other pictures merely showed her legs and skirt, with the pups gazing up toward her face. In person she seemed more urbane, more professorial and older. She had some tropical fish around, but as when an artist finishes with a project, not a dog or a coyote was left.

Mrs. Silver's monograph was the coyotes' welcome to New England. In the West, where fish and game departments tend to be owned by the stockmen the way Maine's Forest Service is controlled by the timber interests, her neutrality might have been unacceptable, but I found surprisingly little interest in these quick beasts among other biologists—certainly no wish to put out a dragnet and kill them, but no sense of delight at the advent of a new personality either. Being myself particularly intrigued by them, I kept trying to put in a good word for them wherever I went. In the coyotes' favor is the fact that they haven't been introduced onto the scene deliberately, as elk and boar were during the millionaire-sportsman years at the turn of the century. Though the boar thrived and persisted in New Hampshire, and though Chinese pheasants, West Virginia wild turkeys and German brown trout are still being stocked, such stunts are out of fashion now. Instead, people speak of a "niche" that the coyotes are migrating of their own accord to fill, which is

212

considered acceptable. Fifteen percent of their diet is woodchucks in season; they also eat mice, rabbits, apples and wild-growing grains, and the dead deer littering the winter woods are a positive godsend to them, so it's a modest role that they play. They're ignored in the regulations, not even being listed as outlaws, and the regional publicists have yet to realize what a drawing card their howls will be around the campgrounds in a few years, as the wilderness otherwise fades.

Eastern coyotes are substantially bigger than their Western brothers, perhaps having picked up some wolf blood in Ontario on their way east. A male may weigh forty-five pounds. (In 1972 an eighty-pounder was killed by a train in northern Vermont.) They have densely salty-peppery coats that reflect back the light, rendering them almost invisible sometimes. Unlike dogs, which can breed any time the bitch comes in heat, both sexes breed only in February. Hybrids of a dog-coyote mating do occur where coyotes are very scarce, and they too acquire this once-a-year limitation on sexual activity, but where the coyotes' biological timing is geared to the birth of the litter during the promising weather of April, with the long summer ahead when the parents can rear the pups, these hybrids for some reason breed only in November—which means first of all that they cannot breed back to a coyote, and secondly that the pups, which are born in the dead of winter, usually are doomed from the start.

I've looked at a dead coyote shot by a farmer while it was pouncing about in his clover field eating meadow mice. It had bluish-gray slanting eyes and curved canines, a rather short tail and a coarsely functional coat that actually felt wild and alive to my hand, like a wolf's. The local game warden had frozen it like a fish in his locker, and yet it still seemed miraculously fluid. Shot through the ribs in mid-twist, its body spun in a dozen planes, its face had scrunched flat and all its muscles were straining for life.

Since her coyote study, Mrs. Silver has been investigating the metabolism of deer, using a temperature chamber as well as outdoor pens. Gilbert in Maine is conducting some of the same experiments but hasn't the chamber. In Vermont, meanwhile, the biologists have been watching what they consider the worst die-off of white-tailed deer ever witnessed by man—something like forty thousand starved to death there in the winter of 1970–71. So instead of studying parasitism or the arcane physiology by which deer adjust to a place that is too far north for them, they have been recording the sorrowful facts of overbrowsing, malnutrition and winterkill.

Deer followed the ax into the shattered boreal forests where moose and caribou had lived. The caribou, wolves, moose and panthers soon were gone and the settlers hunted so hard, both for themselves and the Boston meat market, that by the end of the Civil War the deer had disappeared too. They were supposed extinct in Vermont and for the next thirty years hunting them was banned. In 1878 seventeen privately purchased deer were released near Rutland, the forebears of the present overblown herd. In New Hampshire the situation would have been just as desperate except that the White Mountains furnished more of a retreat. But under protection the deer came back as never before, multiplying as the farmers got used to eating beef. When hill-country farming declined and saplings grew up in the old pastureland, this was another boon for them, adding cover and even some acreage to their range just at the time that summer people were beginning to flood everywhere. Down in Connecticut, in spite of an explosion of human beings, for the past twenty years the deer herd has managed to hold at a population of about seven thousand simply because land that used to be two-thirds cleared farms has become two-thirds scrub woods. In only four years in Massachusetts the herd has increased from seven thousand to eighteen thousand (Vermont's outsized herd is a hundred and fifty thousand).

Yet all this good news pales if four and a half feet of snow lies on the ground, with a crust not yet formed and a wind from the Arctic, and the bone-thin deer have to confront the same skinned boughs that they nibbled last year. The fawns and the gravid does that are going to die eat as much as they can for as long as they can, leaving less for the rest. Climatically, these deer are north of where they should be, and they must winter in the rough waste areas unoccupied by man. Bedding down under some conifers, they wait for the weather to break. If it doesn't they die there in a ball, without ever standing up again. The coons and foxes eat their meat, and the porcupines chew on their bones.

Mrs. Silver observed that a starving deer has eyes as soft and big as a hunter's target. She's masculine-minded on the question of hunting, but not nearly as sanguine as some of the higher-echelon officials I was meeting. They said that since there are more deer in the woods than during the Indians' heyday, everything will get better and better, that even as the game lands shrink, concentrations of food grasses and shrubs can be seeded which will provide more fodder than natural wind-seeding. Mrs. Silver doesn't believe recreation can be equated with conservation in land-use planning, though the attempt is made to pair them together. Recreation is a conflicting interest, and as an appeal or as an industry it has such terrific clout that no conservationist factors can stand up against it. The old farms that once were going back to woods are being bought up and subdivided.

The cost-benefit studies don't stop with dictating which species of fish shall be planted in every body of water. In New Hampshire—as presumably everywhere else eventually—they go on to delineate for the consumer exactly what can be caught where, mapping each lake, specifying at what depth good fishing is likeliest, as well as the bait to be used. Pilot studies are being done on the average number of hours an angler must spend on the larger lakes before catching a fish—a "success-unit," it's called. All this refinement is aimed at the leisure-time market, the customer who sits back on Friday night wondering whether he wants to go bowling or fishing tomorrow. He will have contour charts and "success-unit" statistics for all the nearby lakes, as well as the latest figures on stocking statewide, stream by stream, pond by pond, and whether it's brook trout, which are easy to catch, or brownies, which are hard. He'll tune in the weather report, and if the conditions sound right and he decides not to bowl, he'll make up his mind where to drive.

In Concord one morning at eight o'clock I watched the Fish and Game staff lumber in—musty-looking men, for the most part, of 1930s and 1940s vintage, wearing string ties and flannel shirts. If the sum of much of their activity seemed somewhat absurd to me, I was touched nonetheless by how heavily they moved, each man to his cubbyhole, and by the earnest, sisterly women who did their typing.

I learned that New Hampshire had got the best of its fisher-for-turkey swap with West Virginia because turkeys are so much harder to trap than fishers. The West Virginians needed ten times as long to catch their quota. I learned that opossums, though sluggish, are gargantuan breeders and tenacious of life, and will eat almost anything they can fit in their mouths. They have been migrating steadily northward like some elemental force under the sheltering influence of civilization, but have now been stopped at the White Mountains by the weather; their naked ears and tails freeze off. I was told that the last stand of the Canada lynx in the state is in the high country around Zealand Notch, that it's been years since a marten was seen, and that maybe two hundred moose live in the forests bordering Maine, wandering a bit when they rut in the fall or when afflicted with *Pneumostrongylus,* but that the illegal kill equals whatever natural increase may occur. In 1956 a roaming moose made it all the way down to Ashford, Connecticut, before it was shot.

I sought out David White, the bear man in New Hampshire's Fish and Game Department, bears being loved ones to me. He's a dryly agreeable statistician with short white hair and I liked him, though his job is to draw up some of those consumer reports that depress me. Thus, as applied to bears, he tabulates the kill for every town in the state on a year-to-year and ten-year basis, mapping out kill frequencies and densities per hundred square miles, which the armchair hunter can sit and brood over. He's gone even further; he's also compiled a chart of the foods that the bears shot were feeding on at the time of their deaths, arranged by month, county and town, and so has boiled down into a few tables the sort of accumulated lore of the woods that expert hunters in the old days acquired alone and laboriously over many years.

During hunting season apples and beechnuts are the predominant foods for New Hampshire bears. White noticed that these seem to alternate as the principal crop —beechnuts one year, apples the next—unless a snowfall in May kills the apple blossoms. A student of pamphlets can do a good deal of planning without leaving the house. If it's going to be an apple year, the fellow will know that the bears will fatten and den up sooner; therefore he ought to hunt early in the season and stick to orchards and grown-over fields rather than venturing back on the ridges and into the deep woods. Since beechnut years have proven outstanding for the out-of-staters but during apple years it's the local folk who kill the most bears, if he's from out-of-state and really studies the charts he might want to transfer his hunt somewhere else. There *are* hunters as analytic as this. Two doctors I know use different-sized pellets and x-ray the pheasants, when they shoot together, in order to check the kill patterns and see who's taken the most birds.

Massachusetts, too, which has only a one-week bear season and hasn't had a bear killed in several years, charts some of these things, and Vermont has an ambitious "vulnerability" program that details how the sexes react— when, for example, breeding females are most likely to be shot, information that might be of value in protecting the race as well as in killing it off. In 1955 the bounty on bears was removed in New Hampshire. (It's a state for bounties; until 1969 there was a $10 bounty on tramps.) In 1961 a regulated bear season was established, now a hundred days long. As the pressure on wildlife intensifies, these seasons will shorten and other ameliorative measures can be taken. Poisoning and trapping bears is already illegal everywhere in New England except in Maine. A limit might be placed on the number of hounds they can be chased with, and electronic equipment might be banned from the hunt, because some hunters not only communicate with each other by walkie-talkies, but also attach model-airplane transmitters to their hounds so that they can keep track of them.

Bears are so manlike that a researcher often becomes fond of them and begins employing weighted words like "vulnerable." Most bears are shot during deer season, fortuitously, as they seek to avoid several hunters at different points of the compass. In moving along on a course to escape the first three, they blunder into the fourth. But a lush Indian summer may so disarm them that they seem to walk right into the guns; all over the state the kill of daydreaming bears will suddenly double. On such weekends even the deer mice seem elated. If one has traps set about the house they will all be full, the whole colony having gone out adventuring.

3

Still in fighting trim, I went on to Vermont. I got caught in a squishy snowstorm and had Easter dinner with my next-door neighbors, walking two miles up from the highway, finding eight feet of spring snow piled in front of my door because of what had thawed off the roof. With no foliage, the rock outcroppings of the mountain across the way gleamed wetly. It was sugaring time and we could see thirty good acres of maples outside as we ate, but my neighbors are seventy-five and eighty-five, and twenty years ago when age began to get them down they had the best of the trees logged off for cash, selling hundreds of buckets and taps and a half-mile of pipe. The problem for them up here, as for the people I'd bought my land from, has always been making ends meet. Even though they'd kept cows, there was almost no way to make enough money; they had to make forays to Connecticut and go into domestic service. Karl, born on the farm, had seen some of the final pioneering, grubbing large spruce stumps out of the ground with a crowbar right where I'm lazily letting poplar and birch grow up again, and when he worked on a sightseers' steamboat on Willoughby Lake a few miles away, he saw the swank brand of tourism that preceded World War I. The sawmill and railroad station and store at the bottom of the hill are gone; on my scrap of land alone there are two cellar holes. Sutton, the town to which we pay taxes, is fading away, being one of the northern hill towns that were best suited to raising sheep, which is an industry New England lost soon after the Civil War. The water power, railroads and highways were in the valleys, and these hilltop communities have retained little except their lovely views. But according to the planners who were sent in last year on a government subsidy, even the valley town where we shop will not regain the population it had thirty years ago until 1995, if it is lucky.

The summer people want Vermont to stand still, as rural and serene as they supposed it to be when they bought property, but the natives want jobs, industry and prosperity—not eye-burning neon or Los Angeles or calamity, just the good life of this day and age. Most sell their land with some relief because the rise in land taxes is as panicking to them as the rise in the value of acreage is exhilarating for the speculators. What the summer people have done is to refurbish the tax rolls, financing schooling in the townships that might otherwise have had to be centralized (and perhaps improved). They've made the old farmhouses nice and presentable again, which would be fine for local morale if the houses didn't stand empty most of the time, even as the land itself goes wild in a scraggly way that the lumberman as well as the farmer looks down his nose at. This naturally is what the summer people want, however. They're looking for peace in Vermont, not a livelihood, and so are glad to let the quirky progression of weedy gray birch, pin cherries, goldenrod and bracken fern choke up the corners of a piece of property that is now intended as a retreat, after all—species with which nature herself repairs the wounds and undoes the trauma of logging or cultivation, a process to which the scarred city man is instinctively sympathetic, whether or not he is aware of the botany of it. One result is that the traditional open Vermont landscape of dairy pastures is closing so fast that the state has stopped its reforestation program, whereby old fields a farmer had no further use for were re-planted with pines.

One of the ideas I'd brought with me to Vermont was that in a Republican region property rights must be paramount, but I found this not true. In New Hampshire a landowner cannot legally post more than fifty acres; in Vermont the saying used to be that the only way you could get a snowmobiler off your land was to shoot him, because the law simply did not provide for a blanket posting of land against trespassing as such. Only personally speaking to the fellow would suffice, and the snowmobiler might refuse to stop for a talk. Vermont's conservatism has involved perpetuating a way of life more than property rights, and so the sentimental new city pilgrims who arrive panting for privacy and try to draw around themselves the sort of guard fence appropriate to city living do not win many friends where land historically

222

has been common property—if not for profit then for pleasure, at least—and a poor man could always go tramping across boundary lines for an afternoon's lark.

Land planning, developmental control, the devices of easements, tax breaks, trade-offs—these concepts are being explored in Vermont with more sophistication than I'd realized. The state's Land Use and Development Act of 1970 is among the most advanced in the country, and the Ford Foundation is sponsoring a study of how it works out. It has been a state of farmers (and now of city people who wish they were farmers), so although it had little in the way of a conservation movement until recently and did not receive the early assistance of the Bull Moose conservationists of New York and Boston who worked on behalf of the Adirondacks and the White Mountains, it was land-loving, low-key, skeptical about the American dream and suspicious of any flashy dream merchant who had a promotion in mind—if only because it was too poor a ground for him to operate on in any case. Consequently it has arrived in pretty good shape for the seventies, when no highroller scheme can go forward without thorough review. Even turnpike money has not been overly welcome. In 1936 the voters rejected by referendum a federal proposal to build a Green Mountain Parkway the length of the state, and lately the governor, a conservative named Deane Davis, has turned a cool ear to requests that he approve a new interstate highway that would cross northern New England. In Montpelier some of the officials were wondering if they couldn't finagle permission to use highway funds to buy land for the public on the theory that it was scenery, and in my own town the hunters who hang around the taxidermy shop were complaining that Interstate 91, being constructed north from White River Junction, was wiping out some of the best game territory they knew. Instead of benefiting them, they guessed that any jobs it would bring would go to skilled labor migrating in.

Another notion I'd brought to the state was that fishermen and hunters in their sportsmen's clubs are the "sleeping giant" of conservation, unlikely to recognize the alliance of interest that ought to exist between them and such organizations as Friends of the Earth. This may be true elsewhere, but Vermont never has had conservationist chapters of quite the same type. The Green Mountain Club maintains the Long Trail; the Green Mountain Profile Committee keeps an eye on developments in the crest areas that might mar Vermont's backdrop or skyline; and the Audubon Society tries to preserve certain key nesting areas. Each one sticks to its own task a bit parochially, so that when I'd explored the last pockets of wilderness in the state I found no activists to take my worries to. The people who seemed most knowledgeable and effective were working for the state fish and game or forestry departments, and they had few real allies. The best private cadre of conservationists was the staff of the Vermont Natural Resources Council, a charming group of urban transplants who were accomplishing a great deal on pollution and scenic problems, and lassoing reckless developers, but they were uninformed about the wild lands. It was some of the sportsmen I ran into who knew what I knew and who cared. Unfortunately, sportsmen tend to be humble souls, accustomed to a world in which other people have the whip hand; they are blue-collar and grimace at changes coming their way, not considering it possible to drum up much opposition to the powers that be.

Happily, in a state with a population smaller than Buffalo's, one man can still accomplish a good deal. It's said that the anti-billboard law, another trailblazer (which, unlike Maine's, for example, has been enforced), was brought into being by one devoted proselytizer; and I met two naturalists, on different sides of the state, each of whom, working independently and at first alone, had succeeded in conveying into public hands tracts of five or six thousands acres that meant something to him. In doing so, one of them, Frederick Mold, defeated not only the U.S. Army Corps of Engineers and the state's Board of Water Resources but a liberal Democratic governor, Philip Hoff, and a distinguished Republican senator, George Aiken.

Mr. Mold heads an excellent little museum of natural history in St. Johnsbury, and exercises the ham in him by giving a noontime weather broadcast on TV and by lecturing, with his assistants, to four thousand school children a month. A former New Yorker, he is outspoken, impulsive and owlish, and came here from a museum in Stamford, Connecticut, in 1948. Since then he has raised a $260,000 endowment—a lot for Vermont—by playing golf, going to cocktail parties and drinking people under the table occasionally, he says, disliking some of it but liking the cause. Now he's losing 10 percent of that sum a year in keeping his educational program going in spite of cut public funds. He's a mock-argufier with knotty arms, baggy blue eyes, a heart condition and a short red blunt nose. He compresses his lips, and looking for shockers, says most teachers are "paper tigers" at teaching science; that we will all die like mice if the birth boom goes on; that eventually the pill which women take will be a canceling factor given them once or twice in their lives to permit them to have a baby. He says Alexander Hamilton was right: the people *are* a lost beast.

Still, Mr. Mold is obviously his county's foremost humanist; he worries about unemployment and under-education; says Vermonters are only hired to "pick up the beer cans" on the treadmill of more tourism; speaks of the "snowmobile mentality—the less education you have between the ears the more hardware you need to enjoy yourself." He keeps cedar waxwings and talking ravens, and people phone him when the first spearhead of Canada geese flies through. He has no office; we talked in various lecture rooms when I dropped in. Twenty-five of the kids he has taught have become Ph.D.'s in the natural sciences. He flies to Georgia and Michigan to teach educators, and is a member of the governor's Scenery Preservation Council, but because this high-sounding body has no teeth or budget he's written the governor suggesting that it be abolished. He doesn't walk much in the woods any more, though he has long legs and an outdoor stride. In a chair, lolling tiredly, he is stubby-looking, but he used to delight in accompanying surveyors and timber cruisers on their fifteen-mile strolls.

Victory Bog is the place that Mold saved. Nine million people live within two hundred miles of it, yet in miniature it's a genuine wilderness, with moose, with rumors of mountain lions and a reported wolf that leaves four-inch tracks and must have trotted down from the St. Lawrence River. In the nineteenth century Victory Bog was the haunt of a legendary bear-man (or man-bear) called Old Slipperyskin. Back before Darwin, in the days of the Colonial frontiersmen with their cranky, front-loading guns, it was just such redoubts that were thought to harbor the mammoths and mastodons and saber-toothed tigers whose bones kept turning up but who had not yet been sighted alive. I've met more than one rawboned woodsman who got twisted around and spent a night lost in Victory and loved it for this all the more.

Scientifically, not much of it is a "bog," though you'd better wear boots to your knees, and the Moose River that flows through is sometimes nine feet deep. It's a braided-stream basin stretching between Umpire and Kirby mountains, which the state now owns, and Miles and Temple mountains, owned by two or three paper companies. The last virgin spruce in Vermont was logged off Umpire Mountain in 1940. At one time the town of Victory had its own railroad spur and up to a dozen sawmills and six hundred people; now it has a population of forty-six, more of them old than young. But it's not ghostly or sad. To begin with, it's so wildly beautiful that after many visits I still find it difficult to keep my car on the road when I drive through; I weave around and nearly land in the ditch. Wet moosey sedge meadows spread away towards the mountains. Labrador tea and

227

leatherleaf, with creeping snowberry, velvet-leaf blueberry, bunchberry, checkerberry, sheep laurel and withe
rod grow in the hummocky sphagnum swamps. There are
blackberry clearings with fly honeysuckle and bush honeysuckle, wood sorrel, dogberry and lily of the valley. On the
knolls, mountain ash, mountain holly, mountain maple,
partridge berry and shiny club moss grow. There's larch
and fir, black, red and white spruce, and twisted-stalk,
starflowers, wild sarsaparilla, painted trillium, goldthread
and Indian cucumber root. In the pools there's eelgrass,
and swamp candles, spike rushes, water plantain and
broad-leaved arrowhead flourish at the edges. Thirteen
kinds of wood warbler were spotted in a couple of weekends by an Audubon party, along with green and blue
herons, ospreys, beavers, and wood and mink frogs. Sometimes I stop and poke about, walking up Bog Creek from
Damon's Crossing past five successive ponds, through a
deer yard, to a rapids and a swimming hole, finding
snails shaped like little tubas, butter-yellow butterflies
with black trim, and maybe a nest of pink baby mice. It's
in the deep woods, but once it had twenty homes and a
store, school and mill.

The sun is never quite as bright as it is in Victory.
Rough-legged hawks sail by, and the frogs sound like
untuned banjos, or like muttered conversation broken by
the wind. Salamanders scutter in the mud. I've scarcely
begun the exploring I plan. The state owns twelve thousand acres here, the paper companies very much more,
and as the crow flies, one could walk forty or fifty miles
northeast from Victory to the Canadian border through

magnificently varied, choppy terrain, crossing only a single paved road. With more than six hundred square miles, Essex County has fewer than six thousand people, and most of them live along the Connecticut River, which is the New Hampshire boundary, or at the edge of neighboring counties, in small communities which are picturesque but economically depressed. Victory escapes their haggard air because its people seem at home with the wilderness that surrounds them, as their ancestors were, and are content to put up with a standard of living which is unlike that of people elsewhere. They didn't even obtain electricity until 1963.

When Stewart Udall was Secretary of the Interior and was concerned about preserving the Allagash, his department also considered proposing Essex County as a national wilderness, finding that "92 percent" of it was still wild. Aside from the difficulty of raising money to buy land for the public, the stumbling block in these negotiations is always the problems raised by depleting the local township's tax base. The federal method of getting around this is to pay the town 25 percent of the proceeds of all timber sales. Vermont's Forestry Department pays only 10 percent, but the anti-federal tradition— going back to the Revolution and the War of 1812, when Britain's troops in Canada ate Vermont beef—is still so strong that nearly everybody was against the Interior Department's plan, preferring to see the land, if it ever did pass into the public domain, do so piecemeal and gradually, purchased by the state. There was consistency in this position, because a few years later when the Corps of Engineers announced its readiness, with the backing of Senator Aiken and Governor Hoff, to dam the Moose River at Victory Bog under an old flood-control authorization, Mr. Mold and the local game warden and a humble college ecologist or two were able to mount a withering home-based campaign with their facts and their sentiments and rout these soldiers and gentlemen. The conservative Senator Winston Prouty and the yet more conservative Governor Davis, elected to replace Hoff soon thereafter, then tossed them some timely political clout that they needed, demonstrating again that conservationists now draw a shifting pattern of support that cuts across previous schisms.

Vermont was first seen by Champlain in 1609 from what is now Lake Champlain, which the Indians had nicknamed "the Great Warpath" because it was how they moved from the Hudson to the St. Lawrence to fight one another. Vermont was mainly guerrilla ground—hit-and-run trails and hunting lands. The first permanent white settlement, Fort Dummer, didn't come into being until 1744. By 1760 the white population was just 300 (Maine's was 20,000). But in 1790 it was 85,000; ten years later, 154,000; and in 1810, 218,000. No other Northern or Eastern state was showing increases like this, as the settlers of southern New England recognized a frontier close by where they could obtain land without trekking all the way West. However, in 1816—"eighteen-hundred-and-froze-to-death"—the winter extended into June, when there were still snowdrifts two feet high. More snow fell in July and August, and a hard frost on September 10 finished the rest of the crops and even the hay and most of the livestock. The famous saying about Vermont's climate was born—"nine months' winter and three months' damn poor sleddin'." Emigration became a significant factor for the state.

Potash and lumber were the first industries, as the land was cleared; then raising beef and growing potatoes, quantities of which were sold for starch. Beef was driven on the hoof to New York City and Boston. Even geese, their feet tarred for protection, were driven to freighting points, and pork, mutton, butter, cheese, hay and the various grains were hauled to the cities by teams of eight horses. The Bellows Falls Canal on the Connecticut and the Champlain Canal on the Hudson speeded shipping, but when prosperous, Vermonters didn't forget their shabby beginnings as a territory that was squabbled over by the Wentworths of New Hampshire and the patroons of the Hudson Valley. Not being one of the thirteen original states, from 1777 to 1791 they regarded themselves as a separate republic. At one juncture George Washington spoke of squelching their discontent with an army, and finally Vermont's citizens had to buy off the claims of the State of New York for thirty thousand dollars. Their own state constitution was modeled on Pennsylvania's—that is, on the thinking of William Penn and Benjamin Franklin. It forbade slavery or even apprenticeship bondage, and allowed universal manhood suffrage, freeing voting from any link with property ownership. In 1803 a bill to permit banks to operate in Vermont was passed by the state house of representatives by a close margin, after having been defeated in previous sessions. But the governor and his council refused to concur, giving as some of their reasons: "Banks, by facilitating enterprises, both hazardous and unjustifiable, are natural sources of all that class of vices, which arise from the gambling system, and which cannot fail to act as sure and fatal, though slow, poisons to the republic in which they exist. . . . Banks tend strongly to draw off the dependence of debtors from their own exertions as means of payment, and to place it on the facility of increasing new debts to discharge the old. . . . Banks have a violent tendency, in their natural operation, to draw into the hands of the few a large proportion of the property at present fortunately diffused among the many. The tendency of banks seems to be to weaken the great pillars of a republican government, and at the same time to increase the forces employed for its overthrow. . . . As banks will credit none but persons of affluence, those who are in the greatest need of help cannot expect to be directly accommodated by them. . . ." In 1856 the Georgia legislature, which had been angered by Vermont's annual resolution protesting slavery, proposed that President Pierce employ enough able-bodied Irishmen to dig a ditch around Vermont and float "the thing" into the Atlantic Ocean.

The dark side of all this frontier democracy and tough nonconformism—unintimidated by the winter of 1816 and the floods of 1827, eschewing the McCarthyism of, for instance, New Hampshire in the 1950s—is, of course, the much-bruited eccentricity of some citizens of the state. All other Vermont eccentrics may have met their match in Pardon Janes of Calais. For many years in the 1800s he wore a short pitchfork fastened to one hand so that he need never touch the flesh of another human being. On his rare trips to market for cotton or salt, he held out a pail with money in it at the end of the fork and the clerks made change.

When humor and self-deprecation lighten this streak it gets into bibelot form, reaching the *Reader's Digest.* Then, read by younger Vermonters, the anecdotes are retold and regionalized as curios until even in Victory what one hears is a retread of the published version. But there's no harm in that; it gives some of the true people, while they last, a certain status or celebrity among the tourists and in their own minds, even if for silly reasons, which makes the grueling winters and the poverty and social assistance a little bit easier to bear. One does meet occasional crabbed old regionalist souls in the New England tradition when traveling through the back country, but the best of the breed don't overdo that dry sort of stage business. Instead, they have about them the clear-eyed, mild-browed accessibility of men on the newer frontiers, who are sustained by the joy of a world that is young—men with a generous spread to their mouths, who are free of the bile of the Vermont anecdote, who, having lived all their lives among animals, watching the domestic antics and follies, the perfunctory quick births and solitary deaths, the equanimity of animals, know something of what life may be about and take a long view and are self-possessed.

I'm partial to Vermont, which helps explain why I took

233

so uncritically to its natural-resources people. To get an impression of how things stand, one should talk to a wildlife expert about forestry practices and ask the state foresters about the game situation, and I did this. The foresters said that the beaver were being overtrapped and the bears overhunted, and the game specialists told me that International Paper and the Brown Company were stripping their acreage of trees to the point where soon it might not pay them to keep up with the taxes on it. But this is par, really; everybody more or less agrees with assessments like these.

The chief of forest-land management for the state was Ben Hoffman, a subdued Marylander with a Lone Ranger voice and a strong nose and glance, as rangy as a cowboy. He remembers a timber survey he did a decade ago in the Green Mountains that lasted three months, and this and other euphoric episodes give him a bias that would favor the wilderness advocates, except that he is a practical man and their tendency to condemn all logging activity offends his loyalty to his profession. Sometimes he speaks peevishly of wanting to rub their noses in logging, of logging the very roadsides so that they can't escape seeing the trees downed. On the other hand, he told me with disgust about how Weyerhaueser Company had made a hash of Jay Peak, one of the prettiest mountains in the state, while gouging out a series of ski lifts and runs in a rush to complete an all-season resort before Expo 67 opened in Montreal. I took a great liking to him, and thought him responsive to my subversive suggestions that in all the six million acres of Vermont, *some* land might be left to go wild. By now when I interviewed a man in his position it served mainly as an occasion to plead the urgency of my own views.

The chief of fish and game research, James Stewart, was a lyrical fellow who had helped wield the influence of his department in the fight to save Victory Bog (Fish and Game finally bought the Bog outright in order to keep it from being dammed). I found him quite optimistic, though. He knows fish, and does not see them as a dying flowering-of-life, but as renewable and manageable, however the sport of fishing as a sport declines. Talking of birds, he's a field man, again, and looks at what is actually happening in the skies. Southerly birds like the mocking-bird, titmouse, brown thrasher, cardinal and black vulture have moved north; ravens and wild turkeys are newly back in Vermont; Old World birds like the cattle egret have transplanted themselves. These cheer Stewart up when he sees the spruce grouse disappear, and the falcons and eagles. Vermont is home to a hundred and seventy-five species of birds at breeding time; a hundred and forty more show their colors in passing through. So far most birds have been eminently adaptable to the advent of man, and if the younger laboratory scientists are correct in their gloom and more types of birds begin vanishing with poison in their bones, it will be particularly cruel for biologists out in the field like him.

Right now the bleeding sore for Stewart and his deputies is the famine stunting the deer of Vermont. In other states the game men laugh and speak bitterly of Vermonters as people who "like" their deer so much they want to starve them into the open fields where they can

235

see them. In this case the conservationist streak in the state operates perversely, so that only bucks can be hunted; the voters are too chivalrous to permit a change in the law. Thus 85 percent of the herd now consists of does, and even with a hundred and fifty thousand hunters out in the fall, the number of bucks that they kill is utterly insufficient to bring the deer population into reasonable accord with the winter feed—feed now being destroyed for years to come, as the deer strip even starvation-diet trees like fir and pine. It's a protein-poor diet at best, and the snowmobiles roar into the woods and chase off the last few ounces of fat on the animals' ribs and sweat them into a fever, till they catch pneumonia. Then a pack of house dogs, frisky and plump, discover the snowmobile tracks leading right into the deer yards like an avenue, and run in and finish them off. As the weather warms, the corpses rot to a green color, then a dead blue, and when the bears wake up they sniff out the carcasses, peel back the hides like a banana skin, and eat everything but the teeth and hooves.

One of Stewart's men will go out and within a few hours find forty deer starved to death on top of the snow, without digging down to the lower layers: one deer for every ten acres of winter range (the count across in New Hampshire might be one in thirty acres). It's too cold for most people in the woods, so no one else sees them before they disappear, and when the department asks for a better deer law they meet with frank outrage from citizens who say that they love their deer and denounce these fellows for asking for more hunting rather than less, criticizing

236

them as failures professionally because every year there are fewer deer.

Hubert Vogelmann, a botanist at the University of Vermont, may be the best example of how far one man's voice can carry in a small state. Like most people in the environmental movement he came from out-of-state originally, with an "overview" of what is to follow, but in seventeen years at the university he's acquired enormous influence in determining what concessions will be made to the natural world. Putting it simply, he can go to some nook in the mountains, an ecological community deserving of concern, and hike about inventorying the plants and other delights for an afternoon, and afterwards on state planning maps an admonitory black dot will mark the spot, announcing its special value. He's performed this service, with a helper or two, at two hundred and fifty sites so far. By rallying the Nature Conservancy in Washington for lobbying pressure, he has been able to operate as a Robin Hood within the Green Mountain National Forest also.

I thought Vogelmann somewhat naïve politically, which, oddly enough, is probably a great advantage when he is called upon to give expert testimony and must appear impartial. Speaking to committees of legislators as if they were all men of good will, with no awareness of the factions involved—never dreaming that there are men who would put the interests of a developer ahead of the public's welfare—he estranges no one. Yet he isn't so otherworldly that he just talks about rare ferns and orchids and neglects to stress fishing and hunting when discussing a marsh, for instance, or is concerned only for the Ice Age

237

plant relics that grow on the peaks while forgetting that they are a watershed for each dairy farmer below. Mount Mansfield catches fifty-two inches of rainfall a year, whereas Burlington down below gets about thirty, and the conifer boughs coalesce additional moisture out of the high fogs. These cold forests alter dramatically with altitude. There are eighty plant species at 1,800 feet on Camel's Hump, only fifty-two at 2,600 feet, and seventeen at 3,200 feet. Higher still is sedge tundra and alpine heath. Vogelmann's own research, done in the Sierra Madre in Mexico as well as here, has involved climbing up and down, checking rain gauges, comparing soil temperatures and samples, but recently he's garlanded these scholarly exertions with dramatic rescues of almost whole mountains—such earthy achievements as seeing that sixty-five hundred acres on the north slope of Camel's Hump were transferred from a developer's drawing board to a state park.

Because his name is Hubert Vogelmann I'd expected a pedantic German of advanced middle age, and looked in vain for such a figure in the photographs of terrain that he sent me. In fact, he is called Hub, and is as lithe as a panther, with handsome saturnine lines to his face, a somber look, and a forceful hooked nose. He wears desert boots, looks alert like a highlander, and lives with a picturebook family in a picturebook house on a hundred and fifty acres that are like an arboretum of New England trees, including some huge old undiseased elms. Since he's such a big gun, it's lucky he's so prepossessing, and like Mr. Stewart he's not despondent. The arctic antiques he's tried to preserve on the peaks are being ground to death by hikers and jeeps, but overall, Vermont has been enriched by many invading grasses and much European flora, beginning with some of the daisies and dandelions. A century ago, when sheep were turned loose on the mountains after they'd been cleared of timber, Lake Champlain is said to have turned chocolate-brown; and nothing man is doing now in Vermont is as bad as that. In fact, nothing he will ever do anywhere, unless he perishes trying, will affect life and the face of the earth as much as one shuttle trip of the last ice sheet.

These were sweet people I talked to. And I met several of the Chamber of Commerce individuals who attempt to outflank them, as well. One donnish, well-intentioned fellow owned half a symmetrically lovely mountain, a sort of Fujiyama that he ran skiiers down. At the bottom he was building chalets in clusters (the enlightened way, leaving communal meadows between). He was entertaining his formidable mother for luncheon, and she was very wealthy, slightly testy, and he may have needed a bit of support from her, but she seemed to be giving much of *her* land, down in Connecticut, to the Nature Conservancy.

In June I climbed Camel's Hump and Mount Mansfield. Camel's Hump has a tossing, sea-reeling, camel-like, hat-like loftiness—a real hump to it. It's everybody's favorite mountain—unmarred, nicely structured, a mountain's mountain, set back amid extensive woods and landforms, with the hump a fillip of fun. One climbs up through a belt of maples, a white-birch zone, through fern gardens, past overhanging ledges, to spruce and dwarf fir. I encountered more rabbits and porcupines than people, and up on the hard-won heath and rock I slept for an hour and sunned myself, lying so that the west breeze blew the flies away, looking at Mount Washington and the Adirondacks, until the weather turned milky bluish and wet and cold. Then I took a different trail down through beautifully abundant ferns, with woodpeckered old trees smelling of bracket fungus, to a derelict farmhouse, which leaned dignifiedly, the shingles peeling like fish scales and rose bushes growing wild all around.

Mansfield is a graver mountain shaped like a long ridge. The Indians thought it resembled the head of a moose, and when the moose were gone, the white men said the profile was that of a long-lipped Indian. I swam in a brook that chutes down from Lake of the Clouds along bedrock skidways; I was naked but wasn't observed, and could see the blue heights above. There were very large trees on the banks that the loggers had left alone, maybe because they would have split on the rocks in falling. Seen again from the bottom, Mansfield has a physiognomy containing many of the possibilities of a man's face, at rest and yet not at rest. It makes up a skyline not unlike others in Vermont, but higher, bigger, more expressive.

The Green Mountains are lower and more rolling than the White Mountains and generally have been farmed at some stage, so that they have better soil and more hardwood stands. The federal lands are in the southern sections, comprising worked-out farms that the Forest Service bought for an average of nine dollars an acre thirty or forty years ago—holdings amounting to only thirty-eight percent of the land it was authorized to buy; the rest has now been resettled, or is overpriced. Nevertheless, the Green Mountains aren't receiving the worrisome degree of overuse that the White Mountains are; they get less than a fifth the number of hikers.

When school lets out, the Long Trail does see some action. There are scouting groups of twenty or more, sometimes with no adult keeping up with the crowd of kids in the lead to tell them what they are not supposed to do. This is what the trail is for, to give the kids somewhere to hike, and in its two hundred and sixty miles an enthusiast can choose a wild stretch for himself, where, at worst, if he adjusts his pace, he won't catch up with the scouts who are ahead of him or be overtaken by the troop two miles behind. The Green Mountain Club is discovering it has to hire caretakers and formalize things, however, which is sad for the members who pride themselves on having a narrow trail that is everywhere canopied with trees, a wilderness trail cut "just wide enough and high enough for a tall man with a pack to pass through after a rainstorm and not get wet." Some talk about clearing more paths elsewhere in the state to relieve the crush, but some want to keep quiet about these other spots, lest they too become thoroughfares. (A divorcee in Schenectady will write in to say that she is losing touch with her teenage sons: can't she bring them over and all of them pitch in to "maintain" some piece of the Trail?)

A friend of mine, Richard Smythe, walked south with me on the Long Trail from Hazen's Notch for twenty-five miles. We found that ten miles made a full day in this eastern topography, and that though we'd been snobbish at first about bringing a trail book along, it was an extremely reassuring bit of baggage where water was concerned. Our canteen was small, and we'd thumb through the text again and again to learn where the next spring was. Closer up, Smythe could tell if we were near water by the calls of the birds, having once been an Audubon Society instructor. He began adult life as a tree surgeon but fell out of a tree and struck the ground with his heels so jarringly that he feels the blow still; eventually he switched professions to become a land planner. This involves working with a developer, for example, who has bought six hundred acres of land but then discovers that he doesn't know what to do with it. He's sure that financially he made a shrewd deal, and he has an idea of how many houses he hopes to fit on it, but doesn't know where to set the houses. So Smythe will walk over the land for a period of days until the contours are something of a sculpture to him, figuring out the curves and inclines, the ground composition, which trees should stay and which trees might go, and the scenery each family will have from its windows. In the past year he'd walked over land worth aggregately three million dollars. Since he's a man who loves wildflowers and bird life, it can be a wretched exercise with the wrong client. But there are very few ways of earning a living outdoors that can't.

We bad-mouthed our good wives on the trail, boasted about our children, and told each other how zany we'd been in sexual scrapes twenty years ago. He was carrying some whisky, but I didn't drink; I made a point of swimming in Ritterbush Pond and wading in every brook, but he didn't swim. Yet, though we performed different rituals, we had that sense of tender camaraderie which Army friends know. He looked for his home—a hundred and eighty-six acres of hayfields, nurseries and wildflower knolls—from every high spot, while I looked for other mountains I hoped to climb. I'd let my dog come along, ranging ahead of us until its bad leg went lame—which naturally irritated a birder like Smythe who wanted the woods undisturbed. But he got fond of the dog, seeing how it curled round my head when I went to sleep and accosted whole scout troops with hoarse lion snarls (we were, after all, on what sets up as a wilderness path.)

I admired Smythe for the excitement that kept him awake, up in the fire tower much of the night that we spent on Belvidere Mountain, watching for shooting stars, looking down at the whiteness of an asbestos mine and off at the lights of Montreal. I liked his love for his home, which, since he's a year-round Vermonter, is an enlargement of my own passion for my hundred acres, and liked his fanatic streak, which has led him at times to throttle an unwary snowmobiler who was squashing his seedlings and to learn the warm grainy scent of porcupines overhead so as to locate them faster, before they chew up his trees. He's taught himself to botanize swiftly with his eyes on the ground as he walks along, identifying and filing away the procession of plants, at the same time as he records the roster of birds in the woods with his ears—he recognized forty-five species on our trip.

From Hazen's Notch the trail climbs Haystack Mountain, which botanically is a swatch of Newfoundland, and there we met two barefoot, bra-less girls and a boy named Glynn who had been walking for five weeks from Massachusetts and expected to reach Canada the next day. Apparently the girls hadn't lost any weight, nor their chattiness either, though Glynn seemed to be tiring of the talk. The trail was all ups and downs, boggy with footprints as it descended and rose again to Tillotson Peak through a woods of birch and acid-soil conifers. We saw big toads, too large to worry about snakes any more, and saw elderberry shrubs in flower, lady ferns, goldthread, bluets and ground pine. We heard warblers, and thrushes, finches, vireos, veeries, a ruby-crowned kinglet, the beautiful-voiced white-throated sparrow and the winter wren, a very short bird with a very long song. We watched the sun set on Lake Champlain from Belvidere, glancing back across the curve of the forests we'd covered with a detailed fondness. Smythe slept in the open in the wind and I bedded down in a copse of scrub firs, waking every half-hour to listen and look for a moment like an animal.

Next day, going down Belvidere, we saw some bear tracks meandering, and bees in the mountain maples, and Christmas fern, and fragrant bedstraw, from which the pioneers sometimes made tea. We heard ovenbirds, redstarts, flycatchers, brown creepers, grosbeaks, peewees and phoebes, as well as more species of warbler, and downy and hairy woodpeckers. We found a whole glade of jewelweed, and saw royal fern, spinulose fern, hay-scented fern, New York fern, sensitive fern, and nannyberry, partridge berry, dogbane and shadbush. We crossed the

Eden Road, climbed a ridge and went down again through sucky black mud, then climbed a long mountain, Bowen Mountain, by way of Devil's Glen, which is a fine gorge where there is a waterfall. We dunked our heads in it and soaked our feet to shrink the swelling. Here were ostrich fern and wild sarsaparilla and rock polypody. Smythe told me that the song of the song sparrow is, "Madge, Madge, put on the teakettle-ettle-ettle," and that the white-throated sparrow sings, "Oh Canada, Canada, Canada." The black-throated blue warbler says, "I am lazeeee"; the red-winged blackbird, "Hunk-a-cheese, hunk-a-cheese"; the red-eyed vireo, "See me? Here I am"; the chestnut-sided warbler, "I wish to see Miss Beecher. Pleased, pleased, pleased to meetchur."

The second night we slept in the forest at Basin Brook, where four little springs come together. Our practice, an unsociable one, was to cook a hot lunch at one of the designated shelters, which are empty at noon but sooty from countless campfires and smelly inside and swarm with deer flies. We'd read the logbook and bathe our sweat off, then camp somewhere much more pleasant and peaceful halfway between shelters for supper, building no fire, eating cheese and dried apricots. If everybody did it this way, the fires and general garbage might make the trail a disaster, but we wanted to, and happiness on the trail is in the mind, not the body. Sometimes our chests and bodies felt like the old Pilgrim torture of *pressing*, and Smythe's legs bothered him because of his fall from that tree. We both felt stronger than we'd expected, however, and felt pleased with ourselves. So much energy out of doors is used up simply in nervousness that an older man, more confident and relaxed and yet more disciplined, gains back some of the endurance he thought he had lost when he left his twenties.

The treetops swayed in the wind, a mouse next to us was twittering its alarm, and the setting sun was a red dot through the mindless trees. Smythe talked about the foxes that den in his field, a vixen with a white dot on one hind knee and a dog that is camel-colored. Once he and some friends drove to Newfoundland, all the last day through a huge burn, and just at sunset they reached the beach where they planned to camp for a couple of weeks, and there, floating a mile out in front of them, saw a shining iceberg.

The birds woke at 4:30 A.M. but we went back to sleep for two more hours. Then we climbed Butternut Mountain, seeing spiranthes orchids, past young yellow birches and sugar maples, hearing goldfinches, chickadees and red-breasted nuthatches. Then down to Foot Brook, icy to the feet, and to Davis Neighborhood in the township of Johnson. Where the woods opened out into fields, we heard bobolinks and an indigo bunting. The sunshine was blinding and the landscape fantastically expansive and lovely after the tight horizons inside the woods—farm hayfields rolling away to the blue bulk of Laraway Mountain, and to Whiteface Mountain, much more distant. When somebody told us that three Russians had died in their space capsule, it was a rude jostle.

At home I discovered a family of grouse eating wild strawberries behind my house, and that night heard a flying loon calling as it crossed between lakes. My house is seventy years old and there are three oaks set in front that were planted when it was built, so one can look out the window and see exactly how big a seventy-year-old oak is. My neighbor Karl saw his last movie in 1936, a Will Rogers film, but says that he's sure they've made some good ones since. His heart, sounding like an old sidewheeler to him, kicked up about ten years ago, but he hasn't had any trouble since. At that time he had a dog so smart that he and his wife had to spell out words if they wanted to keep a secret from it. It ate corn on the cob like a bone and, in the winter, maple sugar that they poured out for it on the snow; whereupon Karl, as a practical joke, would sneak around the house and rattle the door, and the dog trying to bark would discover that its jaws had stuck together. When Karl hunted, they especially liked the neck of venison, about twenty pounds, roasted, then the leftovers ground up for hash or sliced cold and lavished with eggy mayonnaise. If he noticed a sparrow's nest in the grass when he mowed his fields, he constructed a shelter of shingles around it.

In winter I head for the heat of New York and hole up, but I live much more intensely here than anywhere else. The whole countryside, in fact, sizzles with creatures that crowd in the meat of their lives during these summer months. The birds fling themselves back and forth from bush to bush, the woodchucks dig and the raccoons cruise. The actual stems of the trees have only a six-week growing season between when they finally finish loosening themselves from last winter's grip and the moment when they must begin "hardening off" for the autumn to come. My knowledgeability outdoors is that of a generalist —which is to say that I know very little. My guidebooks awe me, and, of course, nothing ever quite looks like its picture in a field guide. I'm rather glad not to be a scientist, though, because when there are no more bears left in the woods to study there will still be plenty of bears left in my head. In Vermont a man with a naturalist's bent can find maybe a hundred meadow mice in an acre of hay, and red-backed mice, lemming mice, pine mice, and two kinds of jumping mice in the neighboring woods. Also three sorts of moles and five kinds of shrews. There's the screech owl, horned owl, snowy owl, barred owl, long-eared owl, short-eared owl and saw-whet owl.

I was pleased at how easy it now was for me to re-explore the mountains around my place, not leaning limp-legged against a tree wondering how I would ever get myself home—wouldn't somebody carry me, please? It was nothing to get myself up on top of one for a two-hour stroll, and I loved the new views I got of familiar hillocks, exotically green, heaving and humping like monsters of the sea. I walked to the lonely border of Canada on the Long Trail, and on the Fourth of July tramped to a fire tower which the Green Mountain Club considers the most remote in the state. (It will remain nameless here.) I wondered whether the towerman and I would be alone for the holiday, and found that we were; in fact, he'd had no other visitors for five or six weeks. He didn't know what to make of me; he climbed down from the tower, then scrambled up again skittishly while I slipped off my pack, got a drink, stretched my shoulders and glanced about at the summit clearing, which seemed to abound in soft spots where I could bed down.

Domenic was twenty-four, from Rutland. He had a mustache and wore his hair long as a mop, and since this was his fourth year in the towers, he could look out and see mountains where he'd lived before. He was spooked from being so alone. Most of his day off every week was spent just on the round trip for supplies and in clearing the trail. Since he had no car, once he reached the road he still needed to hitchhike to a grocery store. On rainy days he could sleep late, and would read and draw in his cabin, isolated by miles of drenched vegetation. I liked the one drawing I saw, though he was embarrassed that I saw it: a long-haired nude viewed from the back, with her curves natural ones. He was a man of shy giggles and furtive quick glances, jiggling his legs with such nervous intensity that the floor shook as we talked. He had his Army discharge but no further credentials to recommend him in the world's eyes—no girl, no possessions, no college degree, and when he had tried going to Canada last year, they'd taken him right off the bus (the only passenger who was treated so) and turned him away, saying, "We don't admit just *anybody*." He, for his part, listened to a radio station that played only music, no news, and way up there in his lookout tower, felt frigidly free of the world, just the way that my tree-surgeon friend used to, until his fall. By September, he said, the loneliness that afflicted him in the cabin at night would have become a more settled thing. (He was wrong; he quit in a great rush within the next month.)

We went up in the tower to talk. He pointed out Island Pond, a town fifteen miles away across Ferdinand Bog and the Yellow Bog—a walk no one has thought to attempt for years and perhaps as difficult as any in Vermont; yet the towerman here a decade ago had made it routinely each Friday night in order to go see his girl. The prodigious topography, the Western grandeur, hundreds of thousands of acres of timberland, and the rolling, splendid, numberless mountains that might have been Asian or African and were not to be pigeonholed geographically or in altitude, ranged away to the Suttons of Quebec Province and to the sailing, ghostly-looking Presidential Range, fluttering high in the south. Domenic said he occasionally saw pairs of hawks playing in the air, swooping and grasping at one another, and a pileated woodpecker would land on the frame of the tower and beat it with his bill, giving a crazy laughing cry. Every evening there were gamboling deer in his meadow, since he kept no dogs about. I'd noticed that the glades under the summit seemed full of deer sign, but he said there was only one small herd of them, that they'd scarcely pulled through the winter and still looked starved. He had quite a rabbit herd too, bucking and leaping like little broncos in the moonlight, coming especially to nibble the patch of grass by his door where he peed, for the minerals his body cast off. A bobcat had just set up shop on the summit to make meals of them.

He was glad not to have many human visitors; he spoke with a kind of panic of what happened when trippers came, dropping pop bottles off the tower, chopping up the sawhorse for firewood and stealing the axes. "Uncontrollable," he said. He was afraid one might climb up and push him off. The towermen talked on the radio daily to each other of their troubles with black flies and visitors. Except for that period in the fall when he would have got so used to being alone that he'd feel sure he could go on forever, his favorite season was when he first snowshoed into the mountains in May, bursting to be on his own, finding rugged big drifts and bears and bear tracks on the trail—all contained within the tractable dimensions of Vermont which signify that one is not going to die, but otherwise like the great North. The bears, after all, having been asleep for half the year, are literally rediscovering the world, and one of the most fuddling discoveries they must make for themselves in their rebirth is that, as big and strong as they are, even these far mountains do not belong to them. When Domenic was manning the tower on Stone Mountain he had watched bachelor bears and bear families climb into the apple trees of an abandoned farm down below; jumping on the limbs, they shook out bushels of fruit. He saw a hunt, too, in pantomime, where the tiny-looking bear caught the scent of an even tinier hunter stalking him just in time and flattened down, practically spread-eagling into the grass, and wriggled out of sight.

We leaned into the view. The fire towers of New England are in the process of being inactivated; planes, touring at statistically predetermined hours, will replace them. But the six that we could see had all been connected by a circuitous sixty-mile telephone wire before radios came into use, and we tried to reconstruct its route in the swarm of space. So much space blots the eyes, the mountains in unending ridges and circles simply absorb any perspective.

Domenic kept speaking of Stone Mountain but not really saying why. I didn't find out till I climbed it. There in the tower was a lissome, barelegged blonde of eighteen whom I almost fell in love with myself. She was a student-council girl just out of high school, breaking into the beginnings of womanhood, with a kind mouth, a soft voice, curly long hair hanging over the front of her shoulders like a spaniel's ears, and a confident grounding in life thus far that made her serene in contrast to him. She liked to have her friends visit once in a while but didn't mind when they didn't for weeks at a time and the fog socked in and shut her off except for her father's biweekly arrival with food. Once a jeepload of young men had tried to drive up the mountain after dark to attack her or scare her, she said, but they'd been unwilling to do any walking at all and had tried to winch themselves up the path wherever they couldn't drive. The noise had alerted her and she'd hid in the woods to see the outcome. Still refusing to walk, they wound up breaking their winch and driving back down.

Domenic, after listening to the endearing tones of her voice in the radio reports twice a day, took to hiring a taxi to carry him from where his trail came out of the woods to the foot of her mountain and hiking up for the privilege of spending a couple of hours with her on his day off, taking away her letters to mail (which were mostly to a Montreal rock-music station). The day I visited her she'd been off on a walk of ten or twelve miles to see her nearest neighbor, a widow who lived alone on another farm beyond the abandoned farm with its ruffed grouse, lilacs, blueberries, and orchard trees where the bears played. I liked the brave way she faced me when I suddenly emerged from the woods, and I mooned at her table till nearly midnight drinking her coffee, and the next morning went downhill to look at these marvelous old overgrown pastures myself.

As the summer went on, I climbed the other fire-tower mountains in the forty-by-twenty-mile area that I'd staked out, usually sleeping in the June-grass-and-hawkweed clearing on top, with my dog curled protectively around my head, waving his tail to shoo the mosquitoes off, and the moon out, the trees in the moonlight a mixed silhouette of heart-leaved white birch and spruces with their tops broken off by the snow and wind so that they were as stunted as pitch pine at the beach. On West Pond Mountain one towerman had kept a burro to pack his groceries, and wherever he'd tethered her the grass was particularly lush and sweet.

The trail climbed up through cathedral hemlock groves and parks of witch hobble and maidenhair fern, over numerous brooks, through a beech-maple forest and belts of recent logging, up into ledgy bad footing and softwood growth, to that first abrupt view of the tower, which looked like some queer sort of dynamo or tall telescope, a giddy, four-legged, laddered and bolted steel super-structure a hundred feet above the mountaintop. With the cold winds of early morning blowing and the cold of the heights, the cabin looked enviably cozy to me as my sweat dried and I rested a bit. Though I was glad to meet nobody on the path, I was always disappointed if the towerman himself was not at home. But on Burke Mountain the fellow, famous for silence, went straight to his ladder as soon as he saw me and began to climb. I called to him and tried to talk, but he kept right on climbing. I began to stutter, and halfway up he turned around long enough to lock behind him a gate that he'd built on the ladder. I found myself stuttering even more, like an epileptic, and he glanced down and kept on climbing coolly, until he reached the final hatch, which he closed, leaving me to my fate.

Domenic's domain looked down on the ponds, bogs, glories and ramifications of Paul Stream. On Gore Mountain there was a young German with a seaman's beard who surveyed the complexities of the Nulhegan country: the North Branch, Yellow Branch, Logger Branch, Black Branch, East Branch; and Sable Mountain, Green Mountain, Black Mountain, Meacham Swamp. Each of the towers, unexpectedly man-wrought in such surroundings, somehow had the focus and seriousness of a whole profession personified; such a climb, such a sight from the top, seemed to possess the arduousness of a life's work. The sense that I always had was that the fellow's career was just to gaze out at it all, not looking for anything so particular as smoke.

I went to the dismantled radar station on top of East Mountain which a wood-carver has bought as a kind of eccentric kingdom; and toured with the county forester and the game warden; and visited the sheriff who leads the search if people disappear, and whose territory encompasses all this fine timberland. During the hunting season I drove with Vermont's bear biologist on his rounds—he pulled a tooth from each beast that was killed to extract a cross-section for aging purposes. Usually the bear was hung up on show at the side of the road by the hunter's house, and he would lower it, pull the tooth, and then winch it up on the gibbet again. Still wet from the dew of the chase, the bear would smell doggy and seem to move with some of the ambly looseness of life while he was cranking it down and then up again, as if making a tacit plea on behalf of the rest of the race against the passion of each new spectator to shoot another. The biologist, a young man with a recent M.A., was becoming fond of bears as he went around measuring their vital statistics. He had observed that their average age declined year by year: below six, below five, towards the tender and vulnerable age of four, which is scarcely above puberty and hardly allows for a population base.

These were good men, these officials. I chatted with Domenic's supervisor while he sawed through an unhandy beaver dam blocking a creek in Warren's Gore, and I went to the offices of the St. Regis Company and the Brown Company, which between them own much of the forty-by-twenty miles, in order to meet the foresters who were in charge. Both men were beginning to feel the pinch of the environmental movement. The Brown fellow spoke of it as "socialism" opposing the prerogatives of private ownership, and St. Regis's forester, Fred Cowan, while he did not necessarily disagree with some of the movement's aims, wondered where all these nature converts had been, say, three years ago, or thirty years ago, when he first went into the woods. Nationwide, St. Regis owns or controls eight million acres and is far from admired by conservationists, but in Vermont and New Hampshire, due entirely to Mr. Cowan, its reputation is high, up with that of the Seven Islands Land Company, of Maine, as an ornament of private enterprise. Among fishermen and hunters the axiom is that you can tell when you have crossed into St. Regis lands from those of another paper company just by looking at the color of the streams. The practices it has followed for years—in road-building, in preserving deer yards, in logging with gingerly, selective care on steep slopes and in the vicinity of streams—are essentially the same as what people who seek to legislate these things propose.

I had assumed that the reason St. Regis's land was managed so well, with four generations of trees blithely growing in the forest, was that the company was financially strong enough to be able to think of the future as well as the present. But I decided instead that the reason was Cowan. He's a pungent, devoted man who jumps up constantly from his desk to go to his maps. Trees are his love. As he had to hire more foresters to meet his quotas there was a fall-off in quality, say the wildlife biologists who work in the woods, but they'd had him to turn to. The company knew also that the prettier Cowan kept his 335,000 acres the more valuable they would be for leisure-

time use, and, in fact, had a leasing agent pushing hard
to fill up the loveliest of the valleys, such as Paul Stream
and the trench of the East Branch of the Nulhegan River,
with hunting cabins and summer cottages, both for the
income they would produce and as a blocking action
against any idea that these superb pristine places might
be maintained in the future as wilderness regions for the
public at large. Then, possibly as a result of an ominous
policy decision within the company, Cowan was transferred to a different job in Maine.

By the end of the summer, after canoeing and climbing
and visiting such a great number of people across the
three northern states, I found that what I'd heard in the
beginning was right. There is no wilderness as such left
in New England, nor any wilderness people of the sort
who might miss it either, not even the handful of elderly
hermits who lived in the woods through perhaps the end
of the 1950s, marking the last stage of that earlier existence. I asked everywhere for them, and after trappers who
really knew how to track in the snow in the old style. I
inquired whether there were any Fish and Game personnel
anywhere who in the pursuit of their duties still slept
out overnight in the woods in good weather. No, none.
Human beings adjust to change so swiftly that no change
quite overtakes them. And it isn't a problem of villains,
I found. It's a dilemma whereby the areas designated
officially as wilderness areas become overrun because
everybody gets so nostalgic and enthusiastic about them.
On the other hand, any wild redoubt that *isn't* publicly

identified will soon vanish completely, turned into cash.

There is no solution to this. I learned, though, that everybody concerned does know the measures that must be employed as a stopgap: easements or other tax breaks for the owners of undeveloped land, the loss of revenue to be made up by an expanded system of license fees which would include all outdoorsmen, the hiker as well as the hunter. Already the tax bite is forcing a good many timber owners to sell out or subdivide. Time is so short that there is no time, and yet it's a matter of waiting for the public's wisdom to catch up with the planners, and for all the outdoorsmen to recognize that they must pool their interests and lobby concertedly—the snowmobilers, bird watchers and campfire buffs together, putting aside their squabbles. I learned, too, that I personally will have an abundance of deserted land to roam about in for the next decade or so. In that forty-by-twenty miles, my friend Domenic and the bear biologist (getting fonder and fonder of the creatures whose carcasses he examines) and I will be pretty much on our own, except for the loggers St. Regis sends in. This is the strange twist to what is happening: people are not going to bother to explore what is left. Despite all the fuss about wilderness, people nowadays don't really want to be in the woods all alone. If they did, there would be less wildness in the woods and in the end there would also be more of it. Even faster than the woods go, people are losing their taste for the woods.

HEART'S
DESIRE

Of all the poignant ways to earn a living, one that seems most affecting in this well-clothed age is when somebody undresses and tries to win fame and fortune by presenting to us his body. The "strong back," mocked by the brainy for centuries and now by the machine, is an endangered animal. As for prizefighting—two people bashing each other for our delectation—it's almost too barefaced to be believed. So is the whole carry-over, the outrageous labor relations, the predatory eating—three-pound sirloin steaks—the tax men crouching in the wings, and the stars floating in a balloon in the comic strips to signify a knock-out—that not merely symbolic death, but a near approach, like sniffing too much glue.

In the American Dream one socks one's way to success, and here is a man who is doing just that, bloodying the loser, puffing up his face, leaving him for dead. Fight fans congregate in the arcades under the arena before entering, eyeing each other for sudden shifts of fortune (ups and

259

downs are what fighting is all about), and watching the retired boxers, now rather chapfallen, and the columnists, the gamblers, the tanned well-heeled fellows with their women who like to rub shoulders with the fight crowd three or four times a year. Right alongside the fat ticket holders with rings on their pinkies who've made some sort of K.O. in the world are harried scalpers, who dodge among them, barely eluding arrest, and maybe part of the best of it for some of these prosperous guys in the good seats is knowing that, however much in earnest the victor is, the entire production is a joke on him. He's taken the injunction literally. He's too dumb to know that one can't actually *sock* one's way to success—that isn't how it's done—and so his shambling victory dance in the ring, when he thinks he is "champion of the world," is the dance of a dunce. Even during his moment of victory he's a loser as well; he's getting nowhere, a champion only in Harlem, if anywhere. From the vantage point of the spectator, it's heads I win and tails you lose.

But there are also plenty of likable boxing fans, especially, as with other sports, those who resemble hobbyists. Hobbyists are men who allow a few chinks in their city armor to show, gathering together for the sake of their enthusiasm and revealing, whether diffidently or in raucous tones, something of what they really live for. One hears a combo of them blowing Dixieland down in a cellar, sees them with cameras in Inwood Park, hears about "frog and toad freaks" from a pet-store owner, reads news of medallion collectors deep in the *Times*, and of the volunteers who varnish each new acquisition at the South

Street Seaport. Some cycle, or sing hymns or just explore New York as a hobby—knowing about the chocolate and coffee stores on Christopher Street, the bums who fry slabs of pork over a blaze in a barrel on Gansevoort after the wholesale butchers there close up.

Fifteen years ago boxing fans were like that. They'd go to Stillman's Gym to watch Isaac Logart or Joey Giardello work out—pay fifty cents, chat with the trainers, nod to the fighter himself. These private excursions were necessary for a fan who wished to go far with the sport because it was so corrupt that several of the best fighters were never seen outside a gym—at least not till their sharpness was gone and they wouldn't derail anybody the smart money was in league with. Such wastage might be impossible today because there's less talent around, but the best fighter I ever saw was a light heavyweight named Harold Johnson. Though he was finally permitted to try for the championship in 1961 and won, by then fifteen years had passed since he'd started fighting, and seven years since he'd last fought someone of championship caliber, and he was past his prime. I managed to watch him during the middle 1950's by going to South Philadelphia and finding a certain empty flat over a vacant store in a sunny slum square where this superb dynamo was sparring. He was laughing because of his own speed and strength, even though only three or four of us were witness to what a panther he was. Archie Moore wouldn't fight Johnson for fear of losing the title; the other contenders wouldn't sign with him lest he knock them out of contention; the up-and-comers were avoiding him because he would blight their careers—so that long years of waiting were in the offing. Yet he was at such a peak that he couldn't help laughing.

The gym was also the place to be in the case of dizzy youngsters who were being overmatched and trained up for slaughter. Sugar Hart, another Philadelphia fighter, a welterweight as slim and vain as a girl, was such a one. Just as the isolation of Philadelphia may have helped to smother Johnson's career, so it favored building Hart up. Nobody saw him, but they heard that in Philly he was looking very good. He chalked up knockouts and got on TV, until everybody was willing to fight him—the comers because his name would look fine on a list of victories, and the better contenders because he represented a pay-day they needn't fear. So, very soon, overmatched, he got into some fast company, got smashed and smashed again, till the fanciness, the eagerness, the confidence and the vanity were crushed. But in the gym, among friends, this hadn't happened as yet. Here, for the interested fan, was talent and youth, assurance and innocence, quick feet, stylish hands.

Boxing is a waning sport, not turning silver-plated as so many sports have. There would be no dearth of fans if there were more excellence, but what hope can there be that in the America which we foresee people will trouble themselves to fight for money that can be had much more easily? Fewer fighters mean fewer gyms, and fewer fans in them. The best left in New York is the Gramercy Gym, "Home of Champions," on 14th Street a few doors from

Luchow's, among the diamond buyers and chow-mein places, next to a discount store called Straight from the Crate. Floyd Patterson trained here and later Jose Torres, during the years that their manager, Cus D'Amato, operated it. Yellow, black and red posters paper the walls, announcing historical events starring such luminaries as Frankie Ryff, Sonny Liston, Buster Mathis—fights at the Roseland Ballroom in Taunton, Mass., the Jersey City Armory, the Alexandria Roller Rink, and Sunnyside and Madison Square Gardens.

The Gramercy Gym is two flights up some littered, light-less stairs that look like a muggers' paradise, though un-doubtedly they are the safest stairs in New York. Inside, two dozen bodies are chopping up and down, self-clocked, each fellow cottoned in his dreams. Some are skipping rope, turbaned in towels, wrapped in robes in order to sweat. These are white-looking figures, whereas the men who are about to spar have on dark headguards that close grimly around the face like an executioner's hood. There are floor-length mirrors and mattresses for exercising and rubdowns, and two speedbags banging like drums, and three heavy bags swinging even between the rounds with the momentum of more than a decade of punches. The bell is loud, the fighters jerk like eating and walking birds, hissing through their teeth as they punch, their feet sneakering the floor with shuffly sounds. They wear red shoelaces in white shoes, and peanut-colored gloves, or if they're Irish they're in green. They are learning to move their feet to the left and right, to move in and out, punching over, then under an opponent's guard, and other repetitive skills without which a man in the ring becomes a man of straw. The speedbags teach head-punching, the heavy bags teach body work, and one bag pinned to the wall has both a head and torso diagrammed, complete with numbers, so that the trainer can shout out what punches his fighter should throw. "Bounce, bounce!" the trainers yell.

There are mongooses and poleaxes, men who hog the floor with an aggressive stance, men whose heavy arms flip out of a clinch like a thick tunafish. The room is L-shaped with a rickety ring set in the L, and so crowded that one might infer that the sport is thriving, though most of the young fighters speak Spanish now. Chu-Chu Malave, a promising welterweight of twenty-one with hard fists and a 15–3 record, has girl-length hair that he ties in a rubber band when he is fighting; and he trains in a shirt with Bach's head on it. He is an acting student, lives in the East Village, and seems touching and young. Another boy wears an "Alaska Hiway" shirt and lizard-green shoes. He sucks in a mouthful of water and spurts it out grandly. Everybody is trying to sock his way upwards through life, but they are divided between those who prefer to fight while moving forward and those who like to fight as they move back. Naturally, the arena match-makers will try to pair a man from group A with one from group B.

In the ring the spittle flies when the punches connect and the real rumbles start. Gym fighters sometimes don't look quite as good under the klieg lights, and sometimes are never given much chance to fight anywhere else—the "animals" down in Philadelphia, who are left to rot in their gyms and fight their hearts out where nobody can see them, are still joked about—so everybody likes to look good at least here.

The Gramercy Gym's king is Carlos Ortiz, a blocky lightweight who has been fighting professionally for seventeen years. He was the champ in 1962–65 and 1965–68, retiring the next year, but in 1971 began a comeback. He has fought four or five tune-up appearances in the same number of months, and the word is that although he may have lost his legs, he has not lost his punch. He sports a red headguard, baggy blue sweatpants and an NMU shirt, has a nose that looks bobbed because of all the violence wreaked upon it, and fights as watchfully as a lathe operator bending to a machine. It is perhaps this attentiveness that's so overwhelming. But with the youngsters he is gentle, pulling every punch even as he shovels their resistance aside and swarms over them. (I thought of the legendary way wolf cubs take on their lupine form, licked into shape by the tongues of their mothers.) Then he leaves for the day with a gorgeous redhead with a million curls.

It's a career that's naked to the world—just the simple matter of wins versus losses, the vitality or lack of it observed exactly by a horde of thousands. And there is no disguising the cruelty of the losses; they've watched the man nearly get killed, jeering and pitying him, shaking their heads with a chuckle. Only a series of savage beatings awaits the fighter as he approaches his middle years, the doctors sardonically stitching his eyelids. Maybe this is what makes these personalities so unassuming when you sit down with them. I was eavesdropping on the interviews done by Vic Ziegel, the *New York Post's* boxing specialist, and watching the managers handle their fighters, wiping a hand across the face of a black man to find out how much he was sweating, then slapping him lightly like a horse if it seemed not enough. When this happened, the kids who hadn't yet proved themselves withdrew into a private smile, the dreams of glory someday, when they might cut a swath. Floyd Patterson's simon-pure teenaged face looked out from the wall above this inscription: "Congratulations to America's greatest boxing expert" (unnamed). "Your prediction of my success is a great encouragement to me. I shall try to keep your record perfect."

Walter Seeley is a roofer and a featherweight who commutes every day after work from Long Island to train. He has a victim's gutsy tired face, a bear-it grin, and has suffered only one loss in thirty fights. A career assessment of him would say that not only aren't the fans very much interested in his weight division (the featherweight limit is 126 pounds), but there are very few fighters competing in the same class outside the Far East.

Bobby Cassidy is a left-handed middleweight, a bar owner and marathon runner who also comes in all the way from Long Island. He's had fifty-four fights in eight years, losing just twelve, has had good management and was ranked tenth in his class. His nose, however, looks double-parked, his eyes are recessed, and he bleeds easily. Being left-handed probably helped him early in his career because other young fighters were baffled by that, and he has good fists and good underneath shots, but is not much for strategy. He is black-haired, fun-loving, yet oddly quixotic, and impressed me as a lovely man riding along on a battered wide smile that might carry him through almost anything.

Dan McAloon has milk-white legs, an amused, mustached face, squaring into a beard, and teaches phys ed at a private school. Sometimes he brings his wife and baby to the gym to watch him train. By last year, at twenty-eight, he'd worked up a string of nice showings, including two at Madison Square Garden that earned him a bout with Emile Griffith. Griffith, who is the last of three marvelous Cuban fighters (he was Isaac Logart's protégé, as Logart was Kid Gavilan's), was welterweight champion for a number of years, and gave him a boxing lesson, beating him painfully. Then another former welter champ, Billy Backus, outpointed him badly and humblingly at Syracuse. But he has offers from Italy and the West Coast.

Benny Huertas has been an up-and-down fighter since 1964. Recently he'd accumulated a string of wins, then was knocked out in the first round. Shook up by that, he lost twice more and is only now springing back, fighting well in France. He is another heedful lightweight, weaving, protecting his face like a purse.

Tom Kocan is a dishwasher, a heavyweight with a thin face but an unsettling right hand. Lonely-looking in a lonely sport, he fights best late in a bout when exhausted and loose.

Smoky Roy Edmonds at twenty-four is soft-spoken,

hopeful, endearing. He runs on the horse path in Central Park every morning, fueled by his aspirations. He was sidetracked by two automobile accidents last year but is waiting now for his manager, who is a guard at Sing Sing, to finally arrange for him to appear in Madison Square Garden in a preliminary for the first time.

The gym is a period piece, as authentic as rope, and these people bring it alive. For their pains, their long months of training, they are paid $150 for fighting four rounds at the Garden, and $50 or $75 at the lesser showplaces where most bouts take place. For a six-rounder the fee jumps to $500—$100 or $150 elsewhere—an increase due more to the punishing competition accompanying the jump than the number of rounds. At Sunnyside Garden in Queens, a famous old club where all boxers fight eventually, the men in the main event get about $1000 apiece, as an advance against 10 percent of the gate. The manager takes one-third, and since even wrestling outdraws boxing today, the prices have not changed in twenty years. One night I went to see Bobby Cassidy battle an awkward, stubby rock of a barroom brawler named Gil Diaz, whose middle-aged legs soon gave out and who even before then hadn't dared take the chance of sitting down between rounds. Eight hundred and ninety-five people had paid $4,950 at the Sunnyside box office. The promoter barely broke even.

Beforehand, Vic Ziegel and I ate supper with Cassidy's manager, Paddy Flood, and his previous manager too, an antique dealer named Al Braverman, both of them

enthusiasts and former fighters. A scout from Madison
Square Garden was there, and the *Daily News* man was
expected as well. As the sport sinks, these hands gather
around and retell the myths, the bad-guy stories: how the
best time to pay off your fighter after a fight is as you
walk away from the arena in the dark of the night. You
count his share of the money into his hand, and exhausted,
cut, beaten up anyway, and what with the bad light, he
doesn't know what he is getting. They all seemed like
decent men, however, exhilarated like kids as fight time
approached—this stuff was for the sake of the mystique.
Braverman talked about "the chills" he'd gotten during the
great sequences of a fight last week, though he's been
watching prizefights for forty years. Paddy Flood, Ziegel
and I had driven out from Manhattan with an off-duty
cop, a friend of Flood's who beat the stoplights and drove
up on the sidewalk and made U-turns and used every
other trick to twist through the usual jams. On First Avenue
we saw a man with a chimpanzee in his car and hooted at
him. We saw Johnny Carson, ferretlike in a red sweater,
dodging on foot between the stalled cars. The cop began
telling celebrity stories, and we yelled out the window at
Carson, "Hey, Johnny. Hey, Johnny," until he turned.
Then, happy as clams, we hollered at him, "FUCK YOU,
JOHNNY CARSON!"

Cassidy won by a technical knockout in the fourth
round. I got the impression that the other fighter had been
accepted as a match for him on the assumption that Cassidy
would be able to dispose of him around this midpoint.
Cassidy sat panting, smiling and toweling his face in the

dressing room while we questioned him, adhering to the tradition that one seldom speaks to the loser. Smoky Roy Edmonds had won his preliminary bout by a knockout too, and he and the fellow he'd beaten were placed knee to knee in another dingy, narrow room as we listened to him softly voice his heart's desire about where he wanted to go from here. It wasn't so different from casually congratulating any man who has had some success, except that the smiles directed by the spectators to the loser were rather as if a good joke had been played on him, instead of his having just died in effigy.

That's it, I suppose. Lose in boxing and you are a joke; win and sooner or later you are a joke also. It's a kind of extravagant burlesque of the course of anybody's career, even of life itself. The fighter who fights too long looks into the mirror one day and realizes that his face has gradually been transformed by the pounding into a skull.

MEATCUTTERS

ARE A

FUNNY BUNCH

We all would like a nice light workout in the morning, at least in our idealized image of ourselves. But perhaps better than actually doing exercises is to watch a trim athlete do them for us while we eat cornflakes, eggs and toast. At the M & M Restaurant on Little West 12th Street it is possible to do this, if you're a late sleeper or want to grab a quick lunch. A hamburger is sixty cents, and from 11 A.M. on, two girls, working in shifts and wearing pasties and G-strings do go-go dances on a stage. These are topnotchers, mind you, because at that hour the M & M must be almost alone in offering employment—they are daylighting, as it were—and an unending variety of girls appear, themselves just out of bed, sweating pleasantly even when there is a frost outside, warming to the fresh bright day. The pleasure they take in their bodies is real, just as, at least in our inner eye, we all feel flushed clean by a good sleep. They're as young as we still picture ourselves as being.

For me, it's as if I had knocked at a lovely young stranger's door, finding her undressed and fixing coffee but, with the limber benevolence of morning, quite willing to invite me in, then stretching, flexing, toweling herself, looking in the mirror and swinging her uberous body to jukebox rock. She pulls a lock of hair under her nose for a mustache. The night is just behind us, so there is not the tawdry hunger of a night striptease show, where one is drinking to quiet one's nerves; nor do the sexual contests of bedtime, or else a lonesome, dismal stint of masturbation, lie ahead. In the morning no one's rich and no one's poor, and I'm so absorbed in the girls' setting-up exercises that I'm recharged. After showing me her own delight in her round breasts and her long hair and the triumphal ease of being just twenty in the waist and legs (for it's the morning and the day is new), the lady joins me at the counter for a cool bowl of cornflakes, herself.

The M & M is a small place, nearly buried in the wholesale meatpacking blocks right over by the Hudson. There is a railroad running overhead; huge trailer trucks from Iowa pull in, stalling traffic while they back and park; and there's the smell of the Atlantic too. Calves' skins are heaped on the sidewalk. White pigs, skinned lambs and beef for Schrafft's hang in your path; on the way you feel nobody's going to starve. Breakfast time for the girls or a longhair like me is practically the quitting hour at the market so that the room soon fills up with butchers in white coveralls with rubber sleeves and white hardhats, black men and whites. Some of the girls come down from Harlem, and Geri Miller, the diva of *Trash,* performs, as well as girls bringing their books for school, who put their glasses on to see who claps. Pretty women do the waitressing and also act as barmaid and cashier, and the proprietor, a broad-faced, broad-mouthed, husky man, a member of the Italian Anti-Defamation League, is not about to allow anybody to be defamed. This is New York as supposedly it used to be. Nobody worries that the girls may not be self-sufficient or the men truly heterosexual. I eat and watch the bodies as I would watch the moon and stars if I got up when my neighbor, gulping his late lunch, does. The stars will be with us tomorrow, and so will bodies that make other bodies, like these.

THE MIDNIGHT
FREIGHT TO
PORTLAND

Railroads provided the big bones of American industry and of much of the country's mythology, too, until the current containerized epoch of trucks and the small-world era of planes. Children rushed out and waved and their fathers stood alert when a train steamed through town, sometimes crossing at street level, bringing all traffic to a halt, and maybe stopping to let the passengers off or maybe not, though they would look out of the windows ironically, in any case. Part of the privilege of being downtown was to see them and to watch the train, boiling with noise and momentum, the crew ten feet above the ground, detached-looking and far-sighted even as they loafed. Their travels lasted nights and days—even the gandy dancers were legends—and no writer who seriously pursued the chimera of the great American novel could neglect to learn some of the lore of railroading.

Recently I rode a freight train from Island Pond in northeastern Vermont to Portland, Maine, to see how the trains run; there has been no passenger service on the line, or anywhere else in Vermont, for years. This is the last hundred and fifty miles of the famous Grand Trunk international rail route from Montreal to the ice-free salt-water harbor in Casco Bay, something that the Canadians needed in 1853, when the last spikes were driven with a good deal of fanfare and acclaim. Later, when icebreakers were making more headway in the St. Lawrence, Portland still possessed a thriving year-round port where enormous amounts of Western grain arrived by rail to be shipped abroad. Twenty-six train crews were based in Island Pond to handle the activity; now there are only six. Island Pond is a railroad and sawmill town which does not hide the fact that it has come down in the world, although it's got some dairying going on where the woods aren't too thick and a little tourism. The station is a frowning sooty brick pile with a plaza-sized area left vacant all around. Many of the other local buildings look like old railroad stations too.

Since the 1920s the Grand Trunk's trackage and perquisites have belonged to the Canadian National Railways. Not waiting to go as a hobo, I'd written to the office in Montreal and was received royally. The station agent put me under the wing of Claude Seguin, his brother, the head-end brakeman on the train I rode. Seguin is a loose-cheeked, modest, drawling man with a farmer's emotive hands, an outdoorsman up early for long walks on his days off, who had been helping a neighbor clapboard his house. Like many railroad men, he collects timepieces as a hobby, even buying large restaurant clocks at auctions, cleaning off the grease and putting them up around the house. I asked if he'd seen any hoboes lately. He said not for four or five years, although the crews used to let them ride if they looked decent. "We're just glorified hoboes ourselves, you know."

The engineer was Eddy Boylan, a quick gray active man well past the years when he may or may not have made some mistakes. The seniority system works excellently in railroading, ensuring that nobody who is still trying to prove something will be risking other people's lives. All these men were hefty veterans over fifty years old, with austere, snowy minds and furry, neutral-sounding voices: Joe Vautour, the fireman; Joe Cargill, the rear-end brakeman; and Donald MacDonald, a judgely, stern but witty man who rides in the caboose ("buggy") and keeps the waybills straight.

I was eager to talk, but when the train pulled in we left immediately, as soon as the Montreal crew stepped off. It was dusk, and a full harvest moon—white, not red, in this cold border country—stood low in the sky toward Portland. The leaves were turning but not yet falling, and we entered fir forests, with low deserted mountains and tamarack bogs and bushy round wild islands posted in a series of lakes. The streams were black and shining; the clouds spread into herringbone patterns. I rode alone in the second of three engines, and Seguin or the fireman paid me visits. The engineer drives from the right-hand side of the front locomotive, controlling the other locomotives from there. The fireman, who nowadays, in the post-steam era, functions as a sort of co-pilot, sits at the left-hand window, looking out at crossings which the engineer can't see.

He's there if the engineer gets sick or wishes to eat, in time of hazard, or if the walkie-talkies that the brakemen carry fail and they are dependent upon hand signals. Since he is basically a featherbedder, though, the fireman is mainly supposed to be good company, and Vautour, who has a world-worn face, a furrowed forehead, a buffeted nose, bushy eyebrows and a voice like William Bendix's, fills the bill.

The two brakemen sit watching for sparks, smoke or hotboxes as the train rolls along, one seated facing backwards in the first engine, the other located in the monitor, which is the double-decker compartment on top of the caboose. We were hauling only fifty-two freight cars, considered a light load, because, as it happened, a rail strike was threatened for midnight. I had assumed the President would sign a cooling-off order, but in a pressure play, he was delaying doing that, and since even this spur which angled down from Canada might be affected, the railroad was stripping for trouble.

We ran alongside the Connecticut River for a while after crossing into New Hampshire. At North Stratford the crew "set off" ten cars; delicately waving his light in signal patterns, Seguin hopped off and on and off to turn the switches and uncouple. Between Groveton and Berlin we skirted the Upper Ammonoosuc River through an expanse of national forest. A deer paused dazzled on the track as we rushed toward it, and Boylan turned off the headlight and tooted. Under the moon, the White Mountains showed themselves in rotund grays and navy blues; lots of empty land, a sense of calmness. Every station had a telegraph operator usually wearing an eyeshade and a checked shirt, who stepped outside to wave. In Berlin we hitched onto a switching engine that the railroad wanted hauled out of harm's way to Portland, in case there was a strike. Berlin has a big stone station and a round-the-clock paper plant pluming steam and smoke. The crew was quite worked up about the possibility of the strike and how far they should take the train if one was called, whether they shouldn't just leave it standing somewhere on a siding as soon after midnight as they heard. Apparently they assumed that the railroad would then have the responsibility of hiring a taxi to take them home to Island Pond.

The shaking and the roar, the rumbling wheels, the amalgam of jolts, hisses and shivers, the rocking and big-bopping over the rails were all as intimately familiar to me as my childhood itself. Though I've never been a railroad fan the way some people are, I sometimes rode at the front window of subways and Toonerville Trolleys as a boy, and admired the figure cut by the engineers on bigger trains as they swept by. Even the track-walker hiking through town on his own lonely schedule intrigued me. Just as a man who has wished to be rich and watched rich men for years is not bewildered about how to behave or what to do when his windfall finally does come, so to be up in that engine myself did not seem novel or astonishing. It was about as I'd expected: the majestic height at which we rode, the swath that the headlight illuminated in front, the diesel fumes, the tilty file of telephone poles, the murky train winding behind. The horn's tattoo

278

was properly pristine. In the moonlight the spruces bulged. There was a breezy, box-shaped chemical toilet perched in among the turbines, a water cooler to drink from, and panels of gauges, gears and levers, with stenciled advisory warnings and small red lights. A pull-rope was attached to the whistle, which Boylan jokingly told me I should pull if I had a question. We sat on upholstered jump seats, not so comfortable that you could fall asleep.

Three hours out we were in Maine, a land of redolent sawmills, clusters of cozy houses with lights in the bedrooms, and a night fog that was gathering across the fields. Chill air, crisp moonlight, gunmetal-colored lakes and tumultuous trees—rollicking, big-topped hardwoods against the sky. At South Paris, a hundred miles from Island Pond, we left off another seven cars, Seguin hopping along the catwalks and the cowcatcher area under the engine's nose. The locomotives revved with the whorling, encompassing sound of a ship's engine—electrical, oil-burning sounds. South Paris is a tranquil little county seat, but it has a shoe-manufacturing plant, a tannery, linoleum and sled-and-ski factories, and a berry cannery. Bouncing along catch-as-catch-can, flying a freight train's white flag on our front, we passed on through Mechanic Falls to Lewiston Junction, and set off two cars which contained cereals and one refrigerator car carrying meat. Because of the projected strike, Boyland and the crew detoured two miles with the meat and placed it at the wholesaler's door, where it could be unloaded promptly. Lewiston has a feed mill, a formica and plastics plant, a factory producing bridge girders, and a General Electric facility.

279

At Yarmouth Junction we disposed of three more cars, which were to be transferred to the Maine Central, then highballed swiftly towards Portland, brazenly blaring our horn, through dozens of deserted crossings with flailing signals. The extra work and the fact that we had stopped to inquire about strike news at almost every station had made us very late; it was three in the morning. Crossing a drawbridge outside Portland, we ran alongside an arm of the bay. Since we had just emerged from the North Woods, the smell of the salt water stung our lungs. It was a marvelous arrival, a rank, spacious, open harbor. In the yards next to the water, Boylan simply parked the train, and, each man with his overnight kit, we walked away, leaving it right where it was, to be dealt with later.

We slept in a bunkhouse over the terminal offices, a remnant of Portland's heyday as a port. When I woke up the view was like a Channel town in France, with smudged seacoast weather and Frenchy frame houses spotted on sandy hills. Mewing white gulls had collected on the piers in crowds. Low-rent industry—ironmongeries, beer warehouses and fender shops—was casually clumped about. The groceries featured olive oil. On East India Street a plaque announced that this had been the site of Fort Loyal, built by the English settlers in 1680 and destroyed ten years later by Indians and French. Through the rain I saw an orange-and-black freighter, a lighter and some coastal boats.

Here on the seacoast the crew looked like men out of the woods, slow-speaking, their faces delineated and chunky. They let me look at their noble gold watches, which the railroad inspects every November and May. We breakfasted in a bar where four or five wet prostitutes were having coffee, "too wet to climb on," as the trainmen said. Spread over the wall was a picture of Bobby Orr horizontal in the air after scoring a winning goal, and the talk, perhaps because of me, was mostly of the heroic era of steam, prior to 1955. The brakemen kidded around, saying they had told the janitor at the terminal that I was a reporter for *Time* and that he was cleaning up like mad, scrubbing cupboards that nobody had even looked into since before the era of steam. MacDonald, the conductor, was trying to think of stories I could use. There used to be contests between the engineers and firemen, he said. If they couldn't manage to get along and the engineer demanded more steam, the fireman *gave* him more steam, until he had more than he wanted, maybe, so that the safety valves were popping, and the fireman would make him figure out how to use it. Putting in more water cooled the boiler, but then the pressure died, or the fire itself might die if there was slate mixed with the coal.

As it turned out, the President had never needed to act, because at the last moment the union limited the strike to three breadbasket railroads in the Midwest, whereupon a federal judge issued an injunction. We left belatedly at 2:10 P.M., pulling twenty-six empty cars that were going to Moncton, New Brunswick, to haul the turnip crop and two that were full of canned goods for Minneapolis and Denver. For a while I was with MacDonald. His desk is the main article of furniture in the caboose, though there are also fold-up beds, a wooden bench, kerosene lamps and an oil stove. Each freight car is in its logical order in the train, and its waybill must give a description explicit enough to help the customs men, who hold the train for an hour after it passes Island Pond. MacDonald says he doubts that any of the crews indulge in smuggling now, but back during Prohibition and afterwards, when some of the crews were younger, the Mounties used to hide behind a boxcar in the Montreal rail yards and suddenly jump out and mount the moving engine and search everybody. Luckily there was steam then; they had a firebox where they could throw the contraband.

MacDonald drinks tea from a thermos and carries Preparation H because of the hard benches he sits on and a miniature screwdriver for tightening his glasses. He has a clean, cutting smile that breaks through this methodical exterior, however. His principal avocation seems to be women, or remembering them. The handsome, slicing smile gives him away, paring ten years off his age. Just as caïque captains on the Ionian Sea flash mirrors at the widows who live on the islands they sail past, so does MacDonald wave and give a high sign to some of the lonely ladies of Maine.

At the Maine Central Railroad's yards at Yarmouth Junction we picked up thirty cars—1,750 tons. Several of these were empty grain hoppers which had carried soybean meal; others had brought asbestos and were going back out West for more. The carloads were either potatoes or else wood pulp or rolled newsprint manufactured to the north in towns like Madawaska; the waybills were from the Belfast and Moosehead Lake Railroad and the Bangor and Aroostook. At Danville, we added on eleven more cars and at Mechanic Falls, another one—now we were hauling seventy. Because of the tangled schedule, our caboose brakeman had been replaced by a fairly young man who had worked fifteen years for the railroad, all of them right in the Portland yards. This was to be his first trip up the line—indeed, the first time he had ever left the state of Maine. Yet he was worrying whether we would reach Island Pond on time so that he could catch the return train and not have to stay over.

The coastal drizzle had preceded us inland, and when the wheels slipped on the track, lights on the panel flashed. I was in the second locomotive again as we began to climb out of the Maine flatlands into the mountains before entering New Hampshire. Westbound, the so-called deciding grade of this particular route is at Bryant Pond, close to the state border. Though each of our engines could pull 2,300 tons on the level ground, their limit for this slope (and therefore for the trip) was calculated at 1,865 tons. Besides being high and steep, it was magnificent abandoned country with forests stretching away for miles, with ducks and herons in all the ponds and lots of creeks—lovely back country, of which we got a view uncluttered by motels.

We acquired nine more cars in Berlin, Seguin adroit and cautious as he moved between them, signaling. A "run-off" is a derailment; a "head-on" is a wreck. The "tell-tales," as he said they were called, used to fascinate me; they are the long strings which hang overhead wherever the tracks near an underpass and slap a man who is on top of a freight car to warn him before he is decapitated. It is the nature of railroading that even a minor goof by somebody means that he has to take a long walk, at the least, maybe the length of a hundred cars.

Because of the rain, night settled down around us much faster. The windshield wipers and heater hissed with enough decibels to have alarmed an ear doctor, quite apart from the roar of the diesels themselves, but I found sitting there in the eye of the roar so soothing that I would have been content for another dozen hours. Railroads are the one great exception among our huge machines in that we've finally assimilated them.

Sometimes a hard rain will clean the tracks nicely, but this was a light greasy drizzle. The ponderous train climbed up into Vermont from the trench of the Connecticut River with difficulty, whining around double-reverse curves at five miles per hour, Boylan using his sand judiciously (each drive wheel of a locomotive is serviced by a pipe from a sand reservoir). The roar had become a lugubrious groan, alternating between two notes like a Parisian police car. It's not the number of cars so much as the load in them, and not the load so much as whether the wheels can grip the tracks. All torments end, however. We followed the Nulhegan River up and out, hooting the horn, regaining speed. White cedars, red spruces, and firs and tamaracks—wild north country. Of course the whole experience was definitive. One wouldn't say that riding a night freight is like driving all night in a mufflerless car across the Texas panhandle, but one might say that driving a mufflerless car across the Texas pan-handle all night is somewhat like riding a night freight train. At last, at 9:15 in the evening after seven hours, we pulled into Island Pond again. The Montreal crew took over.

TIGER
BRIGHT

1

Ringling Bros. and Barnum & Bailey circus still tours America, and all the divorced mothers and fathers are glad because it gives them some place to take the kids. The notices that it gets are uniformly friendly and noddly, not like sharp sportswriting or theater criticism, and afterwards the press agent sends out a letter of thanks to everybody concerned. But last year, after seven good weeks in New York City and two in Boston, the circus left for points west with some of its same old impudent alacrity. Zacchini, the cannonball, was fired from his X-15 with a tremendous boom, so that smoke filled the back passageways, and, even before the smoke thinned, twenty elephants, chained in pairs, went rushing past, with that middle-aged, big-footed push to their gait, down the ramp to the street, to the circus train, at least fifty horses hard after them, even before all the patrons were out of their seats. There is no sentiment about how a circus leaves town; it shakes off the dust of your burg just as readily as it quits Kanakee.

I worked in the circus for a few months about twenty years ago and have followed its fortunes with a fond, mournful eye ever since from the distance of the civilian world—the world that with such a flourish is left behind. The circus has nationhood, but there has been the question whether it will survive. The Depression, then the Hartford circus fire of 1944, in which a hundred and sixty-eight people died, precipitated bankruptcies and changes of management, and after recovering from these crises the more mundane problems of budget in a swept-wing economy caused the Big Show to forswear tenting in 1956 and resolve to play only arena engagements indoors. Whereas the old circus used to need three trains, leaving at intervals, in order to travel, now that the acres of canvas and poles, the seats, cookhouse, generator wagons, box offices, sideshow and much of what was the menagerie have been dispensed with, one train is enough. The money saved is more than matched by the loss of so much buoyant tradition and color, but the change may have been necessary in a day when workmen are paid $70 a week instead of $14, as they were in my time, and the youngest dancing girl gets $140, and the greenest clown $165.

Still, the customers keep coming, and in 1967 the heirs and successors of the Ringling family sold Ringling Bros. and Barnum & Bailey for eight million dollars to two pop-music magnates and a former mayor of Houston, who soon got it listed over-the-counter as a growth stock. Their first act of reorganization was to split the show into two separate circuses which can play simultaneously in different cities, the ultimate plan being to expand to four units, all operating at the same time. Only one of the four would have to be staged new each year, with new acts from Europe and new choreography. This one would appear in New York and Los Angeles and so on, while the others hedgehopped, just as road companies in the theater do, carrying the presentations of previous years to smaller cities. Expenses have been pared so skillfully that the main cost of fielding additional units has become the buying and converting of Pullman cars as the railroads abandon them. Apparently a torrent of children fills all available arenas and halls, and more are being built, so that if there really are going to be four Ringling Bros. and Barnum & Baileys, with twelve rings to fill, the only hitch may turn out to be whether there is enough circus artistry left in the world to display in them. Already, with two shows going, the cream has been spread rather thin.

I spent a week with the Madison Square Garden edition of the show, then another week down in Birmingham, Alabama, with the version that was playing there, remembering all the time the grinding fatigue of the life, yet feeling an extraordinary yearning to be with it again. In Birmingham I sat next to an old acquaintance who had once worked in the menagerie taking care of the pygmy hippo and who felt the same way. His home is ninety miles north, near the Georgia border. He needs a cane nowadays and is feeling poorly, his eyes are going bad on him, he has no teeth and is stout in a petrified way, though he was wearing pants so wide that as stout as he was, they must have been hand-me-downs. He said he hadn't worked in

a circus since I had known him—"It takes a mighty good
man to work on a circus and travel and all"—but that for
the sake of his memories he hitchhiked down every year
when the show was in Birmingham. (Yet *I* remembered
him as a man tormented continually, frequently raped,
prison-style, his arms twisted behind his back, nearly
twisted off.)

Before the performance we watched the propman lug
the elephant tubs and the chimp- and lion-act furniture,
the rigging boys stunt in the rigging, the clowns' hyper-
tense terrier snort around the clowns' goose as it ate, the
Roman-nosed, wooden-looking horses, and the browsing
camels, all joints and humps. Then the performance began
as if irrevocably, like a giant aroused—old blondes somehow mustering up a dazzle to their faces, a brave workaday walk turning into a glamorous strut. Squally, heavy-
beat music was played for the elephants, songs from *My
Fair Lady* for the trick dogs; the trainer's whip was a
swagger stick. A *March of the Olympiads* fanfare announced the trapezists, and sweet-swaying ice-skating
music accompanied their clocked twists. I recognized a few
of the old hands, twisty and lame, among the roughnecks
backstage. They didn't look strong these days, but they
were probably very strong. A circus travels and never
stops: this is the point, and it is addictive. The mud, the
heat, the privation, the gypsy allegiances and easy good-
bys, the chaotic glory and whirl, all mix together and fix
a man into the troupe, and as long as he's traveling he need
never stop and take stock; his situation is fluid, in a sense
his life is ahead of him; things may look up. Even if he's

not young, the ashes of his past are well behind him and he's in new country this week, next week, and forever on.

But there's more to it than that. Twice daily the organization builds to its performances, which are created to convey amazement and glee. Formerly a circus hand might go through the year and practically never see a performance because so much was going on outside the big top. Band music accompanied his chores, but he lived with the herds of horses and a horde of wild characters in the satellite wagons and tents. Now that the performance is all there is, he's with the performers, most of whom really light up and come to life when the show gets under way; and it's contagious. Though they may look as wilted and crumpled and sad over breakfast as civilian folk, every evening their faces spread into the same beaming lines that the children wear, and receiving the cheers of thousands, are lifted beyond the expressions of wonder and childhood to the graceful wide grin of a conquering king. Over the years, their mouths enlarge and their faces grow ever more malleable. A man who has just staked his life on his physical skill isn't modest. He stands in the platinum-colored spotlight used only for danger and princes, and casts his head back, throws his arms wide, his body undulating sensuously as the ovation bathes him, and listens to the crowd rejoice that he is alive.

Women performers aren't quite so dramatic. Rogana is a flawless-bodied tall personage who grips the hilt of one sword in her mouth and balances another by its point from the point of the first, with a tray and six glasses balancing on the second sword's hilt. Meanwhile she climbs a swaying ladder and straddles the top, swinging eerily, poising the swords nearly perpendicularly. After this and other feats, she accepts the applause with reserve, withholding some of herself and looking, despite her long legs and black hair, like Babe Didrikson Zaharias; her face is unfortunately masculine, which may be the trouble. "La Toria," who in fact is Vicky Unus—her father stood on one finger in performances for many years—is another slightly sad athlete. Except for her muscular arms she is slimmer but gawkier and shorter than Rogana, and like an exotic, she paints her eyelids white with streaks of black, though she seems timid and at a loss with men. (Rogana is married to a ringmaster.) Vicky Unus does a brave series of vertical arm twists, fifty-two of them for matinées and seventy-two in the evening, while hanging by one hand from a rope above the center ring. The act, an American invention, is plaintive and arduous, although she looks like a young girl swimming as her legs wrench her body around and around in a sort of scissors kick. She's a small girl built like a big one—rawboned, with a swinging walk, a sharp nose, a gaunt masklike face, but terribly human and touching and feminine because of that jerk her legs make. She tapes her wrist where the rope cuts in, wearing Band Aids under the tape and sometimes a cape. In a way, her stunt and her father's before her seem somewhat the same, perhaps because it is such a short distance from what is compelling to what is compulsive, and they both have managed to stay on the side of the angels in this regard. The great Lilian Leitzel did twice as many twists, varying the number according to mood, suffering more torment from the wounds in her wrist, and, full of fire, eventually fell to her death.

Most performers are Europeans from one or another of a dwindling number of circus families. America has not produced many headliners: just some daredevil types and high-wire men, several great clowns and a few bravura animal trainers of the Clyde Beatty kind. Without circus parents to steer them, kids here were going to school when they should have been learning to tumble and flip, so that daredevil stunts and clowning were the only crafts they were still eligible for by the time they left home. Now even the trainers are German and most of the notable clowns have died or retired. Ringling Bros. has started a school for clowns, and scouts seeking young performers who have been painstakingly schooled in the physical arts are going all the way to the Eastern-bloc countries, where the lag of a decade or two has preserved an old-style dedication to the crafts of the past (also they're cheaper to hire). The Silagis, who are Bulgarian teeter-board tumblers, and the Czechoslovakian Poldis are examples. The youngest Poldi somersaults thirty feet into the air from an aluminum swing, a very shy man who locks his heels when he takes his bow so that his legs won't wobble and looks straight out from under his brows at a dot in the audience, as he's been taught to.

The best acts are hard to write about because they are consummate cameos, long-practiced, that an imprecise process like writing cannot reproduce. Furthermore, in this milieu all words are considered venal by the insiders—if not hyperbole, then frankly bilge. Inaccuracies puff every newspaper piece, people hardly know the difference between a straight man and a strong man anymore, and especially now, after the circus has endured years of decline, the truly incomparable feats are often not recognized for what they are. The excellence of Tito Gaona on the flying trapeze is not like that seen in a competitive sport, for instance; it is perfection. His triple, done blindfolded, is done in the single tick of a clock. He elaborates on what can be done, and leaps, finally, to the net, springs unexpectedly high to land sitting up in the catcher's swing, does a lazy man's dive, bounces to grab the trapeze again, does a sailor's dive, a dead man's dive, and a duck dive, toying with his body's limberness. When at last he touches the ground, he keeps right on bouncing, as if the very ground had spring. He gets a shrill, steely ovation, and Antoinette Concello, now in her sixties, who was the greatest woman trapezist and who stands below at every performance—a tiny, quick-looking woman with eyes alluringly deepened and darkened and a long, sly, survivor's face—smiles at him. He reaches exuberantly toward the crowd for his cheers. He has a huge chest and a broad pre-Columbian face.

There are other young men who may carry the show for the next few years: Emanuel Zacchini (the cannonball), Elvin Bale on the single trapeze, and Gunther Gebel-Williams, who constitutes a circus all by himself and is a Nureyev of show business, a man geared for great fame. It's a question whether he will achieve it—what with the circus's low estate in the world—but in Imperial Rome the crowd's accolade for him would have lapped over the rim of the Colosseum like a tidal wave; he would have been installed in public office. He makes marble steps out of his elephants' trunks and ascends and descends. Obviously if he could afford to have fifty elephants he could lead them all, ride into the jungle, as in some fantasy, and live with them there in his sleek gold boots and open red tunic. With his large mouth, large teeth, young-Satan's grin, and a big cross on his chest that bobs as he runs, he seems almost perpetually elated. His first wife, Jeanette, like a deposed queen, and his second wife, Sigrid, direct high-school horses in adjoining rings, and he stands on the ring curbing just between, ready to dart into the thicket of hooves and plumes to enforce their rule.

When he is waiting his turn, Elvin Bale looks like a cockney sharpster with a beaklike nose and pasted hair but once in the air he swings on the single trapeze with absorption and even a kind of onrushing joy. He swings higher and higher, as a child would wish to, pulling, reaching for extra height; he has no implements to encumber his act, just his arms and legs. Then, when he is swinging as high as he can go, he delicately lets himself slide backwards head-down, only halting his fall with his bent heels. He varies these heel catches in every possible way, catching the bar on his thighs in the most dangerous dives, letting the force of the swing hold him there, before slipping farther down as the arc of the trapeze peaks and reverses itself. He squints anxiously for an instant as he hangs by his heels, until, finding that he's secure, he spreads his arms, marking the finish of the feat. He pulls himself up and lolls, gazing into the expanse of the crowd, swinging and grinning. His body, which had been red with tension, turns golden in the spotlights.

In the New York edition of the show, the first half displayed mostly the arts, the second half the thrills, and Zacchini and a girl named Marcia who masqueraded as his wife—his real wife was recuperating from a broken neck—closed the performance. Zacchini, like many thrill men, is no more daredevil in manner than an astronaut and is not a promising subject for an interview; he appears to be a quite ordinary bloke except when alone during his bout in space. He is flat-faced, built like a running back, and looks petted and plump like a mama's boy until the trapeze act, when he begins guying himself up to risk his life. His wife, neatly dressed in a suit, pushes her wheelchair to a good vantage point, and he gives her his wedding ring to hold. Watching Tito Gaona work but wincing and covering his ears when the clowns' firecrackers go off, he chins himself on the bleacher piping, stretching his back and neck, stretching even his mouth; briefly his stolid face contorts into the visage of a man fighting for life.

The cannon is a giant slingshot contoured to fit inside a rocket which emits lots of noise. He and Marcia load themselves into the muzzle. His father, Zacchini Senior, who limps from having once broken *his* neck, stage-manages the buildup and sound effects and watches as they are shot out, separated by an interval of less than a second, soaring so high that they seem to pause in the air —Zacchini's trajectory slightly higher—before following long, logical parabolas down onto a net, landing carefully on their backs, as trapeze flyers do. Always they keep as straight as possible during the flight; they don't ball up. Unlike most performers, their job is *not* to turn somersaults, because any activity in the air might turn them off course.

Before the event, the band stops playing, forebodingly, and Zacchini Senior calls out their names in the voice of Abraham standing over his son. A terrifying siren wails, and there is a thunderous explosion and the astounding sight of two bodies propelled half the length of the hippodrome. As they recover themselves and roll out of the net, the band strikes up, the performers who have been watching breathe easier and smile, the crowd is rejuvenated, and since the circus's purpose is to evoke emotions like this, it seems altogether a fitting end. Zacchini walks toward the cheers with his arms raised high, his head back, as dazed as a man reborn from the grave, his face in a kind of ecstasy, and moving as if he were swimming in cream. In a day of casual death everywhere, we are rejoicing *he lives! he lives!*

Elvin Bale, a subtle man, structures his feat, entering it intelligently, whereas Zacchini, brave and plump, following in his father's footsteps, is just shot off, then rises and runs forward to meet the crowd's jubilation—radiant, reborn. Tito Gaona doesn't risk his life comparably on the flying trapeze, but he sprouts wings on his heels, bounding practically into the crowd to take their cheers. Flying is special, classical, the *haut monde*, though sociable at the same time, going from hand to hand. On the street near Madison Square Garden, raggedly dressed, Tito looks like one of the Spanish-speaking men who push racks of clothes through the garment center, but as soon as he recognizes me he straightens like a man who knows he's considered to be the greatest trapezist in history.

2

It would be more fun to announce the existence of all this talent if the announcement would cause a stir. Instead, the circus remains a private passion for children and loyal fans; among sophisticates it occupies a niche similar to that of primitive art. Even more than the theater or sports, however, it is a way of life. The clowns are odd loners, the roustabouts are sometimes headed for prison or fiery ends, the performers are clannish; yet they all team up with a collection of candy butchers, nightclub girls, homeless Negroes and Germans and cowboys and Indians, and put on a permanent itinerant show.

The elephants and the horses are citizens too, and one mark of the circus man is that he can deal with this jumbled constituency. Gebel-Williams, who in Europe directed his own show, is remarkable for his impartiality. He guides his elephants with his voice and hands, touching and steering them, waving some to circle the track clockwise and others counterclockwise. He also touches the people he's talking to, intent and good-humored like a young general who fights alongside his troops. He's remarkable for being ebullient whether in the ring or backstage, taking the crowd's admiration in stride and seeming, as far as an outsider can tell, to live in a state of direct gaiety. He seems not to have the death wish, so his act is not a conquest of that.

Evy Althoff's tiger is nearly as big as the stallion it rides. Like most big tigers, it's a slumbering, deliberate-mannered beast. Evy wears a silver dress with a snaky motif, combs her yellow hair high, and makes abrupt, idiosyncratic, female movements in giving directions, as if she were guiding a lover, although in fact the tiger was trained by Gunther. She doesn't hurry the two animals but fits herself into their sense of time. Both she and the horse serve mainly as stand-ins while the tiger, well schooled but bored, with a peculiarly humpy run which resembles a wolverine's, leaps through an oily flame, picks its way on and off the deadpan horse, and lies down and rolls on request. The story goes that the first several horses died of heart failure while they were being trained, and even this valorous Appaloosa used to be so drenched with sweat after a session that its color changed from roan to gray. Being placed in the cage was bad enough but was nothing compared with *carrying* the tiger—that momentous pounce when the grisly creature landed on its back, sickening the instincts of a million years.

Evy is the same height and type as Sigrid, Gunther's second wife, except that her face is more compact, less enlightening. Sigrid is pert, freckled and communicative, whereas Jeanette, who is Gunther's stepsister as well as his ex-wife, looks like a smoldering ribald beauty. She's a blonde too, with a mocking mouth, chubby nose, large sidelong eyes, a fleshier body and more of a head of hair.

While the band plays *Carmen,* she rides on a black Friesian stallion, which is accoutered in silver and muscled like a war-horse but glossy and curly in the tail and mane.

Gunther has a rounded, big, forward nose, too sensual to fit a clown, white-blond hair that his ears tuck into, flat cheeks, a mobile face—a cloven-hoofed, urchinish, inspired look—and a swaying, slim walk of quick persistence. His eyes are usually wide open, especially at any sign of trouble; smiling, he dodges into a tangle of animals. He wears brief-skirted gladiatorial costumes and does tight turns in Roman riding; when he needs a whip somebody throws him one as he is passing, and he twitches it, so that it clicks rather than cracks. He's not a mystic, not even a specialist, because he meets people just as easily as wildlife; he likes money, golf, cars, rock music, airplanes. The money is here in America, he says; performances are faster-paced and more sumptuous than in Europe, the audiences are younger, and though he has not become a celebrity, the traveling is hectic and he is still busy learning English. It's curious that he isn't more famous—being at thirty-five the world's leading circus star, the best animal trainer alive. It is not as if we manage without heroes nowadays or that our heroes are noticeably above the level of *The Jungle Book.* Perhaps his position resembles that of an Indian scout and negotiator in the years after most people had lost interest in Indians and considered them virtually extinct.

He was born Gunther Gebel, far from the aristocracy of tightly knit German circus families, in a Silesian city called Schweidnitz in disputed territory which was transferred after World War II to Poland. When he was eleven his mother and he fled from the approaching Russians toward the Western armies—his father was not in evidence—and finally reached Cologne, where they lived on CARE parcels and Hershey bars until she got a position as a seamstress with the Circus Williams, a large, war-devastated show which was headquartered there. Though she didn't stay with the show, Mr. Williams, the impresario, a splendid stunt man in his own right, wound up adopting the boy. Gunther, keen as the orphan Dick Whittington, learned how to juggle and dance on a wire, flip like a tumbler, ride liberty horses and swing from a trapeze. At first he spoke a primitive, comedian's dialect of German because of the border region he came from, but he had coordination and presence and soon could do anything. He had a way with animals in particular, so Mr. Williams encouraged his involvement with them: it was a rarer gift. When he grew expert with horses he began training lions, and when he felt easy with lions he worked with elephants, and then on to tigers.

In talking with Gebel-Williams, I suggested the loneliness of his position in those years might have something to do with his extraordinary responsiveness to animals, but he disagreed. Indeed, there is nothing misshapen or compensatory about his skill with them; it is more an extension of his talent with people. He is charismatic and graceful rather than driven, not even very ambitious professionally. He is inexhaustible and delights in his work, but his talent exceeds his ambition. This might seem to be his weakness if he were set beside the few greats of the past; his strength would be his joy and versatility.

In the postwar havoc Gunther's schooling was hit-or-miss, enabling him to avoid the conventional engineering career he thinks he might have headed for under better circumstances. After five years had passed, his foster father was killed in a chariot race during a performance in London. The next year Williams' only natural son was also killed. Gunther, now seventeen, found himself running a show which traveled all over the Continent and employed more than fifty people. The widow managed business matters and there were family retainers, but Gunther went without sleep, learned to holler orders, hid his uncertainty, and supervised the teardowns, the overnight trips, the struggle to put up the tent the next morning. He was a centerpiece in the performance also, appearing repeatedly, and he married his classy stepsister. Later he encountered Sigrid, who, like him, was not born of the circus elite but was simply a Berliner who came to watch and sat close enough in the crowd. He was like a fish thrown into water; it was the world he had been meant for.

Gebel-Williams is one of the primary trainers, of course, able to prepare an act from its raw beginnings, maybe passing it on to another performer later while he trains a new group of animals. As long as discipline is maintained, the original bunch will keep on doing the chores they have been taught, and if casualties occur the fellow can insert a yearling or two, which will pick up the cues and gradually reach some understanding of what is expected; their quirks can even be exploited to enhance the act.

301

Generally the group deteriorates to a patchwork, but there is a market for it. Royalties are paid by the secondary trainer to the first trainer or to the impresario who employed him and who still may own the animals he worked with. There may be additional owners, as other animals are acquired along the way, or there may be a succession of trainers, many of whom quit for work that is less dangerous and wearying, feeling that they too are somehow penned in with the cats, a sense akin to what jailers feel. Gunther himself, though he is not punitive with them, says that when he finishes a performance now he closes a door mentally on the tigers and doesn't think about them again; this in contrast to his relations with the elephants, who are uncaged and smarter and with whom he continues to chum.

In America, cat acts are divided between those in which a good deal of fighting goes on—"fighting acts"—and the so-called wrestling acts, where a degree of friendship prevails. The trainer may actually rassle around as if the beasts were sumo wrestlers instead of big cats, stumbling under their enormous weight, demeaning both himself and them. Some movie serials used to feature people who dressed up like Flash Gordon and staggered across the set with four-hundred-pound pets they'd raised from cubs; after a seesaw contest they'd "strangle" the dears. Old World trainers like the Hagenbecks, Alfred Court and Damoo Dohtre worked equally closely with their animals but employed many more at once, and with refinement— no child's play or muscle stuff. They were likely to mix in smaller cats, such as leopards, or bears and wolves; the more of a stew of forces, the more complications. Mabel Stark was of that genre. At the end of her life she still appeared in her Jungle Land amusement park in the round cage, at least for the Sunday show, receiving her tigers one by one because one arm hung dead, the other could only be raised as high as her waist, and she could no longer move on her feet except at a wobble. She communed with them, exhibiting them softly and nobly. The fighting showmen, Terrell Jacobs ("the Lion King") and Clyde Beatty, who toured the country through storms of roars, were not really less knowledgeable about the animals they presented, but their style was to cast them as killers, emphasizing the courage and grace of the man, not the beast. Though probably a number of cats rather enjoyed their company, the tumult of scrapping created confusion and quick changes of mood. Make-believe adversaries could turn into real ones if the fun went sour, and with thirty or forty big cats in one cage, the trainer's first job was to head off trouble between the creatures themselves; a whole bankroll could go in one battle royal.

Charly Baumann, another Ringling Bros. trainer, using tigers owned in part by a woman in Germany, gives a smooth, soft-touch performance, although without the fond intensity of some fellows, who wind up lying down at peace with their cats. He wears an expression like that of a martyr already smelling the flames. (It is not the tigers that distress him, however; practically the only time he seems happy is when he is helping the clowns throw balloons to the crowd.) His trademark is one tiger which does nothing at all during the friendly bustle of hoop-jumping and pussy-roll-over-and-sit-up-and-beg that the rest engage in. Working with his back to her, eventually he gets too close, as if by accident, and she clasps his shoulders with awkward paws, and licks his neck vigorously and rubs her lips hard on his head (cats love rubbing their lips). This wins applause, but you can tell Baumann doesn't entirely like it by the way he neatens up afterwards. Sometimes she holds him there longer than he wishes; yet he can't be too rough in extricating himself because he is at her mercy and will be so again during the next show. Clutching him, she powders her nose on his head.

Gebel-Williams doesn't go in for this kind of thing. *He* does the licking, if any is done, his hands approximating the slow tugging motion of a tiger's tongue till the cat begins to jerk its head to the rhythm. But he doesn't pretend that tigers are living dragons either. A fighting act can be as much a distortion as sumo wrestling, since it caters to the image of tigerish tigers and ferocious lions that we cherish from childhood. No animal could go through life leading such an existence of smoke and fire without burning out.

Ringling Bros. has hired still a fourth cat trainer—Wolfgang Holzmair from Germany. Appearing on the same bill with Gunther in Birmingham, he furnished an ideal foil for him, not least because he was very good. The two of them sat for each other as health insurance, the one off-duty just outside the door of the cage holding a club while the other performed. Gunther has his own cage hands from the Circus Williams for this if necessary, but

304

Holzmair—like Baumann and Evy in New York City—
would have been on his own if he had fallen under a
pileup and been mauled.

Holzmair looks like a cut-down Kirk Douglas, with the
same challenging chin. He is as heavy as Gunther is light,
and works three-quarters naked, wearing slave armlets and
leather kilts, an ironic curl to his mouth. He is square-
chested, big-backed, a rough playmate, and has the appearance of sleepy fury in the cage, a Wehrmacht con-
tentiousness, so that when he puts on his tux after his act
he looks like a bouncer relaxing. But his work is his job,
not a daydream, and so he's a little amused by it and does
not seem to suffer, as some trainers do (even the mild-
mannered Baumann), from the incongruity of striding out
of a cage full of lions where he has been braving death and
exercising his formidable will, to lay down the whips, the
dominance, the belligerence, and defer to the performance
director, step around the children in the entryway, side-
step the ballet girls and their husbands, avoid offending
police and arena officials, and speak civilly in the dressing
room. Some trainers can't. They go off in a corner, shout
at the walls and whale about with their whips for half an
hour, as if in a decompression chamber.

Lions are different from tigers, more repetitive and pre-
dictable. They operate as a gang without many independent characters, so that the trainer, keying himself into the
swirl of the group, has fewer variables to keep track of. If
he stumbles the whole cage may come down on him at
once, but if he keeps on his feet and stays with the script,
his flanks and over-the-shoulder area are more secure than

if he were working with tigers. Certain lions are the ministers of war, some are followers, and still others—usually including the males—are noncombatants; the trainer's task is to make the best use of each. But even the ruggedest Amazon develops settled reactions to what the trainer is doing; he can almost depend upon her. In most cases he could work up a lion-lamb Androcles act if he wished, instead of the earthslide-of-roars routine, because for months he has carefully aggravated the warriors. If a lioness is in love with him, so much the better; it will put passion into her raging.

But lions roar too well for their own good and, colored a straightforward, soldierly khaki, are too stalwart-looking to bedeck with hugs. Roaring like motorcyclists, they charge as straight as a white circus horse goes round and round. They're prosaic good citizens and infantry, loyal to friends, martial toward foes. They're like bread and butter, and Gebel-Williams, who learned his fundamentals on them as a boy, finds them a bore. To sit beside him while Holzmair works is like sitting next to a bullfighter watching another fighter whose sensationalized style and whose bulls he abhors.

The fact is that lions and tigers are flesh and blood, not myths, and they can be stopped when they charge by the simple expedient of poking a strong oak stick in their path. If they can't get past that they can't reach the man, and their paws are not faster than his hands, especially when he has a whip. However, tigers also require delicacy. They spit up their food, and will balk and brood. Solitaries by temperament, they seldom defend one another against an

306

attack. Being somewhat faster, a tiger can usually kill a lion of the same weight, though he may take a moment to chew past the mane, but in a brouhaha involving a dozen of each the result will be several dead tigers, as the lions proceed in a pack from one to the next, while the surviving tigers quietly observe. Only the trainer weeps at the result, because tigers, who are so nervous that they are reluctant to breed, will cost him ten times as much to replace as lions would. Lions are pragmatists; tigers are creatures of emotion and mood. Their camouflage of crazy cross-hatched stripes—a knitwork on the head, thick on the back and growing practically mad down on the hips and pant legs—are symbolic of this. Sometimes the spaces between the stripes even have eyes. Tigers are the proverbial hundred flowers. There are no leaders for the trainer to watch; any one of them will stick out a paw and the earth may become his sky.

In Birmingham, Holzmair's lions entered snarling, abused by the cage hands, whirling in a sand-colored blur: there were so many of them that not until the third show could I count accurately. They were long-striding and masculine-looking like the hounds of hell, magnificent as they loped, roaring like pianos being rolled on a hollow floor. There were seventeen: so much barracks furor and collective noise that they spent the remainder of the day asleep to recover their poise. Lions are generous in using their vocal cords and are most impressive when they are weaving concertedly around a space that gives them room to dash and jump. Holzmair kept them moving, letting the sight sink in, then arranged them on pedestals around the

307

cage by fives, so that the geography of conflict was clear-cut for him. There were five lionesses who never ceased to rev and roar, providing a foundation of dramatic rage for the act as a whole; these were the savage ones, his enemies. Five other, vaulting lionesses did the strenuous chores, leaping through flames and so on, claxoning like engines only if asked to. They were more businesslike and less self-assured, not such ideologues. Stamping his boots, wielding two whips, he could stampede them into wild climaxes if he chose to. There were also five modest cats who were of little use except to add bulk to the act. They beefed up the admirable milling swirl with which he be-gan—the one natural display of lions presented as them-selves, like a powerful sandstorm. Once posted on their stools, they didn't move, just pulled in their heads to sullen, intractable humps under the lash. Holzmair kept his back turned to them most of the time, as well as to two tame young cats he never roughed up because they figured in a brief exhibition of wrestling and trust towards the end, when he demonstrated that he knew the sweet-ness-and-light technique as well as the coercive stuff. He tried thrusting his head into the mouth of one, but the opening as yet was too small for the task; the lion gagged as if it were being doped, and he had to work at the mouth as if he were hollowing a melon. The other lion he carried across his shoulders; along with handling the fiery hoop, this was apparently his least favorite interlude. The youngster itself didn't like the procedure either, and grim-aced but didn't dare quarrel when Holzmair caught hold of its throat. Like Baumann with his pet tiger, he could hardly control these two, having never dared beat them, and resorted to tidbits to make them move.

With the motorized brigade Holzmair was in command, persuading the toughest of them to charge while he held the flaming hoop, and not only to leap through it but also through a circle he formed clasping the whip above his head. Whereas Gunther's nakedness, expensively costumed, was sexy, his, clothed like a slave's, set off sadistic reverberations and emphasized the violence of the act—we were supposed to imagine him torn. Yet he was more ferocious than the lions, in fact; they watched him pass with frank apprehension, just as the rest of us might anticipate trouble from a loose lion. His every motion increased the racket; the snarls were a demon's snore. Ears back, faces flat, sweating from their mouths and streaming urine, the lionesses turned themselves into tunnels to roar. Twisting their heads to bellow from new angles, they thudded down off their stools and charged, as big as titans—but so was he. This was man's earliest image of wild beasts and how to undo them; this was how ancient lion tamers sneered and strode. An actor, a primitive, Holzmair carried one stiff prod and one long-distance lash, and most spectacular of all, as a finale he pushed the swarm of them into an ulcerous turmoil and then stood straddling the cage's outlet when the gate opened so that in exiting they had to dash through his legs.

Tigers would fly off the handle if hectored so. Not being creatures of habit, and without the communal bond, they don't weather bullying. Like other cats, they are not overly bright. The reason a house cat cannot be trained to do many things is not only its "independence," it just isn't as smart as a dog. Cats are supremely equipped physically and have a simplified, well-defined personality that enhances their bodies' efficiency. The great cats, too, are miracles of physicality, a special version of the life-force continuous since the Oligocene; and Gebel-Williams from boyhood gravitated to an interpretive role, not putting them down but drawing them out.

Every part of his act is a refinement of the usual manner in which tigers are presented. When they take their places on the pyramid of pedestals to show off their coats, each tiger does not head for the closest perch, but goes roundabout to the farthest, so that the crowd sees an extravagant moil. While some roll over and over on the ground, others leapfrog over them in a simulation of the way a litter plays; and when they vault between springboards, Gunther varies this familiar maneuver by stationing a tiger in the middle and having the rest alternately bound over it, dart under it and dodge around in front— a playful effect that seems almost voluntary, in which no imitative momentum is set up. He encourages a male to waltz to the band music—a matter of boxing with him in a comradely fashion—using the butt of his whip. Horses and elephants are often forced to dance by disciplinary means, but tigers cannot be handled so easily because if they become fearful or fly into a fury they move faster and faster. He coaxes hard enthusiastic swipes out of one cat, then moves to the largest tiger, which lunges up on its hind legs, topping him by a couple of feet, and roars and

lashes at a stick he lifts, jumping awkwardly but awe-
somely toward him as he backs up. Since the tiger looms
grand as a dinosaur, roars like an inferno and is not laid
low as a result, the sight is not offensive as is sometimes
the case when trainers stage heroic scenes.

Gunther's tigers are mostly males, because a male,
though surly and slow, is bigger—*"more tiger,"* as he says,
measuring with his arms. They smell like rye bread
smeared with Roquefort cheese. He chants and sings like
Glenn Gould as he works with them, swinging back and
forth, drawing murmuring rumbles and air-blast roars.
Tigers growl softly but roar far more explosively than lions
do. He spreads his arms wide so the animals have both of
them to keep track of, as well as watching his face; it's
like having two assistants in the ring. He holds his whips
in one hand, butt and lash reversed, and pets tiger chins
with the other, grinning like a lapsed angel, a satyr—it's
a lean V face, the flat planes cut for mischief and glee, or
a big-eyed lemur's, a tree-dweller's face. Singing and chattering, he composes their ladylike lunges into a fluttering
of stripes, touching his forehead with his fingers in a
Hindu salute to acknowledge applause, and kneels the-
atrically while the tigers sit. Throwing sawdust on their
turds so that he won't slip, he pitches his whip like a
jokester, his crucifix bouncing on his bare chest, his eyes
big and round, organizing them into a jungle trot. They
look bulky as bulls, but when he bats them they rise into
a pussy pose, paws up. "Ziva!" he calls, running to one,
mimicking the twitch of her white cheeks and black
mouth, and stroking her rump. "Hubblebay!" he says, and

they all revolve. The band accelerates into a keynote of victory.

Maybe the loveliest moment is when Gunther simply has them walk: not a feat many trainers would consider exciting or could even achieve by the adversary technique. Two leave their pedestals and promenade as they might alongside a water hole. He induces another pair to join them—but counterposed—the two pairs passing in the center of the cage. Then he gets the other four to join in, crisscrossing as in Chinese checkers before lining up in formation like the spokes of a wheel. Round and round they slink, keeping abreast, looking up at him, delaying behind the band to exercise their claws (tigers never "march").

Bidding this group good-by, he welcomes a middle-aged, equable tiger, redder than most, and fluffing and scratching it, introduces two elephants, an African with tusks and an Indian one without. The Indian voices its aversion in squeals, the African is indifferent to the tiger, having perhaps inherited no feelings about it one way or the other. The tiger springs to the howdah that each of them carries, down to the ground and up again, then leaps between them, back and forth, finally mounting a platform near the roof of the cage, and jumps again onto the African's back. Gunther directs all this choreography only by words, sitting at his ease on the ring curbing and watching. The elephants and tiger mount three pedestals and rotate quietly as he talks to them; he tugs on the African's tusks and feeds it a loaf of Italian bread. The band plays traditional Spartan brass, the tiger mounts the African elephant again, and so does Gunther, his face in a Pan-like grin. He sits on the tiger, and leaning over, tugs its tufted chin, rubs its eyes and lips, and has it roar elegantly into his face. Then he and the tiger drop down to the ground, the elephants leave the cage, and he fondles the cat, tickling its black lips and its orange rump. Then he sits lightly astride its hips and rides it across the stage at a lumbering gallop, a sight not often seen.

Combining the elephants with the tiger is an exploit no rival trainer has managed to duplicate in the six years since Gunther first did it. He himself gave up trying at one point. Unlike horses, elephants are much too powerful to hold still, and the Indian elephant went crazy with fear. Gunther says he probably could train anything, "even mice—only you yourself must a little change." The limitations of a tiger act make it come to seem static and stylized as a Noh play; yet he dislikes training other animals. Bears hold their swinging heads inscrutably low, and have tiny eyes and a locking dentition. If he put lions into his act there would be fights, a challenge which doesn't interest him. Nor does he want to try riding a moose or training hyenas or tapirs. Like a gifted young man at a standstill stage, he seems not to have any plans for what he will do with his abilities, only for what he may do with the money he earns. He has a few scars, for which he blames himself. "You get very close to play, but one time it is not possible." He wears a red robe that says "Animal Trainer," and aimless and ebullient, drives his Toronado around town, honking at friends.

The elephants please him. He has one wise female who

runs from a distance and tromps accurately on the teeter-board on which he's poised, flinging him into a somersault to land on her back. "Hup-hup!" he yells, sliding down by way of her trunk and front legs. The *Colonel Bogey March* switches to *Elephant Boogie,* and all twenty elephants rush out in a line for the final parade, clutching each other's tails with their trunks. Gunther runs and runs, directing the herd with his hands and voice, sorting them into different rings as they fly by. They curl their trunks in, wave their ears and perform practically on their own while he talks and talks, directing them. His wife, Sigrid, swings on a rope held by two elephants while the others gnomishly do a jig. When Gunther shouts over the water-fall of applause they all heave themselves up on their hind legs, like whales of the earth, each one balancing herself with her front feet on her neighbor's rear.

The band slides from minor to major key for the finale; the trombones fluff-fluff, the trumpets blow like blue sky, the elephants stomp like mahogany. Shy-seeming skittering people turn into troupers as the lights hit them. All of the stars come out to recapitulate the evening. Alert showgirls ride by on gray horses, and guys in drag wear flapping shoes that extend out like dachshunds in front of them. Tumblers turn cartwheels relentlessly, and aerialists scramble up ladders, their spangled costumes glittering off the ceiling. And they're all smiling because it's the night of the teardown and they're leaving your town.

WALKING THE
DEAD DIAMOND
RIVER

For many years the New Hampshire Fish and Game Department has made a census of ruffed grouse along nine habitat routes, each about forty miles long, representing when taken together every variety of cover within the state. Lately new highways and real-estate schemes in the southern counties have forced the biologists to shift with some of these, and some of the paths have been preempted by motorcyclists or Sunday walkers, so that even if the grouse population in the area hasn't declined, the annual count can't be tallied as scientifically as the censuses of the past; understandably, this is discouraging to the men who do the counting.

Recently I had the fun of walking the wildest, northernmost Grouse Survey Line, which crosses the headwaters of the Connecticut and Androscoggin rivers, country as remote and untarished as any in New Hampshire—owned by several lumber companies and by Dartmouth College. It's country emptier than the much better-known Presidential Range and the other mountains and valleys of the White Mountain National Forest, lying to the south. My companion was Karl Strong, who is the department's senior biologist north of Concord.

This walk used to be made in midwinter on snowshoes, as well as during the summer when the broods of new chicks can be counted, but now that life is softer for everyone, it's done twice in the summer instead. There are three cabins in the course of the forty-two miles where Strong and his partner used to pack their supplies and sleep over, but first they dispensed with their packs, trucking their gear in ahead of time, and now they arrange to drive home each night. In fact, it was lucky for Strong that we did it this way because on one of the nights of our walk, August 24th, a freak killing frost developed that would have wiped out his vegetable garden if he hadn't been at home to hose down everything early in the morning. He raises about fifteen different vegetables, freezing or canning them so that his family can eat them all winter. Gardening is his passion, though one day in June when I talked to him he was on a schedule of waking up every three hours at night to feed an orphaned puppy. He's a reserved, lean, soft-spoken man, pale in complexion like a Scandinavian, not in any sense a softie in appearance but a cold-weather man, and the depth of his affection for living things does not show immediately. In talking to paper-company officials I found he is called "the missionary." When I mentioned this to him he laughed and said that his grandfather was a minister and that, like a minister, he puts in lots of work and accomplishes little.

He's a deer specialist; the grouse census is a job that he does for New Hampshire's bird biologist, who works with ducks and pheasants as well. He's uncannily attuned to deer and astonishes the paper-company foresters because he can actually smell a deer two hundred feet off. A gland in the deer's heel cords gives off a sex scent which Strong describes as resembling the smell of a certain fungus that is found in rotting birch stumps. He can smell porcupines too, but not bears, except for "dump" bears. This Grouse Survey Line is Strong's particular darling. He's walked it himself for fifteen years, watching his body gradually age when measured against its miles and seeing the trail and rivers change as logging and even sport fishing become modern industries. Logging may soon be done with laser beams or thin pressurized jets of water. Already the more technologically advanced companies cut pulpwood with monster-sized timber harvesters that can sheer a tract of forest right down to its roots, and then, right on the scene, the logs can be fed into chippers which dice them into paper-making fiber, chip-sized, to be trucked to the mill like freight. This is not done in New Hampshire yet, but there have been plenty of changes.

Though Strong's grouse path is mentioned in the Appalachian Mountain Club's *White Mountain Guide,* he hadn't been eager to have me accompany him because it is never hiked on, is purposely marked only very obscurely, and could be destroyed for useful game observation if the outdoor fraternity every really discovered it. A path through splendid country that is traversed twice a year, not worn into ruts by a river of feet, is nowadays a great rarity and a precious one. He said I could come along if I could keep up with him, didn't get blisters, and if I recognized to begin with that any account of the New England wilds must be more of an elegy to pleasures now past than a current guide.

We started at Second Connecticut Lake to go to Corn-popper Spring, which is under Magalloway Mountain. The sky drizzled intermittently, the temperature stayed around 45 degrees with the first of the gusty cold front that killed several gardens that night, and we walked with clenched fists and "dishpan hands," as Strong put it. It was miserable enough, but the raindrops stippled the beech leaves beautifully and the firs in the rain looked as gray as steel. My hat was red, which looks black to a deer or a bear but which birds, with their sharp color sense, are alert to, so Strong planned to be extra alert himself.

Once out in the woods, he seemed younger immediately, lighter and gayer than back in town, remarking on the balsam smell in a soft voice that would be well suited to love-making—his wife packs notes into his lunch with the sandwiches—and reminiscing about a day in 1959 when he caught his limit of big fish in a beaver pond that we saw on Smith Brook, using only the naked hook itself, which he had twitched like a fly. We saw a king-fisher plopping from high up to catch a chub there, and a merganser diving. The forests around the Connecticut lakes are a baronial showpiece owned by the power companies that maintain the lakes as reservoirs, but we soon got into bushwhacking country where the tourists don't come. Strong says that by nature he should be a Democrat, believing the Democrats are closer to the Biblical injunction that we must be our brother's keeper, not dog-eat-dog as the Republicans are, but that the tourists are making him more conservative. He walks with quick quiet strides because the grouse try to steal away on the ground if they hear a man at a distance. When he thinks he has heard one of them call, creaky and peeping, he tramps noisily into the brush and claps his hands to scare up the covey so he can count it.

The low country was lush, with raspberry bushes in hoops and flowers head-high. We saw a broad-winged hawk, and saw beaver-work in the sandy-bottomed brook that we crossed and recrossed—Strong said he thought the man who had laid out the trail must have been on snowshoes, unable to see the water. Strong himself made the mistake of blazing it recently with a paint called International Orange, which in some way sets the bears off; nearly every blaze was chewed. Up in the woods, the trail was cool and shadowy till we got into a logging area, where I learned from smelling the birch stumps that white birch is odorless (which is why it is used for Popsicle sticks), that black birch smells like wintergreen (and is a flavor for chewing gum), and that yellow birch has a delicate, mellow, somewhat minty smell. The stumps of the latter were a wonderful yellow-orange inside. We saw one a hundred years old, just downed.

In the rain the skidders, which are a kind of modified, big-wheeled tractor most effective at hauling logs, had churned several hundred yards of poor Strong's trail into a comically gucky concrete-colored soup. The ruts, four feet deep, were running with rain. Slipping like a monkey on roller skates and balancing wildly with his arms, he insisted on walking the route anyway, laughing because laugh was all he could do.

We descended to Smith Brook again, finding a clearing where five bunkhouses and a horse hovel had once stood, near the remains of a log-driving dam and a tote road, trestled and corduroyed. We saw a doe and a fawn, purple trillium ("stinkin' Benjamin") with its wine-colored berries, Canadian dogwood with bright red bunchberries, and a grouse's scrape-hole in a dusty spot where the bird had bathed itself. We saw a brood of three (our count was eight for the thirteen miles that day). Up on Hedgehog Nubble we found the abundant turds of a moose that had wintered there. Moose winter high and deer winter low. New Hampshire has very few moose but if they were anywhere, they would be here. At the turn of the century the last three caribou in the state were sighted and shot close by.

The clouds swelled gray and silver, settling on us. Sometimes the sun poked through, which hurt the eyes in a sky so dark. Strong smoked when we took a break, to let his liver "release its sugar," telling me that's why a smoker stays thin. We saw a waterfall, and moose and bear tracks, and more than one tucked-away valley with ferns, mosses and snapdragons, usually the site of an old hunting cabin with the owner's Army dog tags tacked on the door and some claw marks where a bear, hungry in the spring, had tried to break in. The resident hummingbirds flitted close to my red hat, sometimes half a dozen in the space of an hour, to investigate why it was the same color as their own throats. Up on Diamond Ridge at three thousand feet was a cold fir forest, very remote. Strong hunts from a cabin on Magalloway Mountain, using a muzzleloader to make it a bit harder for himself. Last year he and his friends sighted in on a mama bear with her hackles up and three cubs, and there was lots of black smoke but no kill. He told me how tough it is to pull a three-hundred-pound bear out of the woods, or even one weighing two hundred pounds; they stretch when you pull but they don't move. Boy, he said, they seem smaller, though, when skinned out.

He has no laws to assist him when he advises the timber operators on behalf of the wildlife as to what they should do (nor do they seek his advice—he just goes around offering it). He's always polite, the foresters say, and will come into the offices of the Brown Paper Company and simply tell them, "Well, we blew it," when a key stand of evergreens has been cut and some deer are going to die as a result. The whole forest is wildlife habitat, of course, but he restricts his marking activities to the 10 per cent of the woods where the deer winter, or he wouldn't get anywhere. Even so, and being prudent, he cannot expect that more than about three-fourths of the trees he marks will be spared. Deer must shelter under mature softwood growth like fir or spruce in a snowy climate. The boughs block some of the wind and catch part of the snow, holding it up where it evaporates. Deer don't browse on trees of this sort unless they are starving; instead they look for young hardwood saplings like maple, poplar and birch to gnaw on and peel, not trees of a size yet worth harvesting commercially. But before any other consideration they must have shelter. Rather than freeze in a zero wind or flounder about in deep snow where a dog could kill them, they will stay in a softwood grove and slowly starve.

In the north woods if there were no logging going on there would be few deer, the pickings would be so slim— just a frontier of big trees better suited to the life style of caribou, which eat moss and lichen. But Strong's job is to intercede with the foresters so that a mix of clearings, glades, openings and sizable timber for shelter is left. Although the personnel are getting brisker, more impersonal, the companies, feeling the pressure of the times, make a big stir about "multiple use"—land with game on it, land lovely for hiking—and he can appeal to that. The traditional cutting cycle used to be seventy or eighty years and the best foresters cut only about a seventh of the timber at hand in a decade, so that timber of every age was growing. Now in the rush for "fiber," younger and younger trees are cut, the cycle is down to forty years, and it's increasingly complicated to manage a forest so that the different requirements of dozens of creatures can be fitted in. Rabbits, for instance, thrive in an area five to fifteen years after the woods have been cut, and grouse fifteen to thirty-five years afterwards, but some of the furbearers and birds need much older timber.

The next day we were back at Cornpopper Spring, starting from there by 7 A.M., with the weather even a little colder but the sun a bit brighter, the wind having blown the rain away. We had ten and a half miles to go to Hell Gate on the Dead Diamond River, where the Fish and Game Department has a camp. Strong said he felt like putting his snowshoes on; the only way to get good and warm was to put on a pair of heavy snowshoes. His father came from the lumbering country of Patten, Maine, and he remembers pouring kerosene on a crosscut saw as a boy to make it go through a gummy pine. They hunted together. Then in 1944, while he was a Navy medic, his father was shot in the woods for a deer (an average of five hunters a year are killed in New Hampshire).

The first mile of this section was a logging road now, and for a while further on, alongside a glacial esker, a farmer had taken his tractor and plowed a track of his own so that his friends in their vehicles could reach a vacation cabin he'd leased. We met some loggers, who seemed like direct but limited men, a notch below the state-employed people I was meeting. We stood at the edge of a clearing watching three of them work without being detected by them. Strong's lip curled in amusement; what kind of woodsmen were they? He waited for them to notice us until he got tired and, like an Indian feeling benevolent today, simply walked peacefully away through the trees.

Since grouse usually run before they fly, a windy, disruptive day like this one was bad for hearing or spotting them. They were plentiful because June, when the chicks were new and likely to die of pneumonia if chilled, had been very droughty—a June without storms is not good for the trees but is good for the grouse. Once grown, they are rugged birds and winter right on the scene, eating birch buds and diving deep into the snow to sleep, leaving no tracks on the crust for a fox to follow. Strong said that the foxes were beginning to build up again after a rabies epidemic in 1969. In the previous siege, in 1963, he'd had to take twenty rabies injections in the stomach as a precaution. It's best not to check for rabies in wildlife too often, the biologists say, because you'll find it so regularly that the fewer checks you make the fewer epidemics you discover. We saw both fox and bobcat scats. Fox dung is surprisingly dainty and small-bore, even considering the animal's whippet-thin body. Bobcats, and especially Canada lynx, look leggy, pathetic and light as air, too, when their coats are skinned off. They are dumber than foxes if judged anthropomorphically by their IQ, but are so superbly cautious and stealthy, so hard to see and so wild, that by their own lights they are smart enough. In a lifetime Strong has sighted just three.

Raw deer-season weather. Strong blew his nose with his fingers, and pointed out where his nephew at seventeen had hit a bear with six shots, the bear dashing on till it finally dropped, nipping off strips of its own intestines as they fell out and trailed. (The nephew has never come hunting since.) We watched two hummingbirds feeding on jewelweed in a glade where Strong once saw twenty. We noticed a woodpecker hole high in a stub where two swifts were nesting. In the depths of the woods we came on a deer lick, with well-defined trails homing in like the spokes on a wheel; I heard one deer flee. The mud was white with minerals, and the roots of the trees had been exposed by the hooves. Strong used to lie here in a blind on moonlit nights to observe the goings-on—three or four deer at once pissing and shitting and drinking in the shallow pools, contributing nearly as many minerals back to the lick as they removed.

We picked hatfuls of hazelnuts for Strong's teenage daughters, and saw lots more neon-red bunchberry and bear-chewed blaze trees, but the trampled-looking grass that I would have assumed was another sign of game turned out to be just a casualty of the hard rains. We talked about how most naturalist writers rate poorly with full-time workers in the field, Thoreau, Fenimore Cooper and Ernest Thompson Seton included. But I was wearing Strong's spare pair of rubber boots, and their good fit seemed to represent the friendship budding between us. Doctors, as another group which cultivates the outdoor life, also run into a lot of kidding from the professionals. Strong told me about two who had crashed in the Pemigewasset drainage while flying over the White Mountains one February and, with a surgical saw, tried to cut some green poplars next to their plane to make a fire. They died, which wasn't so funny, but if they had gone to a softwood grove a couple of hundred yards farther off, they could have broken off plenty of dry wood from the dead bottom branches just with their hands.

We were on the grassy banks of the East Branch of the Dead Diamond River, whose headwaters springs ten miles away we had seen the previous day. The day before it had taken me until the late evening to get the bones of my hands feeling warm again, yet now we were sweating already. The temperature was 58 degrees (whenever Strong saw a grouse he took wind and temperature readings). We lunched partly on hazelnuts—a squash-seed taste—overlooking a thunderous sixteen-foot falls and its twisty catch-pool, a stretch where once in the 1950's Strong caught and threw back two hundred fish in a couple of hours. People had hiked in from what was then the closest road, in Maine, to catch four-pound brook trout, but now these holes were empty of fish.

We watched a bulldozer cracking down trees for a winter haul road, which would need no gravel, only the natural mud architectured into shape on the night of the first freeze, whereupon for the next five months the log trucks would roar back and forth on the ice. However, this was a forest whose patterns Strong had helped to create, and even his management plans for the streams—that the skidders not silt up the spawning beds by operating along the banks—had been followed, so what we saw was not agitating to him. We followed the old tote road on the riverbank, used in log-driving days. We'd crossed from the large township of Pittsburg (312 square miles) to the Atkinson and Gilmanton Academy Grant (fourteen square miles of woods, once sold by the aforesaid academy for four hundred dollars). Dartmouth, which owns the adjoining College Grant (forty-seven square miles) near Hell Gate, leases the recreational rights to this land at a dollar an acre annually so that its alumni and guests may feel free to spread out. Like most other state people, Strong resents the exclusion of the general public by these rich guys, but like me he had to admit to being glad that these woods would resemble a wilderness a little bit longer than unprotected forests. On the other hand, in the fall Dartmouth men kill only about seven deer for every ten square miles of land they have, whereas the public on ordinary timberland kills twice that many. This is not favorable news to a man like Strong who on his snowmobile tours finds twenty deer starved to death per square mile in the cramped wintering yards on even the public lands.

We argued about hunting—not that I could sensibly oppose hunting deer, but there are other beasts. I teased him as to whether this predatory "naturalness" he touted so highly wasn't downright dog-eat-dog Republicanism, but he wasn't to be hobbled by consistency, and pointed out again that too many tourists with city ideas were turning him in that direction anyway. Of course, the yearly symbolic deer he killed was like his assiduous gardening or the cabin he'd built for himself on Magalloway, as I understood. He said, though, that wildlife was public property, for all the people, and that therefore he resented anybody who posted his land against the free access of hunters. My answer was that, first of all, wild animals were perhaps the property of no one but themselves, a question I was willing to leave moot if he wished, and secondly that I resented any man's going on any land, public or private, and shooting some creature, dwindling in numbers, whose like I might have trouble ever seeing in a natural state, and then tacking its hide on his living-room wall—*that* concept of private property was offensive to me.

Strong said, Well, if his hunting something really means

327

that you may never see its like again, I agree with you, he ought not to be hunting it, it should be a protected species; that's what biologists like myself are for. What I'd left out of the equation, however, he added, was the fact that many people who post their lands do not do so out of any beliefs corresponding to mine. Rather, they seem to think that in buying a piece of land they're buying the wildlife that lives on it too, along with the pines and the apple trees.

Okay, that infuriated me too; we were agreed. He'd started defining us as conservationist versus "preservationist," but I laughed and said, Look, if *you and I* name-call and can't get along, then what hope is there that the wilderness forces can ever combine? He smiled. I said, Bear in mind too that some of the people who object to hunting are not as ignorant about the woods as you think. What arouses them is not that a deer is shot which otherwise would eventually starve to death, but that the hunter gets such a kick out of killing it.

Do you see hunters butchering cows for kicks during the off-season? Strong asked. It's not the pain, it's the death, and it's not the death but the stalk and the woodsmanship and the gamey wild meat the fellow is after; the completeness of each of these complemented by the others. I understood what he meant, but to be one up I asked why, if the woodsmanship is the heart of the matter, there are so very few archers in the woods—archery requiring woodsmanship of such a high order that it does overshadow the kill. Strong said bow-hunting is just too hard to do for all but that handful of hunters. Success comes

328

too hard, and most hunters are firearms buffs as much as they are woodsmen and enjoy the big bang and the bird-in-the-hand. Besides, he saw no reason why the kill ought to be overshadowed. The naturalness of the kill was akin to all of the other pleasures one felt in the woods, and in no sense skulky or inferior. It was his business to see that no animal was hunted into oblivion if he could help it, but to have a deer herd protected like the animals in a zoo, just to be looked at, never shaken up by a hunting season as by the whirlwind of natural predation—this was not woods or wilderness, he said angrily; this kind of situation would arrive soon enough as it was, as I should know.

We waded the East Branch just above where the Middle and West Branches join, a black-looking shapely knoll in front of us and a high hardwood ridge beyond, all forest land everywhere, with bluish tall firs in the foreground that Strong had managed to save. The day before, I couldn't have believed today would bring prettier country, but it was like parkland in Colorado—forest and wild grasses interspersed. Though I was getting a charley horse, the marvelous ungrudging succession of Valhalla views, of black knolls, green grass and green trees, the forest unrolling, the sandy-banked river bending alongside—and long-legged Strong—put energy into my strides. As he talked, it became evident that this wasn't just Dartmouth country; it was also a private playground for a good many Fish and Game officers. They could get through the gates and camp and fish where no one else could.

Strong talked about his difficulties in the National Forest. There, too, the deer yards received last considera-

tion, and the federal foresters fibbed to him, outmaneu-
vered him or tried to treat him as some kind of hick in
order to escape interference with their timber sales. In
Canada, where he's gone as a consultant, the Crown
Lands are sometimes overcut just as badly. A cord of softwood on the stump is worth $6, and if there are fifteen
cords to the acre, on these vast tracts it begins to add up.

We saw a red-shouldered hawk, a meadow mouse, and
bobcat droppings with a whole little mouse skull intact
in one. There were the tracks of a raccoon that had been
hunting tadpoles, two garter snakes, a goshawk's nest in a
dead beech, and lots of deer prints. Two big red deer
bounded off, showing each other the way with their fleecy
tails. We were in the principal deer yard along the Dead
Diamond now, country that Strong tours during the winter. He said the deer often die with their stomachs full of
non-nutritive wood, having run off their fat during the
hunting season and the season of rut, but if there are loggers working nearby they can survive off the sprouty tops
of the fallen trees.

On a suspension footbridge we crossed to Hell Gate
Camp, four grizzled huts in a breezy hayfield. We watched
a party of Fish and Game recruits being taught how to
disarm a hunter. They had been issued bird books and
were learning how to identify ducks. As a biologist, Strong
has no police duties. Most of the time he wears no uniform, and unlike the wardens who were instructing them,
can drop in on a hunting or fishing camp in the guise of a
hiker; even noticing a violation, he can move on if whatever is wrong strikes him as really not very important.

.   .   .

These hearties do not let you go without having coffee with them. The next morning we were delayed again while pleasantries were exchanged. I met no woodsmen among them but I did meet outdoorsmen who, feet up on the table, relished being here in this kingdom, with the white water hissing outside, instead of down at the office in Concord.

We waded the Little Dead Diamond, still steaming after the frosts of the dawn. It's a noisy, energetic tributary stream, chiseling potholes and digging rock sculptures in rhythmic curves out of the limestone strata above Hell Gate. We followed it uphill. Six or seven years ago Strong used to catch his limit of ten trout here in an hour while he ate lunch, or feed crumbs to as many as twenty that were visible in the clear water. Now he's lucky if he catches three little ones. The spring freshet, loaded with rocks and ice, wipes them out of the fishing holes, and the stream is too precipitous to be repopulated from the main river below. Until recently a new population would always wash down from the gentler stretches—the stream heads at Mount Pisgah—but now these nursery pools too are being heavily fished by people who reach them in rough-terrain vehicles. No surplus exists.

My left leg was swollen tight with charley horses, yet this walk of eight miles through dense, choppy, unpretentious country which had never been settled or farmed seemed like the best scenery of the trip and a kind of climax. It was ambush country; you couldn't see far, but hidden away there were several quite glorious wilderness

331

elms that Dutch elm disease hadn't found. We saw a splatter of tracks left by a sprinting bobcat alongside the stream. The stream popped and sparkled in the sun, pincering past obstructions, cutting a hundred corkscrew twists.

Leaving the Little Dead Diamond, we took its South Branch, ascending toward Crystal Mountain. Usnea moss ("old-man's-beard") hung from the dead limbs in the stands of young fir, a delicacy for the deer. The masses of moss covering the ground which Strong remembered from some of his early visits had disappeared since the last logging, replaced by raspberry thickets. We ate as we walked, and saw traces of every other creature that had been feasting also, every animal one might expect except for skunks, which stay nearer farmland. There was a new beaver dam, the drowning marsh trees turning red. There were firs and alder—maybe good woodcock country—as well as thick overgrowth scrub where the maple trees had been logged. We saw two broods of grouse, the first mother leading two chicks and the second five. It was a lovely high-ceilinged day, platter-blue, good weather for grouse to be out and about. (Our average count for the whole grouse survey was one bird for each mile and a half walked.)

We crossed into Dix's Grant from the Atkinson and Gilmanton Academy Grant, both owned by the Brown Paper Company. Parts of the bed of the South Branch had been preempted by their logging trucks, so it was badly messed up. Where it forked, we turned from the South Branch to Lost Valley Brook, climbing south through a concealed niche in the ridge, a little lost valley indeed, very isolated in spirit, where a decade ago Strong was marking thirty-inch birch, and hemlock and pine forty inches through. Now even the six- and eight-inch pulpwood is being removed. We found a dead shrew with fine-grained gray fur, and lots of deer sign. The skidders had cut ruts waist-deep, partly overgrown, no joke to fall into.

We talked about naturalness again. The Indians, Strong said, thought that one could no more own land than own the stars; that's why they "sold" to the whites so cheaply. We were drinking from the brook and I happened to remember how, in the Book of Judges, God told Gideon to choose an army to defeat the Midianites by taking his men to a stream and picking the ones who drank directly from the running water on their hands and knees, animal-like, not the more civilized ones who lifted the water to their lips. Strong liked that, but I said that maybe it just meant that the beastly fought better. He told me the latest promotional scheme involving his department was to transplant some ptarmigan from Colorado to Mount Washington's tundra and see if they lived. Unfortunately the question concerned not just the ptarmigan but New Hampshire's twelve fragile square miles of alpine ecology. Would the birds choose the rarest buds to eat, and what would the tramping feet of the hunters do?

At the source of Lost Valley Brook we entered a thick, dark, gloomy wilderness forest of pole-sized fir and paper birch that is one of the watersheds of the Dead Diamond and Swift Diamond rivers. The Swift joins the Dead fifteen miles or so below Hell Gate, and the waters of both go into the Magalloway River (where they meet the paved road), then into the Androscoggin, then the Kennebec, and finally into the ocean at Bath, Maine. Even up top here it was swampy, though, with many toad polly-wogs enjoying the bogs; frogs, which start bigger, would be out of the tadpole stage by now, said Strong. We spotted some hawks, garter snakes, hummingbirds, bumblebees, high phloxlike flowers, red mushrooms, and false Solomon's-seal with red berries. Often the ground was cut every which way by beaver channels, like an obstacle course. Moss, muck and sucking mud, bank-beaver holes, wild grasses and sedges, poplars, cattails. The temperature, 60 degrees, up 15 from when we had started, had me wet with sweat. Fourmile Brook, a portion of which was our destination, heads at a pond so remote that it is stocked with trout thrown out of an airplane.

This brook drops away down the ridge at such a steep pitch that the water sounds like a pistoning motor. We found an antique axhead, broad, rusty as ochre. The last go-through by the loggers had been recent, and so the growth was jungly and low, with plenty of the bugs and berries and wetness grouse like, but for some reason the hauling had been done with a bulldozer, not a skidder, and the ground had not been damaged too much. There was a heady honey smell everywhere from the flowers—purple, blue, yellow—and millions of bugs. Big-toothed poplar, willows and birch, moosewood and silver maples, alders, jewelweed and shadbush. More deer sign, more pollywogs; a grouse brood of four, cheeping like chicks, trilling like mice.

Fourmile Brook is a good deal longer than the name in-
dicates, with bad footing, and we spent much time on it
before reaching Fourmile Camp. This is a tin-roofed gover-
ment shack seventeen miles by woods road from the highway, in a clearing surrounded by hills. The wind from the
south carried the smell of the pulp mill in Berlin, New
Hampshire, a smell more fecal than what one encounters
in the actual lavatories at the paper company. If I stepped
off into the brush for a minute Strong said, "Is that you or
Berlin?" It's a nagging, boiled-cabbage, boiled-egg smell
at best, carried also on an opposite wind from the
Canadian mills sixty miles north, or on an east wind from
those of Oxford County in Maine. A wet light snowfall
in the winter seems to sharpen it even more, which for a
man with Strong's educated nose must be disturbing. We
found a bear's droppings, and I remarked how queer it
was that a man's would have affected us as more dis-
gusting. He said the reason might be that compared with
wild animals people overeat so enormously that they
don't digest as much of the fermentable material. Not
being a scientist, I suggested instead that maybe we're so
egocentric we prefer to believe even the badness of some
of our smells exceeds that of other creatures'.

A truck had been left for us at the camp. As we drove
back toward town alongside the Swift Diamond River, we
saw it had turned the color of mud from fresh logging
that day. So had a stream called Clear Stream. Under New
Hampshire's Clean Waters Act a fine of a thousand dollars
a day can be levied for offenses like this, but it hasn't as
yet been invoked.

.   .   .

Samuel Taylor Coleridge is said to have walked as far as forty miles in a day, and Carlyle once logged fifty-four in twenty-four hours on a walking tour. Wordsworth, the champion in this league, was calculated (by De Quincey) to have totted up 175,000 or 180,000 miles in a lifetime of peregrinations afoot. "I have two doctors," said Sir George Trevelyan of English-style walking, "my left leg and my right."

The American brand of walking of course has a different mystique, almost forgotten lately, which dates back to the frontier and has little to do with the daily "constitutional" and therefore should be exercised in a setting so brawny and raw that the mileage can't even be guessed at. Since my own sports as a boy were running and walking, my image of athletic prowess has been a related one, but I was glad to get home to the soft bed and fortifying dinners of the Colebrook House Hotel each of these evenings. I'm lucky I wasn't born a few centuries ago. For the sake of the exultancy I feel in wild places I probably would have tried to get in on some of the exploration, and as I'm not that strong physically, I would have been one of the substantial number in almost every party who died. Even in balmy weather, when I've been alone on a true frontier, a hundred miles from the nearest dirt road, I've had crazy, incongruous sexual fantasies assault me, like a blanket pulled over my head, as if by them I sought to hide from more powerful fears—of grizzlies, illogical avalanches, of twisting my ankle or getting lost. Yet between these bouts with the fantastical, during which my eyes actually shut

336

at times, I was all eyes, all elation and incredulousness, living three days in one.

Strong stretched his legs the next day on the last lap of eight miles. We both hoped we hadn't been chatting so much that we'd spooked any grouse, so he stayed in front of me, letting me see if I could keep up. We went from Fourmile Camp up a steep hardwood ridge which is part of Crystal Mountain, and down the other side. Many squirrel tracks at the rain pools, a red squirrel and chipmunk confronting each other on a short log (the chipmunk the one with the food in its paws), and a rapid goshawk. Goshawks will plunge right into a pile of brush after a grouse, like an osprey hitting the water chasing a fish. Strong said he saw his last peregrine falcon in 1954. In those days he would see up to fifty horses going home at night on their own along these trails from the logging sites.

The ground where we climbed was heaped with slash sometimes five feet high, wet from the night's rains, and the skidders had cut tank traps everywhere, making walking a sweaty struggle. The grouse we disturbed called to each other. The cocks live alone, each in his own territory, to which he tries to drum mates in the spring. The females nest on the bare ground, usually in some slight depression that they find at an elevated place near the base of a tree. They eat catkins, clover, foliage and fruits, but the chicks are not vegetarian; they eat beetles, ants, spiders, snails, flies and larvae, which are richer in protein and vitamins.

In a clearing we found the remnants of a loggers' supply wagon. Spruce had been the climax forest and now that the big old second-growth hardwoods had been removed also, mostly fir was appearing, a short-lived, fast-growing species that buds early in the spring, risking the frosts but shooting up, its root system shallow and its limbs flimsy. Yet a fir woods, too, requires at least forty years to reach a commercially plausible size, and in modern business enterprise who's going to sit around for the next forty years with real estate like this, watching the dragonflies? Every management shakeup brings a change in plans, and Strong in his advocacy position with respect to the land is naturally on the firing line.

Understand that a bear, for example, needs a minimum of about five square miles to forage in for his food supply. This is not counting the extra land he will roam through in the course of a year, which might comprise seventy-five square miles, or more than two hundred if he is hunted hard. The five square miles is an irreducible wilderness area that will grow his food, and although other bears may overlap with him, he will include their territory in his wanderings. A single deer's primary range for feeding is forty or fifty acres. A mink's, in a fertile marsh, may be only twenty, and a raccoon's ten, though, like the deer, they will each ramble a mile or more on occasion, utilizing the foodstuffs and crannies of a much larger acreage, and could not live in a wild state for long if really restricted to such a space. Yet if an acre is now to become worth $1,000 as recreational property, is that raccoon worth $10,000? Is a bear worth $3,200,000? As in the suburbs, a raccoon can parcel together a home out of snips and pieces of people's backyards, but otter, bears, bobcats and so on cannot. I had teased Strong about hunting, but I hoped he knew that the teasing had been a result of my admiration, that I understood that hunting by men like himself was never the villain in wildlife management. Rather, it was the summer people like me, who come crowding in, buying up, chopping up the land after the loggers have skinned off the trees.

A brook going downhill gave us a steady grade to the Swift Diamond. The temperature rose to 80 in the afternoon, from forty-five. Squirrel and deer country, with lots of witch hobble—deer food. We met mosquitoes and saw a rabbit, an owl's feather in the leaf muck, and a woodchuck's tracks (a type darker than the reddish farm chuck inhabits these forests). Seeing a red squirrel chitting at us, bold in the certainty that we couldn't touch him, I had a sudden memory of the chattering exhilaration which as a boy I had felt just after a close brush with death in a car. So must this squirrel feel at dusk when an owl swoops at him and he swerves round a tree trunk and escapes, feeling the wind of its wings.

The Swift, like the Dead, was employed originally for freighting out the virgin softwoods, so that there was no need to build roads into this country at all until, scarcely ten years ago in the case of the Swift, the loggers came back again for the hardwood trees, which don't float as well. We followed the road alongside the Swift for half a mile, then waded it and struck up Nathan Pond Brook, through a narrow wild brushy defile under Cave Mountain, with yellow birch and soft and hard maples and cone-bearing alders ten feet high. The hummingbirds swarmed to my red hat again, and there were goldfinches, purple finches, and blueberry thickets where we stopped to feast, and shoulder-high joe-pye weed, fireweed, goldenrod, and beaver activity and engineered ponds.

Legally as well as perhaps geographically, it is no longer possible just to throw a pack on your back in the Northeast and hike cross-country for weeks, because casual camping has been prohibited. But here in this obscure little bypassed valley bursting with undergrowth the illusion of the old hiking freedoms persisted. Even the vivid fish in their pools didn't give me the feeling of claustrophobia and pity that I often get, looking at trout cramped into a brook. They had space and a churning current and complexity enough in their habitat to baffle a hunting mink.

About the Author

EDWARD HOAGLAND was born in New York City in 1932 and grew up in Connecticut. His first novel, *Cat Man*, set in a circus, was published just as he turned twenty-three, and was followed by two other novels, *The Circle Home* and *The Peacock's Tail*. More recently he has written *Notes from the Century Before*, a journal of travels in British Columbia, and *The Courage of Turtles*, a collection of essays.

Mr. Hoagland likes the wild side of city life and the outdoor wildernesses of the world, and enjoys traveling. He has taught at such colleges as Sarah Lawrence and the City College of New York, and has won several literary awards, most recently Brandeis University's 1972 Citation in Literature. Married and the father of a child, he now divides his time between New York City and Barton, Vermont.